linking processes in educational improvement

concepts & applications

Edited by

*Nicholas Nash
and
Jack Culbertson*

University Council for Educational Administration
Columbus, Ohio
1977

UCEA

The mission of the University Council for Educational Administration is to improve the preparation of administrative personnel in education. Its membership consists of major universities in the United States and Canada. UCEA's central staff works with and through scholars in member universities to create new standards and practices in administrator preparation and to disseminate the results to interested institutions.

UCEA's interest in the professional preparation of educational administrators includes both continuing education and resident, preservice programs. Interinstitutional cooperation and communication are basic tools used in development activities; both administrators and professors participate in projects.

The Council's efforts currently are divided into six areas: developing and testing strategies for improving administrative and leadership practices in school systems; encouraging an effective flow of leaders into preparatory programs and posts of educational administration; advancing research and its dissemination and ideas helpful to those in universities responsible for designing preparatory programs; integrating and improving preparatory programs in specific areas of administration; and developing and evaluating a wide array of instructional materials.

This report was generated with financial support provided by the National Institute of Education. However, the content does not necessarily represent the position or policy of that agency, and no U.S. Government endorsement should be inferred.

Contents

FOREWORD vii

ACKNOWLEDGEMENTS ix

NOTES ON CONTRIBUTORS xi

Introduction 1

Chapter 1   Change Processes at the Elementary, Secondary, and Post-Secondary Levels of Education 7
Douglas A. Paul

Chapter 2   Linking Agents and the Sources and Uses of Knowledge 74
Jack Culbertson

Chapter 3   The Administrator's Role in Educational Linkage 118
James M. Lipham

Chapter 4   Linking Processes in Educational Change 149
Ann Lieberman

Chapter 5   Training and Supporting Linking Agents 189
David P. Crandall

Chapter 6   A Nationwide Training System for Linking Agents in Education 275
Jack Culbertson

Foreword

These papers were prepared as a collaborative effort among the National Institute of Education, the University Council for Educational Administration, and nine federally supported educational laboratories and research and development centers. Centers included those at the University of California at Los Angeles, the University of Oregon, Stanford University, the University of Texas, and the University of Wisconsin. Also cooperating were leaders in the Far West Laboratory for Educational Research and Development, the Northwest Regional Education Laboratory, Research for Better Schools, and the Southwest Regional Educational Laboratory. The major purpose of the volume is to highlight areas of agreement and disagreement within the research, development, and practice communities on the functions and support needs of those persons with a central responsibility for program improvement.

One of the goals of the National Institute of Education is assistance in constructing back-up and support services for schools and school systems attempting to improve educational practice. There are many Institute efforts directed toward this goal, and this volume is related to two of those efforts: the training of linking agents and the interpretation of research for practitioners.

The chapters provide a conceptual base for what was initially called the NIE Cooperative Dissemination and Linking Agent Training Project and what is now called the Linkage Training Service. This project involves the collection, organization, and transmission of information about human resources and linker training materials to linking agencies and programs. We have expected the consultation and training experience of the Linkage Training Service to keep the papers tied to reality, and we have expected the ideas in the papers to assist in describing and making sense of the experience of the linking agents and agencies.

These papers and the process used in their preparation are also related to the NIE Knowledge Transformation Project which encourages the transformation or interpretation of research findings for application in educational practice. The process of interpretation is seen as an on-going consensus-building activity in which there is a broad involvement in the process of writing and revising interpretive products. We are currently supporting work under the direction of Paul Hood at the Far West Laboratory for Educational Research and Development which constitutes a further effort to identify ways in which organizations and people relate in the complex process of encouraging educational improvement.

The chapters also respond to a commitment shared by both NIE and the University Council for Educational Administration (UCEA) to communicate to professors information which can be used in administrator preparation programs. It is hoped that potential and practicing administrators in these programs can make better use of the available and emerging resources and agencies and that professors and universities can function more effectively as linking agents and agencies.

This particular interpretation activity began in June, 1975, with a review of the literature on linking functions and linker training by Philip Piele. That review and the resulting discussions highlighted a number of problems in the available literature: The important system variables which influence change and improvement in schools are not typically related to the functions of linking agents; there is little attention paid to the nature and quality of the information to be conveyed to practitioners; linking tends to be equated with change and with adoption of innovations rather than with support to program improvement efforts; the role of the school administrator in the linking process is often ignored; the functions of information provision, technical assistance provision, and helping the school system build its capacity to assess and improve education are usually seen as separate and unintegrated roles; and finally, there is little research on the functions of the linking agent.

These chapters were planned to address several of the issues identified above. We do not expect them to provide a final statement on any of the issues identified, but we do hope that they will move us a step closer to an understanding of the crucial and complex problems of supporting persons and organizations in their efforts to improve educational practice.

Spencer Ward

Consumer Information Branch
School Practice and Service Division
Dissemination and Resources Group

Washington, D.C. National Institute of Education
June, 1977

ACKNOWLEDGEMENTS

Many persons have been involved in bringing this book to fruition. Comments and suggestions on the papers were made toward improving the content of the papers by the following people as individuals: David Clark, Tom Clemens (deceased), John Colson, W. J. Furtwengler, Alan Gaynor, Gene Hall, Charles Haughey, Ronald Havelock, Paul Hood, Tom Israel, Michael Moncrief, Carnot Nelson, John Peper, Marie Shepardson, Sam Sieber, Stan Temkin, Jim Walter, and Bill Ward. Many others read individual papers and provided significant comments to individual authors. We express our appreciation for their contributions.

Spencer Ward, of the National Institute of Education, who was involved directly in the conceptualization and planning of the effort, made significant contributions throughout the progress of the project, and Larry Hutchins, also of the National Institute of Education, gave critical support when it was needed.

On the technical side, Sandy Conyers, Mary Somerville, Sandy Booth, Ethel McKenzie, Harriet Ferrell, and Sally Kearns — all of the UCEA Staff — devoted countless hours to typing and retyping the manuscript. Frank Sherrill, Becky Livingston, Pete Mueller, and their colleagues managed the actual production of the book with alacrity and aplomb.

We are grateful to all of them for their several contributions.

N.N.
J.A.C.

Notes on Contributors

David P. Crandall (EdD, University of Massachusetts) is the Executive Director of The NETWORK, a non-profit linking agency in Merrimac, Massachusetts, dedicated to promoting the more effective utilization of human program, and information resources by human systems. Crandall has taught at the secondary and post-secondary levels and was associated with the Center for the Study of Educational Innovations. His extensive training and support work with external agents engaged in organizational change and capacity building efforts in schools has been reflected in a range of presentations and publications. A recent example is "An Executive Director's Struggle to Actualize His Commitment to Collaboration," to appear in a 1977 issue of *The Journal of Applied Behavioral Science*.

Jack Culbertson (PhD, University of California, Berkeley) has been Executive Director of the University Council for Educational Administration since 1959. He has taught at the elementary, junior high, and high school levels, as well as at the Universities of California and Oregon. He has been a member of numerous special committees and an adviser to the U.S. Office of Education, the Ford Foundation, the W. K. Kellogg Foundation, among others. Culbertson's publications include an array of books, chapters in books, monographs, and numerous articles in professional journals — all focusing on aspects of educational administration.

Ann Lieberman, (EdD, University of California at Los Angeles) presently serves as Associate Professor in the Department of Curriculum and Teaching at Teachers College, Columbia University, and as Associate Director of the Horace Mann-Lincoln Institute. Her primary interest has been and continues to be translating conceptions of educational change to the field. She also acts as a consultant for several projects which focus on various aspects of educational change. She has taught at the University of Massachusetts and was a Research Fellow at the Institute for the Development of Educational Activity in Los Angeles. Lieberman has written a wide range of papers on issues of educational improvement and has made numerous presentations at conferences and seminars.

James M. Lipham (PhD, University of Chicago) is a Professor in the Department of Educational Administration and a Faculty Research Associate in the Wisconsin Research and Development Center for Cognitive Learning at the University of Wisconsin-Madison. He heads the Administration and Organization for Instruction unit concerned with research, development, and implementation of Individually Guided Education of elementary and secondary schools. He has worked extensively with local schools in the adoption, institutionalization, and refinement of administrative structures which facilitate educational change. Lipham is the author of numerous books, articles and research reports dealing with leadership, decision-making, organizational, and social systems theory in educational administration.

Douglas Paul (PhD, University of Wisconsin) is presently a consultant to several projects related to educational administration and educational change. He has served as an Assistant Professor at the Ontario Institute for Studies in Education and as a Research Associate at the Wisconsin Research and Development Center on Cognitive Learning. The author of several monographs and reports on linkage and change, Paul is currently involved in work on a transactional model of change, on data focusing on academic roles for the utilization of research, among other activities.

Introduction

It is a rare individual, a rare organization capable of altering its behavior in a significant way. In education, as in other complex systems, leaders ideally should reach beyond themselves to other individuals and agencies judged relevant to a proposed change: Tested ideas, useful products, and related services ought to be gathered, organized, and utilized in thoughtful ways to undergird any concerted effort directed at improving performance.

However, at present these various resources are largely unavailable in coherent and useful ways, and the number of individuals and organizations readily and widely available to serve as a "link" between resources and users is very small indeed.

Beyond this environmental ambiguity, educational leaders have difficulty capturing the opportunities which are known because they are pressed continuously to maintain organizational structure and processes rather than to try to improve them — even though there is evidence to suggest that the organizational capacity to change is positively related to both openness to new ideas and to exchange opportunities with those beyond the boundaries of the organization.

In recent decades, scholars and leaders have paid increasing attention to ways in which communication between organizations can facilitate change. One result has been a growing body of ideas and findings about the linking process and the individual or organizational role through which it might be expressed in order to assist organizations and their leaders in acquiring and using ideas and practices in those areas where improvement is seen as desirable. Many see this linking role as one of significance in supporting change, and a new synthesis of the literature on the concepts and applications of linking seems appropriate.

This volume addresses the problems and opportunities through linking within the larger context of improvement, leadership, knowledge utilization and support organizations from a variety of perspectives. The primary focus is on the *improvement* of educational management. This is not to imply that aspects of maintenance are not important, for clearly they are. In fact it appears that maintenance and improvement are not so neatly isolated. The way in which a school maintains its operation has a great impact on both the effectiveness of current programs and the receptivity of the staff to improvement efforts. It should be added that while the literature addressed is often focused around "change," defined as the adoption of a new program which is assumed to be an improvement, a number of studies have suggested that "change" is not necessarily improvement and may have even more of a deleterious effect.

There are all sorts and conditions of linking agents at the national, regional, state, local, and building level. What are the critical differences between internal linkers (within an organization) and external linkers (outside an organization) and the other diverse linking roles of researchers, developers, and trainers in the support of change? What are the problems and opportunities inherent in linking *agencies* as opposed to linking *agents?* The volume recognizes and deliberately treats linking roles from different vantage points in responding to these and other related questions. Specifically, the organization of the book is intended to illuminate primarily the role of those linkers engaged in or providing support for improvement in local educational agencies, either internally or externally.

These differing vantage points do not define a linking agent as serviceably as some readers might prefer. It may be disconcerting to find differences in interpretation of so critical a concept, but it is from such differences that the most useful sparks fly to outline future discussion, thinking, and research.[1] In general, however, there is agreement that a key function of linking agents, whether internal or external to a school system, is *to help those engaged in improvement activities acquire and use relevant ideas, products, and related resources.* In one sense, the linker function is to help bring greater rationality to change-oriented decisions in school systems by increasing the nature and extent of information utilized in decision making. However, a more specific question arises: Who qualifies as an internal or external linker? This question can be answered both from an agency and an individual perspective. Underlying this volume are two assumptions about linking agencies: First, internal linkers, by definition, must occupy posts within educational systems and be concerned about improvement within those systems and, second, there are several key agencies insofar as external linkers are concerned — state education agencies, intermediate service agencies; research and development centers; departments and related units in higher education institutions; educational laboratories; and leagues, networks and related organizations serving multiple school systems.

Not all personnel in school systems or the external agencies listed above qualify as linking agents. What is it, then, that distinguished linking agents in these organizations from non-linking agents? Three criteria appear to be critical. First, linking agents direct their actions at the improvement of individual or institutional performance. Second, they use

---

[1]Readers may note differences from author to author concerning the use of "linking" agent and "linkage" agent. While one may contend the former suggests the process and the latter the manner of the process, in general the terms are meant to be interchangeable.

knowledge or knowledge-based products and services as key instruments of improvement. Thirdly, in order to connect those engaged in change with ideas, findings, descriptions of practices, training materials and other needed knowledge-based products, they must perform boundary-spanning roles. A principal, for example, might span his/her school and an educational laboratory to connect teachers with materials designed to help improve the school's reading program. Or a staff member in an intermediate service agency might link selected individuals in a university with a superintendent's cabinet in order to improve education through a newly designed administrator staff development program.

To qualify as linkers, individuals need, at a minimum, to meet all three criteria listed above. An associate superintendent, for example, could meet the boundary-spanning requirement but be concerned with maintenance rather than improvement. Or (s)he could direct efforts toward changing staff without using knowledge as a means for change. In neither case would the associate superintendent meet the criteria for a linking agent.

The volume is designed to achieve several objectives, the first of which, as already implied, is to produce for educational leaders an up-to-date synthesis on the role of linking agents and agencies in educational improvement activities and, in the process, to identify and discuss important knowledge utilization issues of interest to the research, development, and training communities. The synthesis reflects and, in part, is shaped by the clear and continuing need to improve education, the growing number of linking agents and the more visible role of linking agencies, and the increase in scholarly activity directed at linking roles and agencies and their educational improvement functions. It is hoped that the synthesis will be of value to a range of individuals who have a stake in improving education at national, state, and local levels, from leaders directly involved in educational change to linkers seeking to facilitate the change process and to researchers, developers, and trainers who contribute to educational improvement.

A second objective of the papers is to address the immediate realities which internal and external linkers confront and to shed light on the kinds of organizational, human and knowledge resources available to them. For example, the marginal character of the linkage agent role is depicted, and the attributes needed by linkers for effective performance are postulated. The specific constraints and opportunities shaping linker roles are identified and described. In addition, the macro-system of knowledge uses and linking processes, which offer a resource for linking agents, is outlined. Also treated are the myriad complexities inherent in linking and change processes. It is likely that content on the immediate realities and environmental complexities of linkage will be of special value to agencies and individuals engaged in linking projects and to those with responsibilities for training linking agents.

A final objective of the synthesis is to provide better bases for advancing linking through new plans and developments. The volume not only should provide better frameworks for enabling leaders in schools to obtain resources for improving or changing programs but also should encourage and should provide bases for better cooperation and communication between producers and users of resources. Since leaders in the Cooperative Dissemination and Linking Agent Training Project very early recognized the need for more effective planning directed at improving the training of linkers, the volume gives special attention to this area. More specifically, it presents concepts basic to the design of a more adequate training system for linkers and basic to the collection and development of relevant resources to support the projected system. Thus, the hope is that the concepts presented both will advance new developments and plans and will stimulate new inquiry into linking agents, linking agencies, and their functions. Clearly, such inquiry is needed to illuminate the complex processes of linking and on their role in facilitating change.

The chapters in the book move from the more general to the more specific insofar as linking agents directly involved in change activities are concerned. Douglas Paul in Chapter One focuses upon change within the context of educational organizations. Differing models of change which can influence and/or be used by linking agents are presented. The four models of change discussed are problem-solving; social interaction; research, development and diffusion; and linking strategies related to knowledge utilization. A wide body of literature is drawn upon to produce the generalizations covering adapting units, processes for bringing about change, impingements of change and the effects of change.

Jack Culbertson in Chapter Two treats from a broad perspective the larger environment of knowledge resources and uses relevant to change. The chapter postulates five uses of knowledge which can support those who are directly engaged in change or are providing support for it. Sub-uses for each category of use are described along with outcomes produced. Types and sources of knowledge used, characteristics of users, and their links with other users and linking agencies are also treated. Illustrations from the literature and from practice to illuminate concepts are limited to the field of educational administration; however, it is assumed that the basic concepts elaborated can be applied equally well to other fields of education, such as curriculum.

James Lipham in Chapter Three focuses principally on the role of the administrator in implementing educational improvement. Administrators are viewed by the author as playing a crucial role in the linking process. Among the topics treated are administrative functions, support needs of administrators, and the training required of administrators. The emphasis in this chapter is upon the leadership functions of the administrator rather than upon the maintenance functions. Consequently, both the internal and external linking roles of the administrator are highlighted. Relationships between the local school and external linking agents are also treated.

Ann Lieberman in Chapter Four examines linking agencies and the functions these agencies perform. The discussion is set within the context of "the school as a social system" and the complexities inherent in this system. Featured in the treatment are the understandings, processes and influential conditions that affect agency functioning, and the generalizations presented are documented from an array of studies. Three vignettes of change and linkage in education conclude the chapter.

David Crandall in Chapter Five addresses issues directly related to the external linking agent. He examines the client system served by the linker and some of the resources which can be used in working with clients. A special section on the "host agency" where external linkers reside is presented along with the multiple roles they perform. Stresses inherent in the role are identified and the skill clusters needed for effective linking performance are described, as well as important implementation issues faced by linkers.

In the last chapter, Jack Culbertson depicts, in the form of a scenario, a nation-wide system for training linkers. Cast within a 1985 time period, the scenario also describes the pertinent support functions, as well as the concepts and events which shape the emerging system.

The scenario is deliberately optimistic in view. With the current pessimism surrounding education, many other less hopeful views could have been presented. Thus, the scenario should not be viewed as a prediction of the future. Rather it should be seen as a directional statement designed to provide leaders clues about the ways in which they might address the various facets of linker training in the future.

In sum, the volume synthesizes key concepts and findings about change processes, uses of knowledge in change, the management of change (or improvement), the functions of linking agencies in improvement activities, the attributes and skill clusters needed by external linkers to function effectively, and a national training system for both internal and external linkers.

The book is offered as one means for advancing the training and the functioning of linkers and for stimulating needed new inquiry and development related to the role of linkers in improving education.

J.A.C.
N.N.

1

Change Processes at the Elementary, Secondary, And Post-Secondary Levels of Education

Douglas A. Paul

SECTION I

INTRODUCTION

Face-to-Face Communication Between Helpers, Trainers And Conveyors On One Hand And Users Of Innovations On The Other Is More Effective Than Print Media Alone.

Print media does not afford the reader to question assumptions, gain feedback, or clarify meaning. More importantly in most schools the burden of finding time to read material is placed on the teacher and principal who have little free time. In contrast, face-to-face communication may provide immediate feedback, is usually accompanied by released time, and allows the teacher and principal to question and clarify meaning. In addition, face-to-face interaction allows the sender to instill enthusiasm and excitement and provide encouragement.

> *The Frequency of Interaction Among Helpers, Trainers And Conveyors On One Hand And Users Of Innovations On The Other Should Be Mutually Determined.*

Too little interaction results in feelings of abandonment, whereas too much interaction results in feelings of being invaded. The status of the organization's being helped determines the optimum frequency of interaction. School staff experienced in using outside help may profit from extensive interaction over a limited time period followed by gradual disengagement. In contrast, staff not ready for or willing to utilize outside help may profit from a gradual increase in the frequency of assistance. This strategy reduces feelings of being invaded or feelings of being inadequate.

These are examples of the generalizations presented in this review of change processes in education. An inductive approach was taken to develop the generalizations. Empirical studies were identified, findings were categorized and tabulated, and generalizations were formed based on both the tabulations and on the judgment of the reviewer. Because the studies reviewed did not address all areas of concern, important issues for those involved in designing linking agent training programs may not be covered here. These and other limitations of the review are discussed subsequently.

Reviews of education research findings and summaries of educational literature promise to provide new insights and syntheses. Oftentimes the reviews conclude that there is much disarray, disorder, and disillusionment in a particular area of study. Weak methodologies are frequently singled out as one of the prime culprits for the sorry state of the research reviewed. Gene Glass (1976), in his presidential address to the 1976 annual meeting of the American Educational Research Association, pointed out the need for extracting the knowledge from the information which is buried in hundreds of research studies. He went on to say that to carp on design deficiencies while trying to integrate studies usually results in advancing a few acceptable studies as the truth. These studies tend to be either one's own work, that of students, or of friends. However, this approach takes design and analysis too seriously and results in the discarding of a vast amount of important data. Glass called on the research community to engage in the meta-analysis of research, the statistical analysis of a large collection of analysis results from individual studies.

The initial draft of this review of educational change processes resulted in a labored list of contradictory findings and charges of deficient research designs. The feedback generously given by colleagues, Cooperative Project staff, and NIE personnel pointed to the need for going beyond a traditional review. Issues, relationships, and concepts which hold potential for major theoretical insights should be stressed, and judgments should be made about the findings reviewed. To avoid making judgments about contradictory findings may be scientifically safe on one hand, but it is a disservice to the reader seeking insights, advice, and knowledge on the other. It is hoped that this review of change processes may provide new insights, advice, and knowledge to those concerned with educational change and improvement. In addition, this review should be of use to those involved with studying change processes in that potentially fruitful areas of study have been identified.

The purposes of this review are twofold: to summarize the major models of educational change and to present a series of generalizations based on recent empirical studies about educational change. The first half of this chapter summarizes the major change models in education, and the last half includes a series of generalizations based, in part, on more than 100 studies. Before the summary of the major change models, recognition will be given to major reviews previously conducted on the topic of change and innovation. Then three major dimensions which provide an overarching structure for analyzing the models of change and the findings from the empirical studies are introduced.

Previous Literature Reviews

There has been a variety of comprehensive reviews of the change and innovation literature. A comprehensive review of the change, dissemination, and knowledge utilization literature was carried out by Havelock (1969) and now encompasses an updated bibiliography of over 4000 entries (Havelock, 1972). An equally comprehensive review of change research and findings, although not focusing exclusively on education, has been provided by Rogers and Shoemaker (1971); it is a revision of one of the earliest reviews of the change literature (Rogers, 1962). Over 1200 empirical studies and 300 non-empirical reports were used to generate 100 generalizations about the diffusion of innovations. The growth and magnitude of the change literature may be seen by comparing Rogers' 1971 bibliography of 1500 entries with his updated bibliography of over 2700 entries (Rogers and Thomas, 1975).

Considerable time and energy has been devoted to reviewing the expanding literature on change and diffusion. A large proportion of the research falls outside of education: rural sociology, business and health. Nevertheless, recent reviews of studies involving educational change and improvement are readily available: Fullan and Pomfret (1975), Gaynor (1975), Hall and Alford (1976), Maguire (1970), Rosenau and Hood (1975), Short (1973), and Sikorski (1976).

Three dimensions for classifying and comparing the major change models in education will now be introduced to serve as a broad organizing framework for comparing change models and for presenting the findings from recent empirical studies reviewed in the second section of the paper.

THREE DIMENSIONS OF CHANGE

Three dimensions of change are described below to summarize and compare four major models of change, and they are used to organize and categorize the research findings reported subsequently. These three dimensions were developed inductively, that is, through groupings of findings, rearrangement of categories, and evaluating alternative taxonomies.[1] They are not intended as a model or as a strategy of change; their purpose is to provide a logical and parsimonious set of dimensions for classifying change findings, concepts, and relationships.

Processes

The first dimension is processes of change, the action and modifiers which help describe action as change occurs. There are a number of ways of categorizing the actions which make up change programs. For exam-

---

[1]Alternative categories are discussed in Paul (1975a). See also Kester and Howard (1975) who constructed a similar set of dimensions. They included stages of change, characteristics of innovations, interaction among advocates and consumers, and circumstantial and structural influence.

ple, elsewhere in this book Lipham describes activities such as purposing, planning, organizing, training, implementing, and evaluating. Change process is defined here as one or more activities conducted through one or more modes of communication and taking place over a period of time. The three components which make up process are activity, mode, and frequency, and these are discussed more fully below.

Activities. The activity category represents the energy expended in order to bring about a change program or school improvement. The activity grouping answers the question of "what" activities are carried out. Activities commonly used to bring about change are: *helping* users diagnose problems, initiate improvements, or implement innovations; *training* users to solve problems and use new ideas and technologies; and *conveying* to users information which may be of interest. This certainly is not an exhaustive list of activities, although they were the most frequently studied activities.

Mode. The mode, a term borrowed from the field of communication, is the means by which change activities are carried out. The mode of change may be thought of as answering the question of "how" activities are carried out. Examples include face-to-face interaction or two-way communication and print media or one-way communication. Two-way communication refers to sending messages and receiving feedback. This mode enables the sender to assess the effectiveness, appropriateness, and timeliness of messages. Feedback allows for modifications of message content and format, evaluations of the capabilities of the receiver to understand future messages, and assessments of the needs and interests and receptivity of the receiver. By contrast, one-way communication permits sending messages only without receiving feedback, a situation which makes it difficult to evaluate messages and interference which may be occurring between the sender and receiver.

Frequency. Frequency refers to the quantity of the activity of change. For example, help from external change agents may occur daily in one district but occur only once a year in another district. Even though frequency is a factor that can usually be modified and controlled, it has received very little attention. Frequency is included here because of the logical progression from asking the questions of what and how. The question of when is often ignored, but it is no less important.

Influences

The second dimension has been labeled influence of change, and is made up of three major groups of factors which influence the processes and effects of change: internal organizational factors (endogenous) such as organizational climate, administrative procedures, and staff attitudes and personalities; external organizational factors (exogenous) such as time, funds, and community; and innovation characteristics such as complexity, compatability, and relative advantage.

There are many factors which influence change processes and concomitantly the effects of change; some of these are barriers to change, while others support and facilitate change. The groupings of factors making up this dimension were developed inductively by tallying and arranging the findings from the empirical studies reviewed in section two.

Effects

The third dimension has been labeled effects and it refers to the outcomes of the change process. There is a variety of ways of looking at change outcomes, two of which are listed below. The list by Hall (1974) assumes that the use of an innovation is intended, in contrast to the list by Sieber (1974). Sieber contends that use of an innovation is only one of several outcomes and that "use" has been stressed at the expense of less visible outcomes. Hall's list includes:

    Nonuse (intended or not intended)

    Information seeking activities

    Preparation for use

    Mechanical use

    Routine use (or misuse)

    Refined use (or maladaptation)

    Integrated use

    Renewal activities

These levels of use are not exhaustive but rather represent one view of change. Sieber (1974) was concerned that knowledge utilization was being directly associated with the implementation of innovations. As a reminder that the effects of a change process are not always the implementation and use of an idea or innovation, he listed ten frequent needs and motivations of school staff in seeking information. Conveying information may be seen as a change process which may result in effects quite different from implementation.

Sieber's list includes:

> Legitimating what one is already doing, or has decided to do or not to do
>
> Winning an argument
>
> Satisfying intellectual curiosity
>
> Learning about practices that ought to be shunned
>
> Becoming aware of possible barriers or pitfalls in a course of action
>
> Keeping abreast of what educators are doing elsewhere
>
> Learning about courses at local colleges or fulfilling requirements for courses
>
> Raising awareness of the world of educational R&D, e.g., learning about the existence of a regional lab
>
> Gaining a clearer conceptual map of one's activities or context
>
> Being inspired to higher levels of energy or commitment
> (p. 65)

Another effect which could be added to this list is using knowledge for completing a task at hand.

These effects of change are frequently overlooked, ignored, or accorded little significance. Nevertheless, because they emanate from the realities faced by practitioners of education, they are important outcomes. In other words, these effects reflect a larger world within which teachers and principals operate, a world more complex and dynamic than is con-

TABLE 1.1
DISTINCT STATES OF THE LEVEL OF USE OF INNOVATIONS

Levels of Use	Description
Level 0	NON-USE: State in which the user has little or no knowledge of the innovation, no involvement with the innovation, and is doing nothing toward becoming involved.
Level I	ORIENTATION: State in which the user has acquired or is acquiring information about the innovation and/or has explored or is exploring its value orientation and its demands upon user and user system.
Level II	PREPARATION: State in which the user is preparing for first use of the innovation.
Level III	MECHANICAL USE: State in which the user focuses most effort on the short-term, day-to-day use of the innovation with little time for reflection. Changes in use are made more to meet user needs than client needs. The user is primarily engaged in a stepwise attempt to master the tasks required to use the innovation, often resulting in disjointed and superficial use.
Level IVA	ROUTINE: Use of the innovation is stabilized. Few if any changes are being made in ongoing use. Little preparation or thought is being given to improving innovation use or its consequences.
Level IVB	REFINEMENT: State in which the user varies the use of the innovation to increase the impact on clients within immediate sphere of influence. Variations are based on knowledge of both short-and long-term consequences for clients.
Level V	INTEGRATION: State in which the user is combining own efforts to use the innovation with related activities of colleagues to achieve a collective impact on clients within their common sphere of influence.
Level VI	RENEWAL: State in which the user re-evaluates the quality of use of the innovation, seeks major modifications of or alternatives to present innovation to achieve increased impact on clients, examines new developments in the field, and explores new goals for self and the system.

Adapted by permission of the publisher from G. Hall, S. Loucks, W. Rutherford, and B. Newlove, Levels of Use of the Innovation: A Framework for Analyzing Innovation Adoption. *Journal of Teacher Education*, 1975, 26, 52-56. © 1974 by the American Association of Colleges for Teacher Education.

veyed by measures of the degree to which a particular product or new behavior is used.

Sieber (1975) was concerned with the assumption made by many that utilization of innovations means implementation. He has noted that information may be assimilated as well as implemented. The former is cognitive, whereas the latter is behavioral. Most studies of change deal with implementation of innovations in a behavioral sense and, therefore, the level of use scale described in Table 1.2 is an appropriate and useful listing.

Effects are the immediate result of a change process, as opposed to the hoped-for-result usually associated with, for example, changes in student behavior. However, such changes depend on the degree of implementation and effectiveness of the innovation. In other words, there is a difference between the effects of change processes and the effects of an innovation. The former refers to the degree to which the innovation is implemented and used, where the latter refers to the degree to which the innovation makes a difference in learner or staff behavior.[2] These three change dimensions are pictured in Figure 1.1 as moving left to right over time. In reality there is likely to be much back and forth movement.

Figure 1.1 portrays an underlying assumption about change, namely change processes are initiated and then modified by internal and external conditions and by the nature of the innovation. These modifiers help determine the effect of the change processes. These three dimensions of change are intended to be general enough to incorporate the more well-known models of change and yet have sufficient structure so that comparisons between models can be made. Four change models are presented below and compared in terms of the three dimensions just described.

MODELS OF CHANGE

One longtime observer of and participant in educational change research has observed:

> In approaching the field of knowledge utilization in education, one soon encounters a bewildering array of so-

---

[2]See Appendix A for a fuller discussion of this and related measurement problems.

called models and strategies. Here is one area of educational interest wherein conceptual schemes are as numerous as the schemes of the medieval scholastics, and in my opinion almost as useless. (Sieber, 1974, p. 61)

Sieber went on to suggest that one factor contributing to the confusion about change models is the frequent intermingling of descriptive and normative models. The former describe; the latter prescribe. For a model to be useful it should be capable both of describing and of prescribing. However, ideologies occasionally develop around a particular model or view of change, and the normative capabilities of a model are then emphasized with little regard given to descriptive limitations. To become emotionally committed to a particular view of change is to limit alternative views which may be helpful.

Change is not dominated by linear, sequential, or even rational processes. Nevertheless, a model that puts forth a process for accomplishing change which is linear, sequential, and rational may be highly useful. First, it may identify potentially critical issues for those encouraging change as well as for researchers studying change, e.g., user recognition of problems; second, it may provide a starting place for launching a change process; and third, it may serve as a framework with logically spaced checkpoints for those engaged in the change process.

Compounding the confusion over change models are inadequate conceptualizations about change in education. Baldridge (1974) has contended that unsuitable paradigms for studying change have been adopted, along with a focus on and analysis of the wrong problems. For example, the early stages of change tend to be emphasized, the innovations studied tend to be technical and easily evaluated, and the unit of analysis tends to be the individual adopter as opposed to the complex organization.[3] As if Baldridge's condemnation is not severe enough, Giacquinta (1973) blasted the literature on education change. He contended that: (1) the literature is atheoretical, with little testing of theories or explanations of change; (2) the findings of change studies cannot be viewed with confidence due to inadequate research methods; and (3) the emphasis of studies has been toward precipitating change rather than studying it.

The following four models should be viewed as complementary perspectives emphasizing different aspects of change and involving different sets of assumptions. As suggested earlier, ideologies and concomitant loyalties have developed around the models: Followers of a particular

---

[3]Cf. G. Zaltman, R. Duncan and J. Holbek, *Innovations and Organizations.* New York: John Wiley & Sons, 1973, p. 61, for a list of individually oriented models of change.

FIGURE 1.1
THREE GENERAL DIMENSIONS OF CHANGE

PROCESSES	INFLUENCES	EFFECTS
ACTIVITIES	*ENDOGENOUS*	*LEVEL OF USE*
Examples:	Examples:	Examples:
Helping	Organizational Factors	Non-use (Intentional/
Training	Administrative Factors	Unintentional)
Conveying	Staff Characteristics	Information Seeking
	Physical Configuration	Preparation for Use
MODE	*EXOGENOUS*	Mechanical Use
Examples:	Examples:	Routine Use or Misuse
Two-Way Communication	Time	Refined Use of Maladaptation
One-Way Communication	Funds	Integrated Use
	Community	Renewal Activities
FREQUENCY	*INNOVATION*	
Examples:	Examples:	
Daily Interaction	Relative Advantage	
Weekly Interaction	Compatability	
Monthly Interaction	Complexity	

18   Douglas A. Paul

perspective proclaim its virtues while remaining mute to its inevitable weaknesses. And although no one model is comprehensive enough to satisfy all ideological groups, a complex mosaic does begin to take shape when the models are viewed simultaneously.

Problem-Solving Model[4]

The problem-solving model of change is well developed, has many adapted forms, and enjoys a considerable number of proponents. It grew out of the work on group problem solving and interaction processes such as sensitivity training and T-group sessions pioneered by the National Training Laboratories. The most distinctive components of this model are user centeredness, user diagnosis of problems, and/or emphasis on building user capability to solve problems.

A simplified synopsis of the model would go something as follows: The first stage is user diagnosis of problems, perhaps including the help of outside facilitators. Next, the user, in collaboration with the outside facilitator searches for alternative solutions to the problem; a solution is chosen from a list compiled by the user and/or facilitator and is implemented on a trial basis; if it appears promising, it is then incorporated into the user system. It is important to keep in mind, however, that there is probably much movement back and forth among the problem-solving stages (Thelen, 1967). Early developers and proponents of the problem-solving model of change include: Bennis, Benne and Chin (1969), Lippitt, Watson and Westley (1958); and Watson (1967). A current and well accepted view of the problem-solving model and user centeredness may be found in Fullan's (1972) article on users of innovations.

In terms of the three dimensions of our general scheme, the problem-solving model can be described as follows: Helping and training by an external agent characterize the major activities of the change process on a face-to-face basis in order to promote two-way communication. The frequency of face-to-face contact is high at the initial problem diagnosis stage but then levels off at the later stage of institutionalization to prevent an unhealthy dependency.

Examples of influences on the problem-solving approach are: (1) norms and organizational support for problem-solving, (2) effective leadership for initiating and maintaining problem-solving, (3) staff percep-

---

[4]The problem-solver, social interaction, and research-development-diffusion models presented in the following sections represent divisions used by Havelock (1969) in his review of change literature.

tions of the legitimacy of a problem-solving approach, (4) openmindedness of staff, (5) sufficient time, funds, and absence of community controversy, (6) adequate space for staff to meet comfortably. In fact, capability to solve problems is, in itself, an innovation. The user organization may decide to develop or implement an innovation congruent with and supportive of increased user capability. Such an innovation would be complex. On the Level of Use Scale presented earlier, level VI would be sought. Figure 1.2 depicts the problem-solving model in terms of the four dimensions of change.

Processes for enhancing user capability to solve problems may be considered as aspects of the problem-solving model. Because organizational development (OD) is aimed at building school-wide capability, it may be classified as part of the problem-solving model of change. OD processes focus on social systems as contrasted to individuals (Schmuck, 1974; Schmuck and Miles, 1971). This distinction is important for differentiating among change models; the problem-solving model includes both.

Some recent studies and reports of change programs help illustrate the user-centeredness of the problem-solving view of change. Preliminary findings from the Experimental Schools Program for Small Schools Serving Rural Areas (Kane, 1976) showed that recognition of educational needs, participation in identification of needs, acceptance of change program by staff, and congruence of program with locally identified problems are important at the early stages of a change effort.

Findings from a large-scale study of federal programs supporting educational change conducted by the Rand Corporation (Berman et al., 1975; McLaughlin, 1976) pointed to the importance of centering change efforts on users of innovations rather than on developers or delivery systems. The Rand studies stressed user adaptation and re-invention of innovations to a greater degree than did the early problem-solving research.

An additional revised view of the problem-solving model to include political power has been suggested by Mann (1976). For example, user adaptation of change programs may be better understood as a partisan struggle among power holders. The addition of political considerations to the problem-solving approach was also documented by Maguire (1970) in a study of a planned change project. He found that the structured steps of the problem-solving model had less impact than did informal interpersonal relationships and political considerations.

The League of Innovative Schools In Southern California, initiated by the Institute for Development of Educational Activities (I/D/E/A), is a current example of an adapted problem-solving approach. The League was created by first focusing on the needs and concerns of principals and their

FIGURE 1.2
PROBLEM-SOLVING MODEL IN TERMS OF THE THREE DIMENSIONS OF CHANGE

PROCESSES	INFLUENCES	EFFECTS
ACTIVITIES	*ENDOGENOUS*	*LEVELS OF USE*
Examples:	Examples:	Examples:
Helping users to solve current problems and build capacity to solve future problems	Norms for problem-solving, Leadership to encourage P.S., Staff see P.S. approach and its proponents as legitimate, and staff are psychologically open to new approaches	Information Seeking activities are followed by preparation for use, routine use, and renewal activities. The renewal activities are sought by the problem-solving approach. Renewal and capacity to solve future problems are considered equal here.
MODE	*EXOGENOUS*	
Examples:	Examples:	
Two-Way Communication in order to optimize feedback and build trust	Time for involvement, Funding to support facilitators, and release time, Non-threatening community	
FREQUENCY	*INNOVATION*	
Examples:	Examples:	
Daily or weekly interaction at first but as user capacity develops frequency decreases	Problem-Solving seen as innovation or solution arrived at as a result of problem-solving process. In either case users see benefits (relative advantage), compatibility, and complexity.	

staffs, rather than on a specific innovation or change program. Eventually the schools began helping each other through the league arrangement and implementing a complex instructional and organizational innovation (Bentzen et al., 1974). Lieberman has drawn upon her experience in the I/D/E/A League in the chapter on linking agencies elsewhere in this book. Aspects of the problem-solving model are found in other change programs which have been developed from other perspectives, and these similarities and differences will be discussed subsequently.

Social Interaction Model

The social interaction model of change emerged from the early research on the diffusion of agricultural innovations, such as hybrid corn seeds (Ryan and Gross, 1943), and the early work of Rogers is associated with its development and refinement (Rogers, 1962; Rogers and Shoemaker, 1971). Distinguishing characteristics of the social interaction view of change are the emphasis on (1) communication channels and messages for diffusing innovations, (2) interpersonal influence patterns leading to adoption of innovations, and (3) stimuli for adoption originating outside of the adopting system. The characteristics of the innovation and innovator are given much attention in the social interaction view. There are four essential stages to the model: (1) knowledge of the innovation, (2) persuasion leading to the formation of attitudes about the innovation, (3) decision about adopting or rejecting the innovation, and (4) confirmation from peers that the decision was a sound one.

In terms of the three dimensions of the general scheme, the major activities of this model involve conveying information about innovations through both face-to-face contact and print media. Although face-to-face communication may occur, the extent of two-way communication would not be important. Because the needs and capabilities of the potential user are not a central concern, the frequency of communication may be low at the start, but as more potential users become interested in the innovation, frequency of communication may increase. After the decision to use the innovation has been made, the frequency of interaction generally levels off. Examples of influences of the social interaction model are: (1) organizational support to establish outside contacts, (2) opportunities for travel, attending conferences, and buying journals, (3) cosmopolitan orientation, (4) time to talk with colleagues, (5) funds to purchase products, (6) proximity to sources of new ideas. Because the characteristics of the potential adopter and the characteristics of the innovation are major influences, they have been given comprehensive attention by social interaction researchers. The innovations with which the social interaction model usually deals tend to be observable, technological, and susceptible to evaluation. Proponents of the social interaction approach would consider adoption (the decision to use an innovation) as the major change effect. The qualitative distinctions between levels of use would not be a major issue. Figure 1.2 depicts the social interaction model in terms of the three change dimensions.

The model's applicability to education has been questioned. For example, (1) educational systems and staff are not comparable to farms and farmers — the focus of the social interaction model during its early development; (2) agricultural innovations are easily evaluated, visible, and reliable in contradistinction to educational innovations; and (3) emphasis is placed on the early phases of change — awareness and adoption — rather than the implementation stage which is believed to be a major stumbling block in education (Baldridge, 1974; Havelock, 1969; McLaughlin, 1976). Nevertheless, the social interaction perspective does offer a different and constructive view of the change process as the following three studies illustrate.

Carlson (1965) studied the diffusion and adoption of new curricula in Pennsylvania and West Virginia by examining the social structure of and communication networks among superintendents. He concluded that districts that were early adopters had superintendents with higher peer status than did late or non-adopting districts and that these superintendents tended to influence other superintendents through personal advice giving.

Two recent studies which focused on post-secondary institutions were based on the social interaction model. Brown (1974) investigated the role of opinion leaders and their sources of information regarding the diffusion of community college instructional innovations. He found that opinion leaders were seldom influenced by impersonal sources of information either at the awareness or evaluation stages. Rather personal face-to-face exchanges were the most important source of information not only for the opinion leaders, but also for opinion followers. However, a recent study of the diffusion of four instructional innovations targeted at university professors revealed contrary results. Rogers et al., (1975) found that more than half of the professors requesting more information about some targeted innovations first learned of their existence through a brochure. In addition, secondary diffusion tended to consist of information exchange rather than influence or opinion leadership. And in contrast with findings from studies supporting a problem-solver view of change, the Rogers study found that rate of adoption of the innovations was not strongly related to needs or existing values of the adopters.

FIGURE 1.3
SOCIAL INTERACTION MODEL IN TERMS OF THE THREE DIMENSIONS OF CHANGE

PROCESSES	INFLUENCES	EFFECTS
ACTIVITIES Examples: Conveying information to potential users so that they are aware of new techniques and ideas and will be influenced to adopt them *MODE* Examples: One-Way communication in order to efficiently reach as many potential adopters as possible *FREQUENCY* Examples: At the beginning of the dissemination program few are reached but the frequency accelerates quickly and then levels off.	*ENDOGENOUS* Examples: Support for outside contacts, travel, and conferences, staff with cosmopolitan outlook *EXOGENOUS* Examples: Time to talk and be influenced, Funds to purchase new products, traditions of the community, and proximity to sources of influence and information *INNOVATION* Examples: Products display high levels of Relative Advantage and compatibility, but low complexity.	*LEVELS OF USE* Examples: Information seeking is a primary effect but preparation for use, and then mechanical use which may be a trial of the innovation is also of concern. If adopted then routine use is sought.

Research-Development-Diffusion Model

Although the primary creators of the Research-Development-Diffusion model (RDD) have claimed that their conceptualization of the change process was not intended as a model (Clark and Guba, 1972; House, 1972), it is nevertheless referred to as one. Two critical assumptions of the RDD model are that there is a rational sequence from development to implementation of Research and Development (R&D) products and that the user of R&D products is rational and will cooperate in the installation of R&D products. A synopsis of the model might proceed as follows: Basic research is followed by applied research; these findings serve as a framework for the development of a new technique, product, or design for improving educational practice. The development is produced and then disseminated to a wide audience who receive assistance in installing it (Guba, 1968).

Conveying information about new R&D products characterizes the initial approach of the RDD model. Users then search for help in installing the innovation. Print media and interactive computer searches for new R&D products typify the mode of change, and the frequency of conveying activities is generally higher than the frequency of helping activities. Examples of influences in the RDD approach include: (1) cooperative institutional arrangements between developers, dissiminators, helpers, and users; (2) leadership which encourages utilization of research; (3) R&D products perceived as legitimate solutions to problems; (4) attentive and receptive audience for messages from developers; (5) time to discover and implement new products; (6) funds for learning about and purchasing new products; and (7) absence of community antagonism. The R&D products which serve as innovations may vary in complexity, but they seldom tend to be simple. Fidelity of implementation or routine use is the major concern of the RDD model. Products are field-tested to overcome potential implementation difficulties. However, the RDD model places responsibility for accurate replication of R&D products in the user organization. Figure 1.4 depicts the RDD model in terms of the three dimensions of change.

Linkage Model

The most recent and probably most popular change model in education today is labeled generically the linkage model. An early proponent

FIGURE 1.4
RESEARCH, DEVELOPMENT, DIFFUSION MODEL IN TERMS OF THE THREE DIMENSIONS OF CHANGE

PROCESSES	INFLUENCES	EFFECTS
ACTIVITIES	*ENDOGENOUS*	*LEVELS OF USE*
Examples:	Examples:	Examples:
Conveying information about new R&D products and providing technical assistance to adopters	Norms for using R&D products, leadership supportive of R&D products, staff sees R&D products and developers as legitimate, staff open to new approaches based on scientific knowledge.	Information seeking is followed by preparation for use and then mechanical use.
MODE	*EXOGENOUS*	
Examples:	Examples:	
One-Way communication for conveying R&D product information and one-way communication for providing technical assistance	Time to initiate search for new R&D product information, funds to purchase reports and new products, and community which does not threaten to prevent outside influence	
FREQUENCY	*INNOVATION*	
Examples:	Examples:	
Irregular frequency of conveying information and providing technical assistance. Usually activities are initiated when new products are developed or when funds are provided.	Staff perceives R&D products as superior to existing practice (relative advantage), compatible with current programs, and not so complex as to be impossible to implement	

Change Processes 25

and user of the term linkage in education was Bhola (1965). He advocated a configurational theory of change in which potential adopters of innovations were linked through patterns of communication or interaction with sources responsible for the innovations. More recently the work of Havelock (1969, 1973) is widely viewed as responsible for raising educators' level of awareness about linkage as a process of change.

The emphasis of the linkage model is on the establishment of communication networks between sources of innovations and users via an intermediary facilitating role either in the form of a linkage agent or a linkage agency. Aspects of the former three change models (problem-solving, social interaction, and research-development-diffusion) are incorporated in Havelock's conceptualization of linkage. For example, the needs of users should be sensed by the intermediary agent—an aspect of the problem-solving model; communication patterns should be established — an aspect of the social interaction model; new knowledge and innovations should be transmitted from their source to potential users — an aspect of the RDD model[5]

There is no single model of linkage. However, a recent conceptualization and empirical tests of a promising dissemination and utilization linkage model have been completed by Havelock and Lingwood (1973), Lingwood and Morris, (1976), and Paul (1975). There are five indices which comprise the model:

(1) User Problem Solving and Helping

Focus on helping user groups develop capacity to solve problems and on identifying users to help in dissemination and implementation activities

(2) Need Sensing

Focus on developing mechanisms for regularly determining user needs and for transforming needs into problem statements

(3) Client-Centered Solution Building

Focus on doing research which is directly applicable to users and for exploring problems at the time they are critical for users.

---

[5]Cf. Ronald E. Hull (1974) for an amalgamated view of the RDD and linkage models.

(4) Solution Processing Channels

Focus on producing summaries of research, rewriting findings into language users understand, identifying important users for specific findings, and selecting appropriate channels to reach users.

(5) Micro-System Building

Focus on establishing structures so that users and researchers can work together on joint projects and exchange information.

The model is depicted in Figure 1.5. It begins with user problem-solving and helping on the left and moves clockwise with micro-system building in the middle.

The emphasis of the model is on linking those organizations which can use new research and products of research with those organizations which can provide new research and products of research. In terms of the three dimensions of the general scheme the linkage model includes helping users identify problems and training users for independent problem-solving. Conveying research findings and products is also used, however, and face-to-face contact on a regular basis between users, linking agents, researchers, and developers is supported administratively and organizationally. Written materials are provided in a language understandable to users. The frequency of interaction is sufficiently high so that trust can be established on one hand, but not so high that the parties involved feel unnecessarily burdened on the other. Examples of some major influences are: (1) incompatible language, values and reward systems that separate researchers, linkers, and users; (2) weak institutional support, security, and recognition for linking agents; (3) substantial imbalance between number of users and number of linkers; (4) demand on linkage agents to process both research, subject matter, and change process competencies; (5) organizational structures and administrative arrangements which limit involvement of linkage agents and which limit time for user/linkage agent interaction; (6) no formal training and/or legitimizing of linkage agents; and (7) geographical limitations on the extent of researcher/linkage agent/user interaction.

Innovations are viewed in terms of users' needs and may vary from complex capacity-building programs to providing up-to-date information. The intended effect of the linkage process of change is toward a higher level of use, i.e., refinement of innovation and subsequent renewal of the user organization. An established and regularly operating mechanism for communicating needs and for learning of new ideas can also be an impor-

28 Douglas A. Paul

FIGURE 1.5
DISSEMINATION AND UTILIZATION LINKAGE MODEL

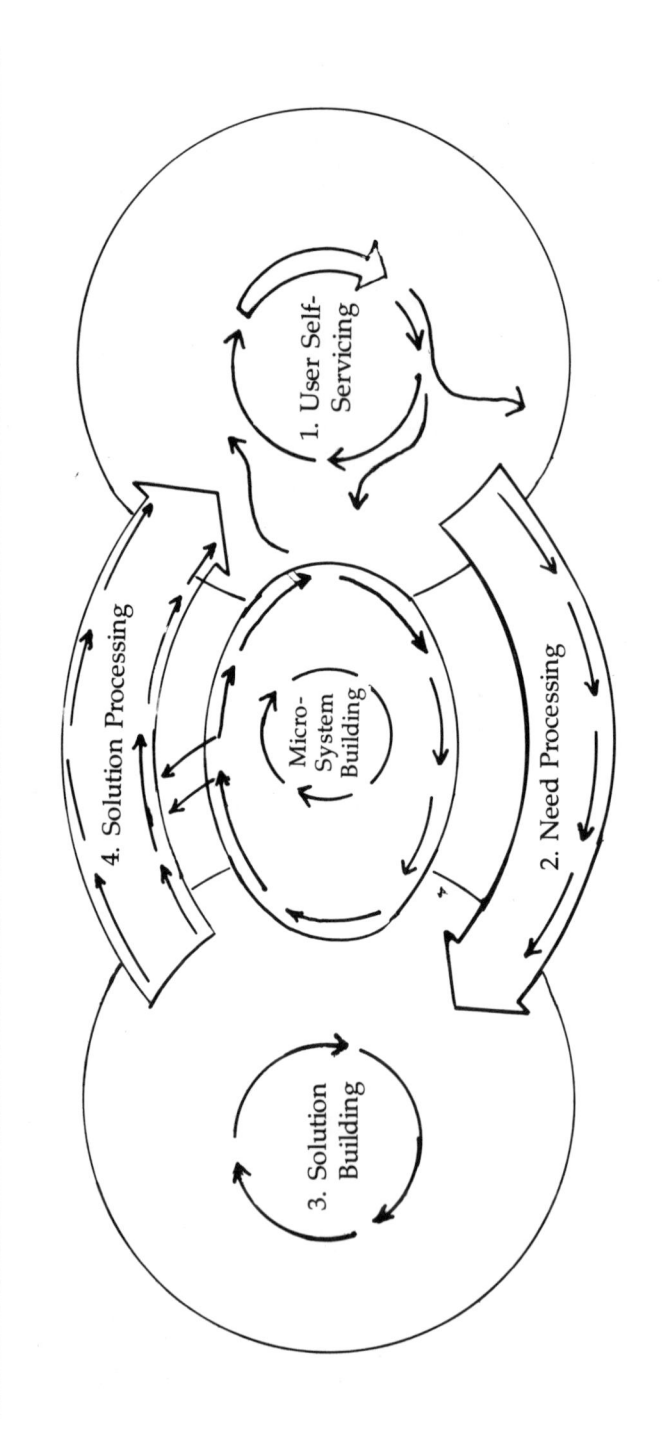

Reprinted from R. G. Havelock and D. Lingwood, *R&D Utilization Strategies and Functions: An Analytical Comparison of Four Systems*. Ann Arbor, Michigan: Institute for Social Research, Center for Research on Utilization of Scientific Knowledge, 1969.

tant linkage effect. Figure 1.6 depicts the linkage model in terms of the three change dimensions.

The Havelock and Lingwood (1973) study which resulted in this conceptualization of linkage focused on the dissemination and research utilization activities of four government agencies including the National Center for Educational Communication. The dissemination and utilization indices (user problem-solving, need sensing, client-centered solution building, solution processing, and micro-system building) were related to such factors as the resource system's organizational support for linkage, researchers' opportunity to work on user problems, and importance of local problems. Organizational leadership supporting dissemination and utilization functions was found to be important as was the importance of adequate opportunities to work on user problems.

These findings were reinforced by a latter study of the research utilization practices of the U.S. Forest Service (Lingwood and Morris, 1976). Replication of the dissemination and utilization indices and modifying factors was applied to an educational research, development, and teaching institution, and similar findings emerged (Paul, 1975). For example, organizational leadership supporting dissemination and utilization activities was stressed as being critical, and the linkage between field agents and faculty and field agents and clients usually depended on idiosyncratic factors, frequent face-to-face interaction, compatible values, mutual respect, and mutual benefit.

There are numerous adaptations and refinements of the basic linkage agent. Two examples are the Concerns Based Adoption Model (CBAM) developed at the Texas R&D Center for Teacher Education (Hall, 1974) and the political linkage model proposed by Lindquist (1974). The CBA model was developed to represent the "dynamic and intertwined process" of change. Underlying the model is collaborative linkage between the user and resource system, and this linkage is based on a mutual openness in communication and mutual benefit from the collaborative association. Linking or adoption agents help the user system implement innovations by assessing the readiness and capability of the user, and based on this assessment, help is provided in contrast to an externally prepared timetable of implementation activities. Interventions are then developed from user needs and are related to the Level of Use (LoU) introduced earlier.

The political linkage model proposed by Lindquist has drawn attention to the governance system in higher education institutions. Since obstacles to academic innovation are great, and academic motivation to change is low, three strategies have been postulated: (1) Increase research and development of academic innovations, (2) strengthen linkages between different individuals on campus as well as between power centers

FIGURE 1.6
LINKAGE MODEL IN TERMS OF THE THREE DIMENSIONS OF CHANGE

PROCESSES	INFLUENCES	EFFECTS
ACTIVITIES Examples: Establishing a cooperative and mutually beneficial collaborative relationship between sources of help and of ideas and users	**ENDOGENOUS** Examples: Norms for involving outside resources, Leadership supportive of R&D utilization, staff perceive facilitators and R&D ideas as legitimate, staff are cooperative and open to new ideas.	**LEVELS OF USE** Examples: Information seeking is entwined with collaboration. Preparation for use and routine use are intermediate steps to integrated use and renewal activities.
MODE Examples: Two-Way communication for establishing trust, learning about needs, and adopting solutions.	**EXOGENOUS** Examples: Time to initiate collaborative relations and establish trust, funds to provide release time, and a community which does not prevent using ideas from outside sources	**INNOVATION** Examples: Staff perceive high relative advantage and compatability. Complexity varies according to confidence of staff. Linkage itself may be seen as an innovation leading to other innovations.
FREQUENCY Examples: A mutually determined frequency of interaction by resource and user staff is supportive of collaborative effort		

and innovation diffusion channels, and (3) develop collaborative problem-solving practices which focus on need for change, for diffusion channels, and for identification of those who can sanction and implement change. These strategies should result in an academic self-renewal program, expensive in terms of time and energy but without which little change in higher education is likely to occur.

SUMMARY

These four models of change represent four different approaches for improving existing school practices, eliminating ineffective practices, and adopting new practices. They are based on different assumptions about what it required to bring about change. These assumptions are reviewed and a new, somewhat controversial view of change, is introduced in the following paragraphs.

One approach for comparing the four models of change was to describe them in terms of the three dimensions of change. However, another approach is classifying them in terms of the three strategies for changing proposed by Chin and Benne (1968). The three strategies are described as follows:

Empirical-Rational Strategy: Assumes men and women are rational and that they will make rational decisions. Changes are adopted if they can be justified rationally and if they are shown to be in one's best interest.

Normative-Re-educative Strategy: Assumes men and women are heavily influenced by and committed to socio-cultural norms. Men and women hold attitudes and values supportive of these norms and have commitments to them. Change in practice comes about when people change their socio-cultural norms and thereby change their attitudes and values which supported the old norms.

Power-Coercive Strategy: Assumes men and women will comply with those with more power and thereby change. The power may be legitimate and represent formal authority, e.g., laws and policies. Conversely, the power may be coercive regardless of perceptions of its legitimacy.

These three strategies have been turned into three images of practitioners that designers or initiators of change hold implicitly (Sieber, 1972). These images are the rational man, the cooperator, and the powerless functionary. If an empirical-rational strategy is undertaken, then its initiators assume that practitioners are rational. If a normative-re-educative strategy is begun then practitioners are considered to be cooperators. A power-coercive strategy assumes that practitioners act as powerless functionaries. The four models of change are summarized in terms of the following three assumptions.

The problem-solving model assumes that practitioners need considerable support, help, and training to overcome established norms unsupportive of self-renewal and capacity building orientation. A normative-re-educative strategy and a view of the practitioner as a cooperator underlies the problem-solving model. The rationality of practitioners is necessary, but it is not as critical as their attitudes and values. Practitioners are clearly not viewed as powerless functionaries.

The social interaction model assumes that practitioners need information and persuasion in order to evaluate the change and to overcome resistance to change. Using information reflects an empirical-rational strategy and using persuasion reflects a normative-re-educative strategy. The practitioner is assumed to be rational and cooperative — rational because new information about better practices is being disseminated to him/her with the expectation that it will arouse interest and search activities, cooperative because opinion leaders and/or field agents will approach the practitioner to persuade, influence, and convince him/her about the need, advantages, and effectiveness of the change. But also there is an implicit assumption that extensive marketing will result inevitably in adoptions of new products regardless of need. In a sense this represents a view of practitioners as powerless functionaries at the mercy of advertisers, salespersons, and opinion leaders.

The research, development, and diffusion model assumes that practitioners need sound information and knowledge about new practices and R&D based products. An empirical-rational strategy is used whereby R&D information and products are made available to practitioners. It is assumed that practitioners are rational and, therefore, presentation of new information will set off a chain of logical reasoning, the result of which is a decision to adopt a new research-based product. The information may originate from preparation programs, journals, or ERIC, for example. To achieve efficiency, initiators of this approach may rely on federal or state legislation and/or rules and regulations to bring about

FIGURE 1.7
MODELS OF CHANGE IN TERMS OF CHANGE STRATEGIES AND ASSUMPTIONS ABOUT PRACTITIONERS

Models of Change	Empirical-Rational Strategy *Practitioner viewed as Rational*	Normative-Re-Educative Strategy *Practitioner viewed as Cooperative*	Power-Coercive Strategy *Practitioner viewed as Powerless*
Problem-Solving	**Moderate** e.g.: analysis of needs and selection of best solution are rational approaches	**High** e.g.: establishing user groups to identify problems and build solutions is a cooperative approach	**Low** e.g.: enforcing laws, rules, and administrative policies are seen as detrimental to the development of self-sufficient problem-solving
Social Interaction	**High** e.g.: evaluating compatability and relative advantage of innovations are rational approaches	**Moderate** e.g.: being open to the marketing of new products and being willing to be persuaded to use them reflects a cooperative approach	**Moderate** e.g.: being influenced by peers to adopt innovations and being bombarded by advertisements renders the user with little will power to defend against unneeded innovations
Research, Development, Diffusion	**High** e.g.: implementing R&D products based on their superiority to present conditions is a rational approach	**Low** e.g.: being concerned with needs and dispositions of users is viewed as unnecessary and/or inappropriate	**High** e.g.: adoption of textbooks by legislative enactments, passing laws, and expecting top-down flow of change all assume little power on the part of the user to respond or prevent
Linkage	**Moderate** e.g.: instituting collaborative arrangements between R&D community and practitioners is a rational approach	**High** e.g.: establishing collaborative relationships is based on a cooperative view of both the R&D and practice communities since the collaborative effort should be mutually satisfying	**Low** e.g.: enacting laws is seen as counter-productive to the establishment of trust and mutually satisfying and beneficial relations

change. Laws and regulations reflect a power-coercive strategy and imply that practitioners are powerless. However, the goal of the RDD approach is the narrowing of the gap between the discovery of new ideas and their uses. Sometimes narrowing the gap may be achieved more quickly by passing new legislation, but acceptance of laws and regulations need not imply powerlessness on the part of practitioners but rather acquiescence to a belief in an expeditious approach to change.

The linkage model assumes that practitioners live within a user system comprised of socio-cultural norms which are different from the system involved with creating and developing new techniques and practices. Interaction between these two incompatible systems is achieved through a collaborative, reflective, and sensitive linkage relationship. This approach reflects a normative-re-educative strategy, since the practitioner and researcher are assumed to be cooperative parties in the linkage relationship. The linking agent spanning the boundaries of the two systems may use normative-re-educative or empirical-rational strategies to bring about closer collaboration. It is unlikely that power-coercive strategies could be used since the linking agent — and most linking agents — lack formal authority or power. Figure 1.7 depicts the four models of change and the three strategies and concomitant views of practitioners.

Figure 1.7 permits a comparison of the models of change and fulfills an heuristic function. The results of the comparison point to a strategy of change which is frequently ignored by researchers: the power-coercive. Except for the occasional moderate use of power-coercive strategies based on the RDD model and the implicit use found in the Social Interaction model, the models ignore power as a mechanism for change. However, change in education has frequently been brought about through power-coercive strategies. School integration is one notable example; others include legal decisions involving teacher unions, students rights, and due process. The community control movement of the late 1960s (e.g., Ocean Hill-Brownsville) and recent citizen reluctance and, in some cases, refusal to pass school budgets are additional examples. One reason for the lack of attention given the power-coercive strategy may be the rational academic bias of model developers on one hand and on the other the persistent belief that educational decisions are not political. Regardless of the reasons for ignoring power-coercive strategies, the fact remains that such strategies are among the most effective and powerful in education today.

This section of the review of change processes will close with a recent and provocative view of knowledge production and utilization called the configurational view by its developers Clark and Guba (1974). The configurational view is aimed at reorienting educational policy from empirical-rational strategy (termed the system view) to a transactional collegial-

TABLE 1.2
EMPHASES DISTINGUISHING THE CONFIGURATIONAL VIEW FROM THE SYSTEMS VIEW

Factors	Systems View	Configurational View
1. Structure	Centralized	Decentralized
2. Functions	Linked, sequential	Independent, disconnected
3. Roles	Discrete	Overlapping
4. Agency status	Hierarchical	Co-equal
5. Goal orientation	Known, shared	Emergent, idiosyncratic
6. KPU orientation	Primary	Peripheral
7. Authority-Responsibility	Delegated	Negotiated
8. Motivation	Extrinsic	Intrinsic
9. Institutional behavior	Nomothetic	Transactional
10. Interaction	Synergistic, permanent	Symbiotic, temporary

Reprinted from E. Guba and D. Clark, *The Configurational Perspective: A Challenge to the Systems Field of Educational Knowledge Production and Utilization.* Washington, D.C. Council for Educational Development and Research, December, 1974.

based strategy (termed the configurational view). The architects for the configurational view contend that most educational institutions are not primarily concerned with the production and utilization of knowledge (KPU). In fact, KPU is an often ignored peripheral concern. They go on to suggest that disappointment with many of the "Great Society" programs of the 1960s is due, in part, to the centralized, hierarchical, extrinsically based nature of the programs. These and more descriptors of the systems and configurational view are listed in Table 1.2.

The implications of the configurational view have yet to be adequately identified and discussed. This new view of change has been briefly introduced in the hope that it will stimulate discussions about the implications it holds for federal policy in the area of knowledge production and utilization.

In this section a foundation was constructed for the generalizations and inferences about to be presented in Section II. Previous reviews of change literature were presented in order to establish a broad perspective concerning research in this area. Three dimensions of change emanating from previous research and from the empirical studies cited in Section II were proposed. The dimensions provide a succinct means for classifying the wide variety of research on change, and they fulfill an heuristic function by suggesting overlooked issues and relationships. The four models of change were described and compared using the three dimensions. Studies associated with the models were cited, and a summary of the models was attempted by using conceptualizations about change strategies and images of practitioners.

SECTION II

INTRODUCTION

In this section over 100 empirical studies completed since 1970 have been analyzed in order to provide the basis for a series of generalizations and inferences about change. These generalizations and inferences do not distinguish between elementary, secondary, and post-secondary levels in education. However, studies dealing exclusively with the post-secondary level are summarized in Appendix B where a rationale for considering the differences between institutional levels as a matter of degree rather than substance is also presented.

The studies summarized here were identified according to key words in their titles[6] or according to references in the change literature. Studies published before 1970 were eliminated because of the many fine reviews covering earlier periods. An extensive search for empirical studies revealed that the vast majority of this work on educational change is being done at the doctoral level in departments of educational administration, curriculum, and general education. In addition, sponsored government research has been conducted by private firms such as Rand Corporation and Abt Associates; selected educational laboratories and R&D Centers have published studies on change in education.

The studies were reviewed and their major findings summarized. Those factors which received considerable attention by researchers formed the basis for a grouping of findings. The groupings fell into three broad dimensions: processes, influences, and effects. Within the process dimension three categories were used to subdivide the findings: (1) *activities*, such actions as helping, training, or conveying, (2) *mode*, the means of communication such as face-to-face, one-way, or two-way, and (3) *frequency*, the amount of interaction between change facilitators and the target system.

Within the influence dimension three categories divided the findings: (1) factors internal to the organization (administrative practices, structure, staff attitudes, staff personality), (2) factors external to the organization

---

[6]Keywords were: change (-s, -ing), diffusion, dissemination, implementation, innovation, link (-age, -ing), organization (-al).

(time, funds, and community), and (3) factors associated with innovations (their complexity, compatibility, and relative advantage).

The summary and grouping of findings did not produce subcategories for the dimension of effects. Most studies treated effects as a dependent variable with little differentiation among possible levels of use.

Most of the studies focused on attempts to use an innovation, the factors which hindered or helped the use of an innovation or the dissemination of information. For the most part, the remaining studies focused on facilitating activities for encouraging and helping schools and teachers learn about or use innovations. A wide range of institutions and institutional levels was represented: elementary, secondary, post-secondary institutions, school district, R&D centers, and state education agencies. In addition, interorganizational arrangements between institutions were studied in a number of cases.

Generalizations and inferences were drawn from the studies; if the generalization or inference is strongly supported by a number of studies, then it may be considered "firm," "moderately speculative," or "speculative" in that order. These judgments accompany each generalization. Immediately following the generalization or inference, a rationale and citations supporting it are given.

GENERALIZATIONS AND INFERENCES

Process Dimension

> External Change Agents May Bring About Greater Awareness of Innovations and Change, But They Must Overcome Resistance. [*Firm*]

External change agents may stimulate, collect, and provide sufficient human and technical resources to facilitate the adoption of innovations. Because teachers have few linkages with outside groups, the external change agent can be an important source of information. In this role the external agent acts as conveyor of information. However, the agent must overcome either covert or overt resistance. For example, covert resistance may take the form of ignoring offers for help, a situation which may be countered by repeating and infusing the target with messages. Overt resistance may take the form of sabotoging new programs and diluting the efforts of outside agents. Without sufficient legitimacy in both terms of political power and programmatic need, there is little that the external agent can do to combat widespread over resistance.

Support: Corwin, 1972; Keller, 1974; Kiser, 1973; Naumann-Etienne, 1974; O'Connell, 1971; Richardson, 1974; Wyner, 1974.

> The Perceived Legitimacy of Change Agents Is a Major Influence On the Effectiveness of Entry Into the Target System and Working With Staff In the System. [*Firm*]

The question of legitimacy concerns change agents located inside or outside a system, and it also includes sources of information. For example, central office staff may be seen as legitimate change agents by some teachers but not by others. Faculty from teacher education institutions may be seen as legitimate sources of on-site assistance or as meddlers trespassing on school grounds. Superintendents in one state may perceive the state education agency (SEA) as a legitimate and primary source of new ideas, whereas superintendents in another state may perceive the SEA as a source secondary in legitimacy to their own district. Superintendents tend to rate professors as more credible sources of information than fellow superintendents or professional associations. The question of legitimacy helps to explain why teachers seem to work well with other teachers, viz., mutual legitimacy and concomitant credibility, trust, and shared values.

Support: Baron, 1972; Bowens, 1975; Farag, 1970; Hartgraves, 1973; Korba, 1975; McCoy, 1975; McKeique, 1976; Paul, 1974; Prafad, 1971; Stephens, 1975; Trent, 1976; True, 1974; Tushingham, 1974; Weigle, 1975.

> When Outside Agents Advocate a Particular Innovation, Their Legitimacy Decreases. [*Moderately Speculative*]

If change agents are identified with a solution to a problem prior to entering the user system, then legitimacy, credibility, and trust with the user will be delayed or even precluded. The user system may believe its problems to be unique enough to deserve a customized solution, and it also may be suspicious of outside agents entering the system with ready-made solutions before the agents are aware of the needs, concerns, and characteristics of the system. As trust and legitimacy develop, then ready-made solutions and innovations may be needed and introduced.

Support: Sieber et al., 1972.

> Teachers Work Best With and Rely Most On Fellow Teachers in Information Sharing and Collaboration For Change. [*Firm*]

It appears that teacher collaboration for change can be effective. However, group composition is a critical issue, that is, a mix of teachers and administrators or outside consultants may create tension and suspicion among teachers. Fellow teachers have more credibility and are able to elicit greater trust and reduce discomfort.

Support: Carr, 1974; Goodridge, 1975; Herring, 1973; Keenan, 1975; Perry, 1975; Sieber, 1972.

> However, Hierarchical Support May Be Critical. [*Moderately Firm*]

Although teachers work well with fellow teachers, their efforts may prove insufficient unless hierarchical support is provided. In other words, formal authority may be needed to legitimize teacher efforts, to provide resources, and to furnish necessary coordinating activities.

Support: Berger, 1973; Pitman, 1974.

> Teachers May Be Reluctant To Get Involved With Linking Agents Unless There Are Direct and Concrete Benefits. [*Moderately Speculative*]

Since teachers have little extra time or spare energy, they are reluctant to take on commitments which involve additional demands on their time, or on their physical or psychological energy. However, student teachers represent concrete benefits which may result in teacher release time and sharing of the workload. Consequently, faculty who act as linking agents and who also have student teachers are in a better position to gain teacher support, interest, and cooperation than linking agents without comparable benefits.

Support: Paul, 1974; Phelps, 1974.

> Teachers Will Tend To Rely On Their Own Experience For Curriculum Ideas Rather Than Use Curriculum Guides Prepared by Central Administrative Staff, Ideas from Principals, or Ideas from University Courses. [*Moderately Firm*]

> Conversely, Facilitating Activities Promote, Encourage,

and Stimulate Teacher Use of Curriculum Ideas and Information Developed or Furnished Outside of the Teachers' Classroom. [*Moderately Firm*]

Producing and providing information and curriculum guides are not sufficient for assuring their use. To influence positively the amount and extent of use of new knowledge, one must engage in facilitating activities. These activities range from providing sufficient amounts of help in using new curriculum guides, fashioning new information so that it is accessible, interpretable, and understandable, to training teachers, providing encouragement, and stimulating confidence. The need for facilitating activities is based in part on built-in resistance users have to new curricula and information, based on their need to protect themselves from information overload, to protect their limited time and energy, and to protect themselves from difficult, esoteric, or unworthy techniques.

Support: Havelock and Lingwood, 1973; Keenan, 1975; Louis, 1975; Poll, 1970; Sieber et al., 1972.

Training Activities, If Properly Applied, Increase the Likelihood of Successful Implementation and Continuation of New Programs. [*Moderately Firm*]

Properly applied training activities explicitly deal with such issues as new roles and functions stemming from an innovation, detailed procedures and specific techniques associated with a particular innovation as opposed to general principles, and entire staff involvement in training as opposed to partial involvement.

Support: Bassi, 1974; Clark, 1974; Gross et al., 1971; Hunt, 1975; Robeson, 1974; Vance, 1974.

Face-To-Face Interaction and Two-Way Communication Are a Most Effective Mode of Conveying Information. [*Moderately Firm*]

Face-to-face interaction allows mutual needs to be determined, messages to be adjusted according to reactions, and mutual influence to occur. These are characteristics of two-way communication, and they are absent from alternative modes of communication such as print media. Encouragement and support may be stimulated and nurtured through face-to-face interaction. This may be especially important at initial stages of change where resistance may be high and confidence low. Because it allows users to evaluate senders of information on one hand and it allows senders to demonstrate nonadvocacy of specific innovations on the other, face-to-face interaction also helps to develop legitimacy.

Support: Brown, 1974; Ebner, 1973; Hood, 1973; Keenan, 1975; Paul, 1974; Sieber, 1972; Vold, 1975.

A Mutually Agreed Frequency of Face-To-Face Interaction Will Help To Optimize the Effectiveness of Helping Training, or Conveying Activities. [*Moderately Speculative*]

Agreement over the frequency of interaction depends on the needs and status of both parties. For example, staff from a school need and want daily help for a semester with implementing an innovation, but facilitators have only one day a week to provide help. A year later the status of the school has changed. Now they only need and want help one day a week. In another instance, the staff or principal of a school may feel invaded if the frequency of interaction from facilitators is too great vis-à-vis the school's status or needs. In other words, the school (1) may not be ready or prepared to accept frequent help even though it may need it, (2) is ready to accept frequent help, but does not need it, or (3) is ready only to accept a lower frequency of help even though it needs more help.

Each Individual School Has Its Own Optimal Frequency of Interaction Curve Which Varies Frequently.[*Speculative*]

FIGURE 1.8
CURVILINEAR RELATIONSHIP BETWEEN
INTERACTION AND FREQUENCY FOR SCHOOL A

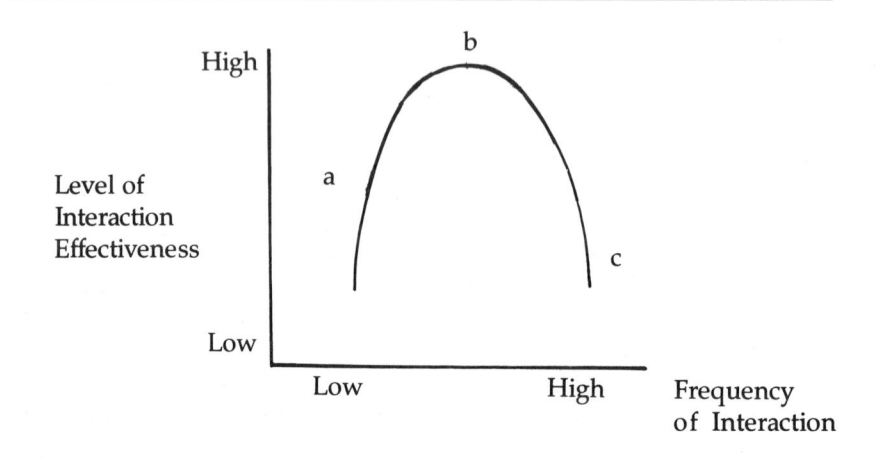

The curvilinear relationship between the frequency of interaction and the effectiveness of the interaction is partly a function of the status and needs of a school which vary over time and from school to school. An individual profile showing the optimal frequency of interaction reflects the status and needs of school A for a specific point in time as shown in Figure 1.8 which represents a hypothetical school. At point "a" there is not enough interaction with linkage agents, at point "b" there is an optimum amount, and at point "c" there is too much interaction. However, prior to the initiation of outside facilitative relationships, some schools may have established norms for problem-solving. The status of these schools is different from schools without these norms, and the two different schools should be treated differently. Figure 1.9 represents the frequency of interaction with a hypothetical school B that has pre-established norms for problem-solving. The status of these schools is different from schools without these norms, and the two different schools should be treated differently. Figure 1.9 represents the frequency of interaction with a hypothetical school B that has pre-established norms for problem-solving. In this hypothetical school at point "a" there is a fairly high level of effectiveness even though the frequency of interaction is low, because the school is already solving problems. At point "b" an optimum level of interactions is reached much earlier than in the previous hypothetical school because the second school was capable of using help earlier. At point "c" the school is beginning to suffer from too much help.

FIGURE 1.9
RELATIONSHIP BETWEEN INTERACTION AND
FREQUENCY FOR SCHOOL B

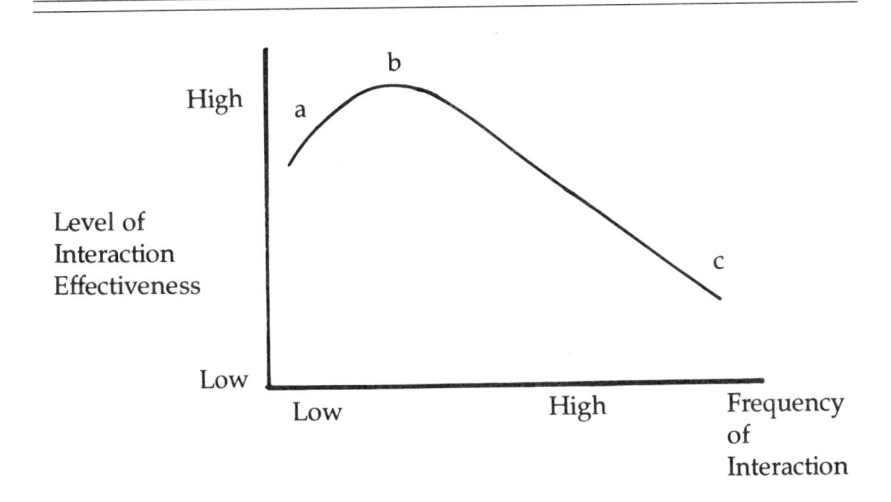

What is too much interaction for one school may be optimal for another school. And what is too little interaction one year may be too much interaction another year. Sensitivity to the frequency of interaction is called for on the part of linkage agents and principals and teachers.

Support: McKeigue, 1976; Paul 1974; Tushingham, 1974; Wyner, 1974.

Influence Dimension: Internal and External Organization

Factors and Characteristics of Innovations

> An Open Organizational Climate May Facilitate the Introduction and Use of an Innovation, But It Does Not Assure Introduction and Use. [Firm]

The organizational climate of schools, commonly measured by the Organizational Climate Descriptive Questionnaire (OCDQ) developed by Halpin and Croft (1963), is one of many factors which influence the degree and extent of change. Taken alone, it is not a sufficient explanation of the variance in the extent of change. Merely supporting the notion of an open climate is not enough to bring about the capacity to initiate and carry through school improvement programs.

Support: Behrmann, 1975; Berman et al., 1975; Brown, 1975; Cahoon, 1974; Christian, 1972; David, 1975; Gridley, 1975; Jarman, 1974; Montgomery, 1975; Rasmussen, 1975; Trent, 1975; Swirsky, 1975.

> Involvement and Participation In The Decision-Making Process By Those Affected By A Change Program Will Be Beneficial. [Firm]

Involvement, participation, and decentralization influence the success of change efforts. Involvement and participation are usually the result of decentralized organizational structure, i.e., decision-making authority is more diffuse than in a centralized structure. Widespread participation of staff at the early stages of a change program will help to create commitment to and identification with a change effort. In addition, extensive involvement provides opportunities for program planners to assess the extent to which school needs, as perceived by staff, are addressed by the change. On the other hand, widespread participation and a decentralized structure may inhibit coordination and control which are necessary for the implementation of new programs. In other words, a loose organizational arrangement may facilitate awareness of needs and commitment to change, but a tight organizational arrangement may be needed to implement the change. This notion is discussed more fully by Zaltman et al., (1973) and Duncan (1976).

Support: Bowers, 1975; Kane, 1976; Michaletz, 1974; Reynolds, 1971; Skor, 1974; Sullivan, 1974.

> Leadership For Change Is Important, But It Is Not Sufficient To Counteract All Barriers To Change. [*Moderately Firm*]

Most principals probably see themselves as change agents — among their other roles. However, leadership for change is often found to be missing. There are organizational conditions which influence the effectiveness of leadership, for example, norms for problem-solving and clarity of project goals. Leadership which promotes, supports, and shows concern for participation during the change process will influence the level of satisfaction among the staff, a situation which in turn results in positive reactions toward the change.

Support: Berman et al., 1975; Cahoon, 1974; Havelock and Lingwood, 1973; Jones, 1973; Miller, 1973; Paul, 1975; Smith, 1972; Starling, 1973.

> Increased Vertical And Horizontal Communication Facilitates Change. [*Moderately Firm*]

Increased communication at the early stages of a change effort can result in greater awareness of the program, more frequent and open discussions of needs and solutions, and greater commitment to change. At later stages of the change process, increased horizontal communication can allow staff to better coordinate among themselves, to learn from each other, and to provide psychological support to each other. Increased vertical communication can result in feedback being sent to change program coordinators and designers who in turn can assess the status of the program and make necessary adjustments.

Support: Edwards, 1973; Howes, 1974; Roberts, 1975.

> Linkages Between Organizations Such As Schools and Colleges Should Be Accompanied by Extensive Communication And Flexible Arrangements. [*Moderately Firm*]

Without extensive communication, parties to interorganizational arrangements may become disinterested in the program or suspicious. Suspicions may arise from speculation that one party to the program will behave in its own self-interest at the expense of others. Extensive communication may also limit the substitution of personal goals and objectives for cooperative organizational goals.

Support: Florio, 1973; Pohland, .970; Winkelpleck, 1974.

> Recognition of School Needs and Congruence Of the Change Program With the Needs Facilitates Change. [*Moderately Firm*]

Recognition that solvable problems exist is a first step toward successful change and school improvement. The solution or innovation should address the needs that have been recognized, and conversely, if teachers do not perceive the need for a particular innovation then its implementation is doubtful.

Support: Kane, 1976; True, 1974; Vance, 1974.

> Experience In Past Change Programs and Expectations For Future Programs Influences the Change Process. [*Moderately Firm*]

Past experience in federally funded change programs provides opportunities for learning about the preparation of plans and proposals, the requirements for reporting progress, and the techniques for evaluating program success. In addition, positive expectations for future change and innovation contribute toward successful programs.

Support: Daft, 1974; Kane, 1976; Whiting, 1972.

> Accurate Perceptions and Expectations Which Are Mutually Agreeable Between Organizational Levels (Intra-Organizational) and between Organizations (Interorganizational) Facilitate Change. [*Moderately Firm*]

Lack of agreement among groups involved in change efforts results in misunderstanding, frustration, and conflict. For example, disagreements over barriers to change or the extent of change have been documented among principals, teachers, central office staff, and external groups. Such widespread disagreement and conflicting expectations are themselves barriers to change.

Conflicting expectations between organizations involved in a change program are also serious, as the more organizations involved, the greater the likelihood that misperceptions will develop. Misperceptions in turn can lead to dissatisfaction with the interorganizational effort and a corresponding lowering of expectations for the program, and weakening of coordination and cooperation.

Agreement over expectations for change programs and understanding of concerns facing the various staff groups of the various organizations involved can be facilitated. For example, greater frequency of communication, recognition of different goals or shared goals, and resources which are complementary rather than competitive are three factors which influence intra- and interorganizational agreement and cooperation.

Support: Abraham, 1974; Blumenkrantz, 1975; Chapey, 1975; Evans, 1973; Paul, 1974; Schumacher, 1975.

> Positive Attitudes Toward Change Facilitate the Change Process. [*Moderately Firm*]
>
> Positive Commitment Toward Change Facilitates the Change Process. [*Moderately Firm*]

Attitudes and commitment toward change in general and specific innovations in particular influence the change process. In addition attitudes are themselves subject to influence. For example, attitudes of principals toward change are influenced by the attitudes of superintendents. However, positive attitudes or commitment are not sufficient in themselves to bring about a successful change effort, but widespread negative attitudes or lack of commitment toward change or a specific innovation might be sufficient to prevent successful implementation.

Support: Bettas, 1974; Brantley, 1975; Edwards, 1973; Gridley, 1975; Kendall, 1973; Loffredo, 1974; Newman, 1975; Peterson, 1974; Richardson, 1974; Roberts, 1974; Roberts, 1975; Sutter, 1974; Washington, 1974.

> The Orientation Of Staff Will Influence the Change Process. A Systemwide or an Organizational Orientation Will Have a Positive Impact, Whereas a Classroom or Self-Centered Orientation Will Have a Negative Impact. [*Moderately Speculative*]

An organizational orientation encompasses concern with performance of an entire school or district, collaboration with other professionals for school improvement, and the improvement of individual expertise to help with improvement efforts. The orientation of staff may change over time; for example, at early stages of change staff may demonstrate

48   Douglas A. Paul

self-centeredness and an egocentric orientation. But as the staff becomes comfortable with and knowledgeable about the change, then concern may shift toward organizational issues (see Hall's Concern Based Adoption Model, 1974). This shift may be difficult to bring about because of the nature of schools and the expectations of teachers. Teacher autonomy, lack of interdependence among teachers, vague educational goals, and satisfaction based on student rather than adult contact act together to promote a classroom-centered orientation.

Sieber's (1968) analysis which found schools to be isolated units with rewards for teachers derived from classroom activities reinforces the idea that staff orientation influences change. Words such as isolated, alienated, and lonely are used to describe teachers (Schmuck and Miles, 1971), and the role of teaching is characterized as being carried out invisibly with minimal differentiation according to teacher ability or integration of common functions (Miles, 1967).

An organizational orientation implies that staff are concerned with the school as a whole, interact with colleagues on schoolwide problems, and strive for integration and differentiation of roles in order to bring about school improvement. Rewards are centered on schoolwide activities and peer assessment rather than classroom activities and student reactions.

Support: Carr, 1974; Keenan, 1975; Knopke, 1975; Magee, 1975.

>   Personality Characteristics Influence Change Processes:
>   Open Mindedness and Experimenting Personality Types
>   Have a Positive Influence On Change. [*Moderately Firm*]

Although personality characteristics are difficult to define and measure, they appear to influence the change process in some—but not all—instances. In all likelihood the extent of influence is mediated by other factors such as role status and administrative practices. Examples of personality characteristics positively associated with change include venturesome, imaginative, creative, experimenting, accommodating, less anxious, openminded, concern with societal well-being, less dogmatic, and less conservative.

Support: David, 1975; Hansen, 1975; Hodgkinson, 1974; Swirsky, 1975; Townely, 1973. (See also Rogers and Shoemaker, 1971).

>   The Availability Of Time To Plan and Implement School
>   Improvements Influences the Change Process. [*Moderately Firm*]

Time is money, and in education approximately eighty percent of the school budget is for personnel costs. Therefore, time, money, and personnel are entwined. To assert that change activities take time to prepare, initiate, and complete is also to conclude that funds are necessary to purchase teacher release time. Conversely, the lack of adequate time to learn about new techniques, to discuss implementation problems, and to assess and revise innovative programs is a major barrier to successful change. Organizations with stable resources are able to provide time for personnel to devote to change activities.

Support: Banfield, 1975; Bowens, 1975; Robeson, 1974; Vold, 1975.

>Availability Of Funds Influences the Change Process, But the Motivation Of Districts Requesting Funds May Have a Stronger Influence. [*Moderately Speculative*]

Although, as noted above, funds and time are related, the availability of funds does not assure that they will be used to provide time for change activities, and even if time is provided there are no assurances that it will be used effectively. This is one reason why some studies have revealed that increased funding did not always make a difference with respect to the implementation of innovations. The Rand Studies (Berman et al., 1975) concluded that funding was not a major factor in successful implementation; more important was the motivation of districts seeking federal funding. Intrinsically motivated districts tended to implement programs well. They were aware of problems to be solved regardless of the receipt of federal dollars. Extrinsically motivated districts tended to implement programs poorly; they were opportunistic in their requests for federal dollars. The proportion of districts intrinsically motivated toward federal funding is unknown, but in one state 40 percent of the districts which were rejected for ESEA Title III funding implemented the proposed program nevertheless.

Availability of funds for initiating new programs is, however, associated with successful implementation. As school budgets become tighter, and as slack resources become more scarce, then the availability of funds is likely to become more critical.

Support: Berman et al., 1975; Jarman, 1974; Melby, 1975; Richardson, 1974; Sullivan, 1974; Vance, 1974.

>Boards of Education Appear To Be Either Passive or Negative Regarding Change Programs. [*Moderately Speculative*]

Boards of Education do not tend to initiate change. They will overlook innovations (i.e., be passive) that cause little or no controversy in the community. Community controversy will stimulate negative board reaction.

Support: Cobb, 1974; Hampson, 1971.

Communities and Parents Are More Likely To Prevent Change Than They Are To Promote Change. [*Moderately Speculative*]

Community and parent groups are difficult to energize; their involvement with school affairs is difficult to maintain. Instances where involvement of parents is sustained show a positive effect on the school program, but instances of negative community reactions to a proposed or implemented change appear to have a greater effect. Attitudes of parents toward specific innovations may not be influenced by increased participation in school programs. In other words, regardless of public relation efforts, their minds are made up about certain innovations. An innovation which serves to antagonize a community has little chance of being implemented. The implementation of a neutral innovation (one that does not antagonize the community) will proceed with little influence from the community.

Support: Hampson, 1971; Kopeck, 1976; Pinch, 1975; Vance, 1974.

The Physical Configuration Of A School May Influence The Implementation Of Innovations. [*Moderately Speculative*]

Some innovations work better in certain facilities, e.g., team teaching in flexible space schools. Not all innovations are influenced by the school facilities, but those that are require careful assessment of current building space and physical layout. Otherwise spatial considerations can prevent successful implementation. For example, an innovative instructional program may call for cross-grade grouping where two grades share instructional activities and perform in groups of various sizes. However, if the two grades are located in distant classrooms, then disruptions may occur when pupils walk through the halls to the other classrooms. The noise and disruption may be enough to dampen enthusiasm for and prevent implementation of the innovation. A different physical configuration may have reduced walking distance and the concomitant noise and disruption.

Support: Meyer, 1971; Paul, 1974; Vance, 1974; Walker, 1975.

Perceptions Of The Characteristics Of Innovations May Vary From Group To Group, And Disagreement Hinders Implementation. [*Moderately Speculative*]

The users of an innovation may perceive its attributes quite differently from the developers or disseminators of the innovation. This has serious implications because the developers hold certain expectations for the users based, in part, on their perception of the attributes of an innovation. The lack of agreement over the attributes of a specific innovation can result in misunderstandings, frustration, and conflict. For example, a developer may feel that a particular product is easy to understand and is compatible with existing practices and behaviors in schools; however, teachers may perceive the product as complex and incompatible with prevailing practice. In order for the two groups to work together effectively, they should become aware of the differences in their perceptions of the product.

Support: Evans, 1972.

The Relative Advantage, The Compatibility, and the Complexity Of Innovations Influence Their Implementation. [*Firm*]

The attributes of innovations influence the degree to which they are accepted and the degree of successful implementation. Relative advantage refers to the degree to which an innovation is perceived as better than the idea it supersedes. Compatibility refers to the degree to which an innovation is perceived as consistent with past experience, existing values, and needs. Complexity is the degree to which an innovation is perceived as difficult to understand and hard to use. Teachers may perceive an innovation as having partial compatibility. For example, a new curriculum which included changes in content and practice was partially implemented: Changes in existing practices were rejected, but changes in curriculum content were accepted. It is usually easier to substitute one content for another, but it is much more difficult to change behavior—one reason why innovations which are not complex are more readily implemented. They usually require only substitutions of content rather than changes in practice, roles, or behaviors. It may be, however, that behavioral change has a greater impact on school improvement than content change.

The balance between complexity and compatibility presents a dilemma for developers of innovative products and programs. On the one hand, simple, compatible, and easily substituted innovations are more likely to be implemented successfully, but on the other hand, complex, incompatible, behaviorally based innovations have greater impact. Clearly, a middle ground must be reached between trivial innovations easy to implement and significant innovations difficult to implement. Propositions related to the above generalizations are:

> The Greater the Relative Advantage Of An Innovation, Then the Greater the Likelihood of Implementation.
>
> The Greater the Complexity Of an Innovation, Then the Less Likely It Will Be Implemented and the Less Likely It Is Trivial.
>
> The Greater the Compatibility Of an Innovation, Then the Greater the Likelihood Of Implementation and the Greater the Likelihood That It Is Trivial.

Support: Brantley, 1974; Clinton, 1971; DeArman, 1975; Goodridge, 1975; Hall and Kester, 1973; Haughey, 1974; Howes, 1974; Newman, 1974; Rivera, 1975; Smith, 1972; Starling, 1972; Swirsky, 1975; Wyner, 1974. (See also Rogers and Shoemaker, 1971.)

> Organizational and Administrative Factors Mediate Influence On Implementation In Addition to the Influence Of the Attributes Of Innovations. [*Moderately Speculative*]

The attributes of an innovation comprise only one dimension of the complex mosaic of change. Other factors may bear more influence than the attributes of an innovation. For example, the influence structure of a school may have a greater impact on the principal's decision to try particular innovations than do the attributes of the innovations. In other words there is a variety of factors to be taken into account for understanding change.

Support: Littleton, 1970.

Effects Dimension

Little has been said about the effects dimension explicitly; nevertheless, it has been treated implicitly in the preceding inferences and generalizations. To say that an activity is effective is to imply that a higher level of use will result, in contrast to another activity. The effects dimension has, therefore, been treated as a silent dependent variable throughout most of the inferences and generalizations.

> Incomplete Implementation Of Innovations Is More Common Than Complete Implementation. [*Moderately Firm*]

There are many factors which impinge upon the degree of implementation. Some factors promote complete implementation, while others hinder it, and still others push for functional adaptations. For innovations involving changes in teacher behavior and roles, the probability for complete implementation is low. If the change process does not take into account user needs and concerns and is not based on a mutually agreeable frequency of face-to-face interaction, then the probability of complete implementation is low. In addition, organizational, administrative, psychological factors, and factors related to sources all influence the degree of implementation.

Support: Brantley, 1975; Ebner, 1973; Gatney, 1974; Reynolds, 1971; Rivera, 1975; Wacaster, 1973.

SUMMARY

A series of generalizations and inferences about change in education has been presented organized according to an inductively developed framework. This framework consists of three major dimensions: change processes, influences of change, and change effects. All the studies reviewed here focused on one or more of these dimensions.

The first dimension comprised change processes including such activities as helping, training or conveying. The manner in which the activities were conducted and the frequency of interaction were also part of the first dimension.

The second dimension included a wide variety of factors which influence change activities and change effects. These factors can be grouped according to internal and external organizational factors and characteristics of innovations. Factors within organizations which influence change tend to be centered on organizational structures, administrative practices, attitudes, and personality characteristics. Factors outside of the organization undergoing change tend to be centered on resources such as time and funds. Characteristics of innovations such as complexity, compatibility and relative advantage make up the third grouping of factors which influence change processes and effects. In addition, the characteristics of innovations influence and are influenced by the internal and external organizational factors.

The third dimension included the effects of change processes which are viewed as a function of change processes. And change processes are viewed as being influenced by internal and external organizational factors and characteristics of innovations. The influencing factors act as mediators of both processes and effects.

Implications for practice emanate from the generalizations and from the basic logic underlying the framework. The generalizations and inferences speak for themselves. The basic logic of the framework suggests that energy introduced into a system, regardless of its source, will be mediated or influenced by system and non-system factors. Over time the mediation will produce an effect that deviates in some degree from the idealized state envisioned at the start of the intervention. There are so many factors which enter into the picture at any one time that expectations for achieving the desired effects without deviation are unrealistic. This multitude of factors is not to suggest that program objectives are useless. Rather, what is being suggested is a broader range of understanding to help explain why program effects vary from organization to organization and from one time period to another. By picturing change programs in terms of the three dimensions of processes, influences, and effects an heuristic perspective is provided to those responsible for initiating change programs.

Implications for research are centered on the need for a systematic analysis of empirical studies dealing with change in education, health, and related people processing institutions. The meta-analysis approach suggested by Glass (1976) is one means for achieving a logical and empirical synthesis of findings. Such a synthesis would lend itself to comparative studies, model building, and middle-range theory development.

APPENDIX A

Measuring Implementation

Measuring where a particular innovation lies on the continuum from non-use to renewal is a critical methodological problem and challenge. Measures of implementation tend to be unreliable, conflicting, or not subtle enough (David, 1975; Ironside, 1973). In addition, self-report measures for determining implementation have been found to conflict with observational measures (Behrman, 1975; Fullan and Pomfret, 1975).

Output measures such as test scores are sometimes used to index the effect of an innovation. The scores of the innovative school are usually compared to the scores of a control school, and frequently little difference is found. The finding of no significant difference may be the case even when the innovative school has implemented the innovation. One reason for the lack of difference is that the control school may be performing similar activities as the innovative school; the only difference is that in one school it is a new activity and in the other school it is a routine activity (Loucks, 1975; Smith, 1972).

The measurement of change and innovation factors is difficult and if done properly, time consuming. Fullan and Pomfret (1975) have critically reviewed studies of implementation and have concluded that (1) user perceptions are not adequate measures of implementation, (2) questionnaires for assessing degree of implementation are of doubtful validity, and (3) principals' knowledge of degree of implementation is of doubtful value. They suggest careful observation of extent of implementation rather than relying on questionnaires. Hall (1975) also stressed this point and has since developed comprehensive instruments to measure implementation. In addition, Fullan and Pomfret have identified three characteristics of implementation that deserve study: structural, behavioral, and knowledge characteristics. Structural alterations correspond to changes in formal arrangements and physical conditions. They are easily defined and relatively straight-forward to measure. Behavioral changes are difficult to measure, yet they form the base of implementation. All key factors (including students) involved with the implementation of an innovation should have their roles defined and relationships between roles defined. Degree of knowledge about implementation features is the third implementation characteristic discussed by Fullan and Pomfret. This corresponds to knowledge of the objectives, content, and philosophy underlying an innovation. Although acquisition of knowledge is not a sufficient measure of implementation, it does provide a broad orientation for the behaviorally based measurement of implementation.

Four levels of effects have been distinguished by Charters and Jones (1975): (1) early intention and commitment, (2) changes in the formal arrangements and physical conditions, (3) changes in role performance of staff, and (4) changes in learning activities in students. Figure 1.10 illustrates the four levels of program change as described by Charters and Jones.

FIGURE 1.10
FOUR LEVELS OF CHANGE

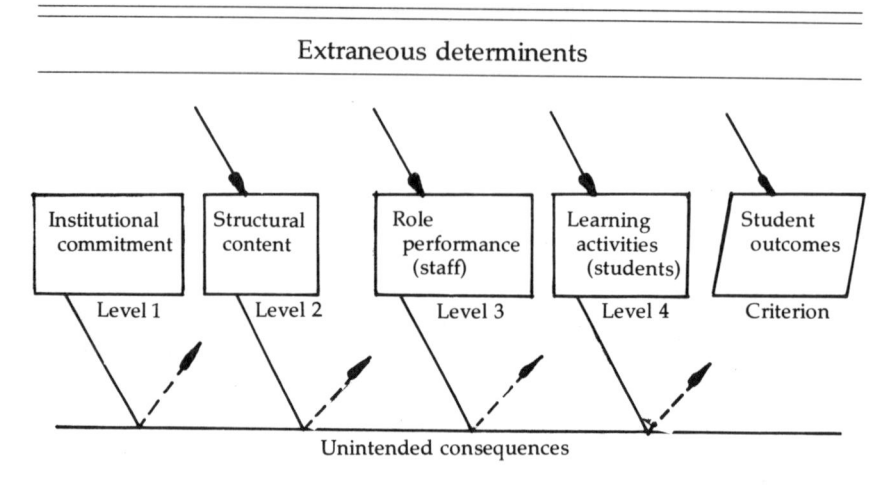

Extraneous determinents

Institutional commitment	Structural content	Role performance (staff)	Learning activities (students)	Student outcomes
Level 1	Level 2	Level 3	Level 4	Criterion

Unintended consequences

Reprinted by permission of the publisher from W. W. Charters, Jr., and J. E. Jones, On Neglect of the Independent Variable in Program Evaluation. In J. V. Baldridge and T. M. Deal (Eds.), *Managing Change in Educational Organizations*. Berkeley, California: McCutchan, 1975. © 1975 by McCutchan Publishing Company.

To evaluate the effectiveness of implementation efforts by measuring student outcome is to assume that the four levels of change have been successfully achieved. This is seldom the case. In addition, measuring student behavior also assumes that the change being implemented makes a difference in student outcomes. In other words, the effectiveness of the change itself and the effectiveness of the implementation process are two separate questions. Implementation may be successful but the change unsuccessful. However, it is more likely that implementation is partially carried out, and concomitantly the change is partially successful. One way of measuring implementation involves determining the extent to which the four levels of change have been achieved.

Some examples from various studies illustrate the pitfalls and difficulties involved with measuring implementation and associated dependent variables. A study set out to measure teacher acceptance of a variety of innovations in relation to a typology of innovation attributes. Acceptance, the dependent variable, was measured according to one questionnaire item: degree of experience the respondent had with the innovation. The problem with this approach is that prior use, i.e., experience, does not necessarily mean cognitive acceptance; conversely, cognitive acceptance does not necessarily mean prior use. Perhaps a more direct approach for determining the reaction of teachers to an innovation would be to construct an index based on the attributes of the innovation. High compatibility and relative advantage on one hand and low complexity on the other are likely to be a basis for high acceptance.

A second example stems from an attempt to identify innovative teachers. In this case, principals were asked to identify innovative and traditional teachers so that their receptivity toward change could be compared. There was no difference between the two on the receptivity scale. This result was probably due to the predisposition of the principal to identify traditional teachers as innovative, i.e., teachers who represent stability, reliability, and who cause little trouble. An alternative approach for identifying innovative teachers would be to interview students using a check list of behaviors considered innovative — individualizing instruction, for example.

A third study illustrates the difficulty with measuring implementation using questionnaire items. In a school district teachers, principals, a project director, a federal program manager, and the superintendent, all of whom were involved in change programs, responded to a questionnaire. There was little agreement among respondent groups for the items used to measure implementation. These items were: (1) percent of project goals achieved, (2) extent of change in behavior, (3) extent to which the project has been implemented as planned, and (4) degree to which the project was difficult to carry out. However, these items show there was concern by the researchers for developing an accurate measure of the degree implementation based on changes in behavior and goals.

To ask a respondent to reflect objectively upon the degree to which his or her behavior has changed due to an innovation or to ask the project manager to assess the percent of goals achieved expects too much objectivity and reflection by those emotionally, behaviorally and politically involved with the change. An alternative approach might involve observation check lists expressly tailored for the change. The results of the observation could be used to validate questionnaire items, and this was one of the recommendations for measuring implementation put forth by Fullan and Pomfret (1975).

In summary, implementation and associated dependent variables are difficult to measure. Faith in questionnaire items for measuring implementation is unfounded and unfortunately widespread. Certainly, careful observation of implementation is called for because of the complexity of the change process.

APPENDIX B

Studies of Post-Secondary Education

Empirical research has been carried out on dissemination and change in post-secondary institutions, and by and large the differences between elementary, secondary, and post-secondary levels are a matter of degree rather than fundamental differences. A number of examples support this view.

Central administration directives stipulating adoption and implementation of new curricular practices were not followed in two community colleges and two vocational education centers; the staff gave lip service to the new curriculum, but they did not implement it (Davis, 1976). The lack of staff participation in the decision to adopt the new curriculum was one reason for its failure, and lack of staff participation is a common theme throughout studies of change, regardless of institutional level.

The effects of dissemination programs on faculty does differ somewhat between post-secondary and lower institutional levels. For example, awareness of new curricula may be effectively achieved through a print mode of communication. In one instance journal articles were successful, and in another instance a brochure was successful (Kinerney, 1975; Rogers et al., 1975). However, face-to-face contact and two-way communication are also important. At two community colleges opinion leaders relied upon colleagues for awareness information and conferences and journals for evaluative information (Brown, 1974). Although staff at the post-secondary level may rely upon print media more often than their counterparts at lower institutional levels, nevertheless, they place considerable emphasis on face-to-face contact at the later critical stages of change, viz., adoption and implementation.

The orientation of post-secondary faculty appears to be similar to that of lower institutional levels. A major change in curriculum at a school of nursing revealed that staff were primarily concerned with personal issues and changes in their own instructional methods. Concern with the school as a whole, its standards, or drive for improvement was minimal (Knopke, 1975). The autonomy of faculty on one hand and the lack of interdependence on the other results in an individualistic orientation. In addition, disciplinary orientation prevails at many post-secondary institutions, i.e., status, rewards, and identification with one's discipline and associated peers.

The lack of an organizational orientation is similar among institutional levels, but there is a difference across the levels. The lower the level, the greater the orientation on student welfare, with rewards emanating from students. The higher the level, the greater the orientation on the discipline with rewards emanating from peers.

Leadership is a critical factor influencing change at the elementary and post-secondary levels. A comparative study of department chairpersons at a major university also revealed that leadership was an important factor. Innovative departments tended to have chairpersons who were able to influence political events, were capable of obtaining outside funds, and coped well under pressure. In contrast, chairpersons from low innovative departments reported major differences of opinion between themselves and colleagues and avoided people and responsibilities in order to avoid pressure (Davis, 1975). The role of department chairpersons in regard to change is centered on supporting and facilitating rather than on initiating and implementing. The role of the chairperson in post-secondary institutions is somewhat analogous to the principal in elementary and secondary institutions: Both can support and facilitate change. The impact of personality characteristics on receptivity toward change has been investigated at the post-secondary level in a study at a major university. The status of university personnel found was to be related to receptivity rather than to their personality. High status respondents reported high resistance to change, and conversely, lower status respondents tended to be more receptive. In addition, the level of risk associated with a change was related to the status of respondents and their receptivity or resistance. High status and perceptions of high risk went hand in hand as did low status and perceptions of low risk (Kazlow, 1976). In other words, the higher the formal status of respondents, then the greater the perceived risks due to change. The greater the risk, then the greater the resistance to change.

Studies of elementary and secondary institutions revealed that misperceptions and misunderstandings within and between organizational units lead to frustration, conflict, and poor coordination. Misperceptions and lack of agreement may also result in resistance to change. A study of the diffusion of innovations from their source to their intended users illustrates a similar relationship for post-secondary institutions. Innovations developed by a national center supported with federal funds were diffused to systems at the post-secondary level. A study of the perceptions of the intended users of the innovations and the developers disagreed about the characteristics of the innovations, e.g., their complexity, compatibility, efficiency, utility, trialability, preliminary use without commitment to implement, and visibility (Evans, 1973). These differences resulted in misunderstandings, frustrations, and low levels of adoption.

The misperceptions between the developer organization and the user organizations resulted in user resistance to adoption. The user organizations probably inferred that the developer was unaware of local needs and concerns because of their inaccurate characterization of their products. In other words, if on one hand the developer claims that a particular innovation is compatible with the user system, is efficient, and has low complexity, and on the other hand the user claims the opposite characteristics, then the user is likely to conclude that the developer is unaware of the user's problems and/or characteristics.

The studies cited here suggest that the differences between elementary and secondary levels on the one hand and post-secondary levels on the other are a matter of degree. Basic issues and problems appear to be shared by all levels: need for participation, need for multiple modes of dissemination, need for an organizational orientation, need for strong leadership, need for less risk associated with change, and need for perceptual agreement between groups involved with change. Although differences between institutional levels may be a matter of degree, in at least two instances the degree of difference is great. Faculty autonomy and power are much greater at the post-secondary level. Decisions over course content can be made independently in contrast to the narrow latitude of decision making associated with elementary and secondary teachers. The strong addition of academic freedom at the post-secondary level supports the practice of faculty control over courses. Also, universities are unlikely to consider institution-wide innovations, whereas school districts frequently do. A counterpart to the autonomy and power of the central administration in a school district is missing at the post-secondary level. Their power is diffuse, and consequently initiation of institution-wide change is limited. The post-secondary level may be characterized by individual faculty as the primary unit for adopting innovations. And the innovations at the post-secondary level may be characterized as course specific, in contrast to innovations requiring institution-wide support and involvement. The empirical studies of change at the post-secondary level are too few from which to generalize. Nevertheless, the suggestion that the differences between the institutional levels are not a matter of kind but rather of degree provides a jumping off point for future study and comparisons.

Post-secondary institutions have many of the same characteristics as their elementary and secondary counterparts. The technology is mostly large group instruction carried out independently, goals are diffuse and vague, vulnerability to outside criticism is high, and indices of efficiency and effectiveness lack consensus and acceptance. That many of the same kinds of problems hinder change at the post-secondary level should, therefore, come as no surprise.

REFERENCES

Abraham, T. J. *Curricular Change: A Study of the Relationship between a University and Three Selected Secondary Schools Teaching East Asian Studies.* Unpublished doctoral dissertation, Columbia University, 1974.

Baldridge, J. V. Political and Structural Protection of Educational Innovations. In S. Temkin and M. Brown (Eds.), *What Do Research Findings Say about Getting Innovations into Schools: A symposium.* Philadelphia: Research for Better Schools, 1974, 3-45.

Baldridge, J. V., and Johnson, R. *The Impact of Educational R&D Centers and Laboratories: An Analysis of Effective Organizational Strategies.* Stanford, California: Stanford University, 1972.

Banfield, B. *Latent Culture as a Force for Change and the Change Process in Operation.* Unpublished doctoral dissertation, Columbia University.

Baron, J. J. *An Investigation of the Consultant's Role as an Agent of Change in the High School English Program.* Unpublished doctoral dissertation, University of Illinois, Urbana-Champaign, 1972.

Behrmann, A. A. *An Analysis of the Leadership Characteristics of the Elementary Principal as Related to Innovative Practices in Selected Elementary Schools in Michigan.* Unpublished doctoral dissertation, Michigan State University. 1975.

Bennis, W., Benne, K., and Chin, R. (Eds.). *The Planning of Change* Holt, Rinehart and Winston, 1969.

Berger, G. *Roles, Role Sets, and Role Partners of Prime Movers in Selected Case Studies of the Curricular Change Process.* Unpublished doctoral dissertation, Columbia University, 1973.

Berman, P., McLaughlin, M., and others. *Federal Programs Supporting Educational Change,* Vol. I-V Santa Monica, California: Rand Corporation, 1975.

Bettas, G. *An Analysis of Teacher Attitudes and the Implementation of Selected Innovative Programs in Open Concept Schools in the State of Washington.* Unpublished doctoral dissertation, Washington State University, 1974.

Bhola, H. S. *The Configuration Theory of Innovation Diffusion.* Ohio State University, School of Education, October, 1965.

Blumenkrantz, D. *An Interorganizational Analysis of Coordination of Services between a Public School System and Selected Social Agencies in One Community.* Unpublished doctoral dissertation, Rutgers University, 1975.

Boucher, D. *A Study of Factors Affecting The Initiation of Innovative Academic Programs at Selected Universities.* Unpublished doctoral dissertation, Texas Tech University, 1975.

Bowens, G. E. *Orientation for Change in an Urban High School through Human Resource Development.* Unpublished doctoral dissertation, Harvard University, 1975.

Brantley, P. S. *Implementing Classroom Innovation: A Case Study of the Relationship between Teacher Receptivity, Degree of Implementation and Selected Innovation Variables.* Unpublished doctoral dissertation, Ohio State University, 1975.

Broman, W. *The Relationship of Administrative Processes of Public Secondary Schools.* Unpublished doctoral dissertation, State University of New York at Buffalo, 1974.

Brooke, J. *A Survey of Social Researchers' Attitudes toward Utilization.* Bureau of Applied Social Research, Columbia University, 1973.

Brown, L. J. *Identification of Sources of Information Affecting the Diffusion of Instructional Innovation among Instructional Faculty at Two Community Colleges.* Unpublished doctoral dissertation, United States International University, 1974.

Brown, W. H. *Management Skills: A Model for Change.* Unpublished doctoral dissertation, Duke University, 1975.

Cahoon, A. R. *Managerial Behavior under Conditions of Mandated Change in a Canadian Bureaucracy: An Empirical Study of the Relationships among Job Satisfaction, Organizational Climate and Leadership Change Styles.* Unpublished doctoral dissertation, Syracuse University, 1974.

Carlson, R. Summary and Critique of Educational Diffusion Research. In *Research Implications for Educational Diffusion.* East Lansing, Michigan: Michigan Department of Education, June, 1968.

Carlson, R. O. *Adoption of Educational Innovation.* Eugene, Oregon: The Center for the Advanced Study of Educational Administration, 1965.

Carr, R. *The Organizational Orientation of Teachers and Change in Elementary and Secondary Schools.* Unpublished doctoral dissertation, University of Iowa, 1974.

Chapey, G. D. *Interrelationships among Secondary School Administrators' Problem-Solving Behavior, Personal Motivation, Social Motivation and Perception of the Rate of Adoption of Change.* Unpublished doctoral dissertation, Fordham University, 1975.

Charters, W. W., Jr., and Jones, J. E. On Neglect of the Independent Variable in Program Evaluation. In J. V. Baldridge and T. M. Deal (Eds.), *Managing Change in Educational Organizations.* Berkeley: McCutchan, 1975, 341-53.

Chin, R. and Benne, K. General Strategies for Effecting Changes in Human Systems. In W. Bennis, K. Benne, and R. Chin (Eds.), *The Planning of Change.* New York: Holt, Rinehart and Winston, 1969, 32-59.

Christian, C. F. *Organizational Climate of Elementary Schools and the Introduction and Utilization of Innovative Educational Practices.* Unpublished doctoral dissertation, University of Nebraska, Lincoln, 1972.

Clark, D. L., and Guba, E. G. A Re-examination of a Test of the Research and Development Model of Change, *Educational Administration Quarterly,* 1972, 8, (3), 93-103.

Clark, J. N. *Locus of Differences in Perception of Barriers to Educational Change by Groups within the School Organization and Groups in the School Environment.* Unpublished doctoral dissertation, University of North Carolina at Chapel Hill, 1973.

Clark, N. E. *Effects and Change: A Study of the Impact of the Elementary and Secondary Education Act, Title III, in California.* Unpublished doctoral dissertation, University of Southern California, 1974.

Clinton, A. *A Study of Attributes of Educational Innovations as Factors in Diffusion.* Unpublished doctoral dissertation, University of Toronto, 1971.

Cobb, J. *The Social Network of Influence in the Adoption of an Innovation: Community Education of Webb City, 1965-1972.* Unpublished doctoral dissertation, University of Oregon, 1974.

Cooke, R. A., Duncan, R. B., and Zaltman, G. *Assessment of a Structural/Task Approach to Organization Development in School Systems.* Paper presented at the Annual Meeting of the American Educational Research Association, Chicago, 1974.

Corwin, R. G. *Reform and Organizational Survival: The Teacher Corps as an Instrument of Educational Change.* New York, John Wiley & Sons, 1972.

Daft, R. L. *The Process of Organizational Innovation: An Empirical Study of Thirteen High School Districts.* Unpublished doctoral dissertation, University of Chicago, 1974.

David E. B. *The Relationship of Length of Teacher Tenure to Teacher Openness to Curriculum Innovation.* Unpublished doctoral dissertation, University of Virginia, 1975.

Davis, D. E. *The Consequences of Adopting an Educational Innovation: A Study of the Impact of the Illinois Occupational Curriculum Project Manuals.* Unpublished doctoral dissertation, University of Illinois at Urbana-Champaign, 1976.

Davis, J. H. *Selected Perceptions of Chairmen in High Innovative and Low Innovative Departments.* Unpublished doctoral dissertation, University of Florida, 1975.

DeArman, J. W. *Investigation of the Abandonment and Causes of Abandonment of Innovative Practices in Secondary Schools in the North Central Association of Colleges and Schools.* Unpublished doctoral dissertation, University of Missouri-Columbia, 1975.

Duncan, R. B. The Ambidextrous Organization: Designing Dual Structures for Innovation. In R. Kilmann, L. Pondy, and D. Selvin (Eds.), *The Management of Organization Design Volume 1: Strategies and Implementation.* New York: Elsevier, 1976.

Ebner, W. C. *The Diffusion, Adoption, Implementation of a Nationally Recognized Innovative Program in Special Education.* Unpublished doctoral dissertation, University of Southern California, 1973.

Edwards, F. H. *A Study of Affective Change in Elementary Schools Implementing Individually Guided Education.* Unpublished doctoral dissertation, University of North Carolina at Chapel Hill, 1972.

Edwards, J. K. *A Study of the Factors Influencing the Internalization of Innovations by Teachers within a School System.* Unpublished doctoral dissertation, Miami University, 1973.

Etzioni, A. Human Beings Are Not Very Easy to Change After All, *Saturday Review,* June 3, 1972, 45-47.

Evans, D. J. *Perceptions of Analytical Innovations by Maryland Community College Business Officers and Members of the National Center for Higher Education Management Systems at the Western Interstate Commission for Higher Education (WICHE).* Unpublished doctoral dissertation, George Washington University, 1973.

Evers, N., Fruth, M., Heffernan, J., Karges, M., and Krupa, W., *IGE Implementor's Manual* Madison, Wisconsin: Wisconsin Research and Development Center, April 1975.

Farag, V. E. *The Intra-Organizational Diffusion of an Innovation: A Case Study of the Itinerary of an Innovation within a Public School System.* Unpublished doctoral dissertation, University of North Carolina at Chapel Hill, 1970.

Florio, D. H. *Organizational Cooperation for Educational Development.* Unpublished doctoral dissertation, Northwestern University, 1973.

Fullan, M. Overview of the Innovative Process and the User, *Interchange,* 1973, 3, 1-46.

Fullan, M., and Pomfret, A., *Review of Research on Curriculum Implementation.* Toronto: Ontario Institute for Studies in Education (Prepared for National Institute for Education NIE-P-74-0122) April, 1975.

Gafney, L. J. *A Program of Organizational Innovations Directed toward Independent Learning in a Traditional Secondary School.* Unpublished doctoral dissertation, University of Pennsylvania, 1974.

Gaynor, A. K. *The Study of Change in Educational Organizations: A Review of the Literature.* Paper presented at the UCEA-Ohio State University Career Development Seminar, Columbus, Ohio, March 27-30, 1975.

Giacquinta, J. ·B. The Process of Organizational Change in the School, In F. Kerlinger (Ed.), *Review of Research in Education.* Itasca, Illinois: F. E. Peacock Publisher, 1973, 178-208.

Glass, G. Primary, Secondary, and Meta-Analysis of Research, *Educational Researcher,* 1976, 5, 3-8.

Gridley, G. C. *Dimensions of the Use and Design of an Innovative Program in Fourteen Schools Related to Implementation and Effective Use.* Unpublished doctoral dissertation. University of Texas at Austin, 1975.

Goodridge, C. G. *Factors That Influence the Decision to Adopt an Educational Innovation: IGE.* Technical Report No. 376 Madison, Wisconsin: Wisconsin R&D Center, December 1975.

Gross, N. C., Giacquinta, J. B. and Bernstein, M. *Implementing Organizational Innovations: A Sociological Analysis of Planned Educational Change.* New York: Basic Books, Inc., 1971.

Guba, E. G. Development, Diffusion and Evaluation. In T. Eidell and J. Kitchel (Eds.), *Knowledge Production and Utilization in Educational Administration.* Eugene, Oregon: Center for the Advanced Study of Educational Administration, 1968, 37-63.

Guba, E. and Clark, D. *The Configurational Perspective: A Challenge to the Systems Field of Educational Knowledge Production and Utilization.* Washington, D. C.: Council for Educational Development and Research, December, 1974.

Hall, D. C. and Alford, S. E. *Evaluation of the National Diffusion Network: Evolution of the Network and Overview of the Research Literature on Diffusion of Educational Innovations.* Menlo Park, California: Stanford Research Institute, 1976.

Hall, G. and Loucks, S. *A Developmental Model for Determining Whether or Not the Treatment Really is Implemented.* Austin, Texas: Texas Research and Development Center for Teacher Education, 1976.

Hall, G., Loucks, S., Rutherford, W., and Newlove, B. Levels of Use of the Innovation: A Framework for Analyzing Innovation Adoption, *Journal of Teacher Education.* 1975, 26, 52-56.

Hall, G. *The Concerns-Based Adoption Model: A Developmental Conceptualization.* Research and Development Center for Teacher Education. University of Texas at Austin, February, 1974.

Hall, G. *The Effects of Change on Teachers and Professors: Theory, Research, and Implications for Decision-Makers.* Research and Development Center for Teacher Education, University of Texas at Austin, November 1975.

Halpin, A. and Croft, D. *Organizational Climate of Schools.* Chicago: Midwest Administration Center, 1963.

Hamann, J. *A Survey of Innovations, Factors That Bring about Innovations and Strategies for Change.* Unpublished doctoral dissertation, University of Minnesota, 1971.

Hampson, D. *Influencing the Curriculum Change Process: A Case Study of a Selected School District.* Unpublished doctoral dissertation, Stanford University, 1971.

Hansen, D. E. *Exploration of the Interrelationships between Teacher Related Factors Identified as Critical to Planned Change.* Unpublished doctoral dissertation, Wayne State University, 1975.

Harris, R. *The Relationship between Autonomy and Innovativeness among Elementary School Principals.* Unpublished doctoral dissertation, Cornell University, 1974.

Hartgraves, W. R. *Relationship of Principal and Supervisor Leadership Variables to the Implementation of an Innovation as Influenced by Organizational Variables.* Unpublished doctoral dissertation, University of Texas at Austin, 1973.

Haughey, C. *Federally-Funded Innovation in School Systems: ESEA Title III Project Persistence in Pennsylvania's Local Educational Agencies.* Unpublished doctoral dissertation, University of Pennsylvania, 1974.

Havelock, R. G. and Havelock, M. *Training for Change Agents.* Ann Arbor, Michigan: Institute for School Research, Center for Research on Utilization of Scientific Knowledge, 1973.

Havelock, R. G. Locals Say Innovation is Local: A National Survey of School Superintendents. In S. Temkin and M. Brown (Eds.), *What Do Research Findings Say about Getting Innovations into Schools.* Philadelphia: Research for Better Schools, 1974, 73-98.

Havelock, R. G. *Bibliography on Knowledge Utilization and Dissemination.* Ann Arbor, Michigan: Institute for Social Research, Center for Research on Utilization of Scientific Knowledge, 1972.

Havelock, R.G., et al. *Planning for Innovation through the Dissemination and Utilization of Knowledge.* Ann Arbor, Michigan: Institute for Research, Center for Research on Utilization of Scientific Knowledge, 1969.

Havelock, R. G. and Lingwood, D. *R&D Utilization Strategies and Functions: An Analytical Comparison of Four Systems.* Ann Arbor, Michigan: Institute for Social Research, Center for Research on Utilization of Scientific Knowledge, 1973.

Hering, W. M. *Some Effects of Change Teams on the Dissemination of New Curricular Materials.* Unpublished doctoral dissertation, University of Illinois at Urbana-Champaign, 1973.

Hodgkinson, W. K. *Values as an Affective Measure of Teacher Orientation to Innovation in Education.* Unpublished doctoral dissertation, Pennsylvania State University, 1974.

Hood, P. *The Relationship between Purposes for Seeking Educational Information, Sources Used, and Type of Position of the User.* San Francisco: Far West Laboratory. September 1975.

Hood, P. How Research and Development on Educational Roles and Institutional Structures Can Facilitate Communication, *Journal of Research and Development in Education*. 1973, *6*, 96-114.

House, E. *The Politics of Educational Innovation*. Berkeley: McCutchan, 1974.

House, E. Responses to Clark and Guba: The Logic of Revisionism, *Educational Administration Quarterly*, 1972, *8*, (3), 104-106.

Howes, N.J. *Change Factors Related to the Institutionalization of the Multiunit Elementary School*. Unpublished doctoral dissertation, University of Wisconsin. Madison, 1974. (Also Technical Report No. 319, September 1974.)

Hull, R. A Research and Development Adoption Model. *Educational Administration Quarterly*, 1974, *10*, 33-45.

Ironside, R. The Fall 1972 Follow-up: A Process Evaluation, *Supplement to The 1971-72 Nationwide Installation of the Multiunit/IGE Model for Elementary Schools*. Durham, North Carolina: Educational Testing Service, 1973.

Jarman, W. V. *Interrelationship of Innovation, Organizational Climate, Educational Wealth, and the Superintendent*. Unpublished doctoral dissertation, University of Tulsa, 1974.

Johnson, L. *The Relationship of Selected Teacher Characteristics and Selected Factors to the Diffusion of Innovation in History*. Unpublished doctoral dissertation, Ball State University, 1973.

Jones, J. E. *A Case Study of a Selected Elementary School under Conditions of Planned Change*. Unpublished doctoral dissertation. Syracuse University, 1973.

Kane, M. B. Interim Summary Report, Executive Summary No. 2 for Evaluation and Documentation of Experimental Schools Program for Small Schools Serving Rural Areas. Cambridge, Massachusetts: Abt Associates, Inc., April, 1976.

Kazlow, C. *Resistance to Innovations in Complex Organizations: A Test of Two Models of Resistance in a Higher Education Setting*. Unpublished doctoral dissertation, New York University, 1974.

Keenan, C. E. *Channels for Change: A Survey of Teachers in Eleven Chicago Elementary Schools*. Unpublished doctoral dissertation, University of Illinois at Urbana-Champaign, 1975.

Keller, C. *The Diffusion of Innovation within One Michigan School System Using a Communication Flow Inventory*. Unpublished doctoral dissertation, Michigan State University, 1974.

Kendall, L. R. *The Principal's Attitude towards Educational Change and Teachers' Perceptions of the Organizational Structures of his School*. Unpublished doctoral dissertation, University of Northern Colorado, 1973.

Kester, R. J., and Howard, J. *Evaluating the Process of Educational Change: A Model and Its Application*. Paper presented at the Annual Meeting of the American Educational Research Association, Washington, D. C., April 1975.

Kinerney, E. *The High School Geography Project in Relation to Instructional Practices in Introductory College Geography: An Upward Dissemination of Educational Innovation*. Unpublished doctoral dissertation, University of Maryland, 1975.

Kiser, K. J. *Explorations in Organizational Change: A Case Study of a Federal Intervention Program.* Unpublished doctoral dissertation, The Ohio State University, 1973.

Knopke, H. J. *University Faculty and the Implementation of Change in Health Care Education.* Unpublished doctoral dissertation, University of Wisconsin-Madison, 1975.

Kopek, H. D. *The Relationship between Certain Community Norms and Innovation in Selected Elementary Schools.* Unpublished doctoral dissertation, State University of New York at Buffalo, 1976.

Korba, W. L. *An Unobtrusive Experiment to Test Source Credibility and Heterophily Tolerance in the Diffusion of Innovation.* Unpublished doctoral dissertation, University of Connecticut, 1975.

Ladouceur, J. *School Management Profile and Capacity for Change.* Unpublished doctoral dissertation, University of Toronto, 1973.

Lindquist, J. Political Linkage: The Academic-Innovation Process, *Journal of Higher Education,* 1974, *45*, 323-343.

Lingwood, D. and Morris, W. C. *Research into Use: A Study of the Forest Service Research Branch.* Ann Arbor, Michigan: Institute of Social Research, Center for Research on Utilization of Scientific Knowledge, 1976.

Lingwood, D. and Morris, W. C. *Developing and Testing a Linkage Model of Dissemination and Utilization.* Paper presented at the Annual Meeting of AERA, Chicago, April 1974.

Lippitt, R., Watson, J., and Westley, B. *The Dynamics of Planned Change.* New York: Harcourt, Brace and World, 1958.

Littleton, V. C., Jr. *A Study of the Factors Contributing to the Predisposition of Elementary Principals to Try Selected Innovations.* Unpublished doctoral dissertation, University of Texas at Austin, 1970.

Loffredo, M. *A Study of the Relationships between Various Personal Characteristics and Perceptions of Iowa Public School Principals and Their Attitudes towards Educational Innovation.* Unpublished doctoral dissertation, University of Iowa, 1974.

Loucks, S. F. *A Study of the Relationship between Teacher Level of Use of the Innovation of Individualized Instruction and Student Achievement.* Unpublished doctoral dissertation, University of Texas at Austin, 1975.

Louis, K. S. *Linking Organizations and Educational Change: The Case of the Pilot State Dissemination Projects.* Unpublished doctoral dissertation, Columbia University, 1975.

Magee, Sister P. *Anxiety of Professional Personnel Prior and Subsequent to Adoption of Innovation.* Unpublished doctoral dissertation, University of Wisconsin-Madison, 1975.

Maguire, L. M. *Observations and Analysis of the Literature on Change.* Philadelphia: Research for Better Schools, 1970.

Maguire, L. M., Temkin, S., and Cummings, C. P. *An Annotated Bibliography on Administering for Change.* Philadelphia: Research for Better Schools, 1971.

Maguire, L. M. *A Comparison of a Planned Change Effort of a Regional Educational Laboratory to the Lippitt-Watson-Westley Model.* Unpublished doctoral dissertation, Temple University, 1970.

Mann, D. For the Record. *Teachers College Record.* February, 1976, 77, 313-322.

McCoy, M. *Teachers' and Principals' Perceptions of Supervisors as Being Helpful in Implementing Innovations in Selected Elementary Schools in Florida.* Unpublished doctoral dissertation, Florida State University, 1975.

McKeighe, J. E. *The Involvement of Rhode Island State Education Agency Services in Local Education Agency Innovation.* Unpublished doctoral dissertation, Columbia University Teachers College, 1976.

McLaughlin, M. Implementation as Mutual Adaptation: Change in Classroom Organization, *Teachers College Record.* 1976, 77, 339-351.

Melby, A. C. *Midwestern Suburban Superintendents' Perceptions of Factors Influencing Recent Curriculum Change.* Unpublished doctoral dissertation, Indiana University, 1975.

Meyer, J. *The Impact of the Open-Space School upon Teacher Influence and Autonomy: The Effects of an Organizational Innovation.* Stanford Center for Research and Development in Teaching, Stanford University, October, 1971.

Michaletz, J. E. *A Comparison of the Perception of Two Groups of Elementary School Principals Concerning the Exercise of the Leadership Role Effecting Change.* Unpublished doctoral dissertation, Loyola University of Chicago, 1974.

Miles, M. Some Properties of Social Systems. In G. Watson (Ed.), *Change in School Systems.* Washington, D. C.: National Training Labs, 1967, 1-29.

Miller, E. M. *Feelings and Views of Oregon Principals Regarding their Roles as Change Agents.* Unpublished doctoral dissertation, University of Oregon, 1973.

Montgomery, H. J. *An Examination of Some Factors of Change in Selected Schools of a Suburban Elementary School District.* Unpublished doctoral dissertation, Loyola University of Chicago, 1975.

Naumann-Etienne, M. *Bringing about Open Education: Strategies for Innovation and Implementation.* Unpublished doctoral dissertation, University of Michigan, 1974.

Newman, E. F. *Forces Affecting the Maintenance of an Innovation: Flexible/Modular Scheduling in a Senior High School (Volumes I and II).* Unpublished doctoral dissertation, University of Michigan, 1974.

O'Connell, R. H. *A Diffusion Model for the Colamda Project in Colorado.* Unpublished doctoral dissertation, University of Denver, 1971.

Paul, D. The Diffusion of an Innovation through Interorganizational Linkages, *Educational Administration Quarterly.* 1976, 12, 18-37.

Paul, D. *The Diffusion of an Innovation through Interorganizational Linkages.* Unpublished doctoral dissertation, University of Wisconsin-Madison, 1974. (Also Technical Report No. 308, July 1974.)

Paul, D. *A Conceptual Framework for Studying Knowledge Utilization.* Paper presented at the Annual Meeting of the American Educational Research Association, Washington, D. C., 1975a.

Paul, D. *A Comparison of Research Utilization Roles between Faculty and Field Center Staff.* Unpublished report, Ontario Institute for Studies in Education, 1975b.

Peoples, C. *Comparison of Organizational Climates of An Innovative and a Traditional High School.* Unpublished doctoral dissertation, Pennsylvania State University, 1973.

Perry, W. R., Jr. *The Use of Teachers as Change Agents: A Case Study.* Unpublished doctoral dissertation, University of Massachusetts, 1975.

Peterson, A. C. *An Examination of a Set of Presuppositions on a Philosophy of Human Nature and Perceptions of Change by Teachers in Traditional, Transitional, and Innovative Schools.* Unpublished doctoral dissertation, George Peabody College for Teachers, 1974.

Phelps, S. S. *Cooperative Teaching Centers: Exchange of Services as a Key to Institutional Linkage.* Unpublished doctoral dissertation, Wayne State University, 1974.

Pinch, J. H. *Parent Involvement with Curriculum Change in a Public School.* Unpublished doctoral dissertation, Michigan State University, 1975.

Pincus, J. Incentives for Innovation in the Public Schools. *Review of Educational Research.* 1974, 44, 113-144.

Pitman, J. C. *Training for and Implementation of a Team Approach to Planned Educational Change: An Historical Study.* Unpublished doctoral dissertation, Duke University, 1974.

Pohland, P. A. *An Interorganizational Analysis of an Innovative Educational Program.* Unpublished doctoral dissertation, Washington University, 1970.

Poll, D. *The Study of Selected Factors Related to the Implementation of Centrally Prepared Curriculum Guides.* Unpublished doctoral dissertation, Northwestern University, 1970.

Prasad, R. *Educational Change and Role of Central Administration: A Case Study.* Unpublished doctoral dissertation, Stanford University, 1971.

Rasmussen, R. H. *The Relationship of Organizational Climate and Individual Attitudes toward Change to Teachers' Perceptions of Organizational Receptivity to Change.* Unpublished doctoral dissertation, University of New Orleans, 1975.

Reynolds, L. J. *Problems of Implementing Organizational Change in the Elementary School: A Case Study.* Unpublished doctoral dissertation, University of Oregon, 1971.

Richardson, C. L. *Diffusion of a Professional Innovation among Public School Districts in Texas.* Unpublished doctoral dissertation, University of Houston, 1974.

Rivera, P. R. *A Study of the Development and Implementation of the Curriculum Innovation World Cultures in the Baltimore County, Maryland Public Schools (1968-1973).* Unpublished doctoral dissertation, University of Maryland, 1975.

Roberts, E. N. *Changes in Organizational Climate Associated with Implementation of an Educational Management System in a Large Urban School District.* Unpublished doctoral dissertation, University of Southern California, 1975.

Roberts, J. *Belief Systems of Innovative West Virginia Public School Superintendents.* Unpublished doctoral dissertation, Ohio University, 1974.

Robeson, R. L. *The Diffusion of Educational Innovations through the Explicit In-Service Training of Teachers.* Unpublished doctoral dissertation, University of Maryland, 1974.

Rogers, E. M., and Thomas, P. C. *Bibliography on the Diffusion of Innovation.* Ann Arbor, Michigan: University of Michigan, Department of Population Planning, School of Public Health, 1975.

Rogers, E. M. and Shoemaker, F. F. *Communication of Innovations: A Cross-Cultural Approach.* New York: Free Press, 1971.

Rogers, E. M. *Diffusion of Innovations.* New York: The Free Press of Glencoe, Inc., 1962.

Rogers, E. M., Agarwala-Rogers, R., and Lee, C. C. *Diffusion of Impact Innovations to University Professors.* Ann Arbor, Michigan: University of Michigan, Department of Journalism and Program in Mass Communication Research, 1975.

Rosenau, F. S., and Hood, P. *A Literature Review for Diffusion of Educational R&D Products/Processes.* San Francisco: Far West Laboratory for Educational Research and Development, 1975.

Ryan, B., and Cross, N. C. The Diffusion of Hybrid Seed Corn in Two Iowa Communities, *Rural Sociology.* 1943, *8*, 15-24.

Sailer, W. *A Study of Communication as It Relates to the Leadership Styles and Readiness for Innovation of Elementary and Secondary School Principals.* Unpublished doctoral dissertation, New Mexico State University, 1974.

Schermerhorn, J. *Determinants of Inter-Organizational Cooperation: Theoretical Systhesis and an Empirical Study of Hospital Administrators' Felt Needs to Cooperate.* Unpublished doctoral dissertation, Northwestern University, 1974.

Schmuck, R., and Miles, M. (Eds.). *Organizational Development in Schools.* Palo Alto, California: National Press Books, 1971.

Schmuck, R. Some Uses of Research Methods in Organizational Development Projects, *Viewpoints.* 1974, *50*, 47-59.

Schumacher, S. A. *Political Processes in Education: A Case Study of an Interagency Curriculum Evaluation and Diffusion Project.* Unpublished doctoral dissertation, Washington University, 1975.

Schumer, A. B. *An Educational Change Model: Pre-service, In-service Continuum.* Unpublished doctoral dissertation, University of Massachusetts, 1973.

Short, E. C. Knowledge Production and Utilization in Curriculum: A Special Case for the General Phenomenon, *Review of Educational Research.* 1973, *43*, 237-302.

Sieber, S. Organizational Influences on Innovative Roles. In T. Eidell and J. Kitchel (Eds.), *Knowledge Production and Utilization in Educational Administration.* Eugene, Oregon: Center for the Advanced Study of Educational Administration, 1968, 120-142.

Seiber, S., Louis, K., and Metzger, L. *The Use of Educational Knowledge: Evaluation of the Pilot State Dissemination Program.* New York: Columbia University, Bureau of Applied Social Research, September, 1972.

Sieber, S. Images of the Practitioner and Strategies of Educational Change, *Sociology of Education.* 1972, *45*, 362-385.

Sieber, S. Trends in Diffusion Research: Knowledge Utilization, *Viewpoints.* 1974, *50*, 61-81.

Sieber, S. *Knowledge Utilization: A Conceptual Paper.* Unpublished Concept Paper (typewritten), 1975.

Sikorski, L. *A Study of the Current Status of the Implementation of Science and Mathematics Materials at the Pre-College Level in the National Sciences, Social Sciences, and Mathematics.* San Francisco: Far West Laboratory for Educational Research and Development, April 1976.

Skor, C. *Implementation of Change and Selected Organization Variables.* Unpublished doctoral dissertation, Yeshiva University, 1974.

Smith, M. A. *A Comparison of Two Elementary Schools Involved in a Major Organizational Change: Or You Win a Few; You Lose a Few.* Unpublished doctoral dissertation, University of Oregon, 1972.

Snell, J. *A Study of the Penetration and the Desirability of Certain Selected Educational Innovations in New York Elementary Schools.* Unpublished doctoral dissertation, Indiana University, 1975.

Starling, W. M. *An Unsuccessful Attempt to Implement an Educational Innovation: A Case Study.* Unpublished doctoral dissertation, University of Oregon, 1973.

Stefoneck, T. Educational Planning and Evaluation: A Local District Perspective, *Information Series.* Madison, Wisconsin: Wisconsin Department of Public Instruction, 1976, 5.

Stephens, K. G. *The Process of Educational Innovation: A Participant Observation Analysis.* Unpublished doctoral dissertation. University of Illinois, Urbana-Champaign, 1975.

Sullivan, J. J. *A Study of Selected Factors Related to the Successful Institutionalization of Educational Change.* Unpublished doctoral dissertation, University of Massachusetts, 1974.

Sutter, W. *A Study of the Innovativeness of Teachers and Administrators in Selective Schools in Relation to Change-Oriented and Status-Oriented School Districts.* Unpublished doctoral dissertation, Illinois State University, 1974.

Swirsky, D. M. *Teachers' Perceptions of Organizational Climate and their Acceptance or Rejection of an Innovation in Classroom Practice.* Unpublished doctoral dissertation, Columbia University, 1975.

Temkin, S., Brown, M., and Dougherty, J. *Linkage Models for Dissemination and Diffusion.* Paper presented at the Annual Meeting of the American Educational Research Association, Chicago, 1974.

Thomas, J. Why Review the R&D Model of Innovation? *Educational Administration Quarterly,* 1975, 11, 104-108.

Thelen, H. A. Concepts for Collaborative Action-Inquiry, In G. Watson (Ed.), *Concepts for Social Change.* Washington, D. C., National Training Labs, 1967, 37-46.

Townley, J. L. *Personality Characteristics of Innovative Teachers as Measured by the Cattell.* Unpublished doctoral dissertation, University of Southern California, 1973.

Trent, P. J. *A Study of Organizational Climate and Dynamics of Change in an Elementary School: An Anthropological Approach.* Unpublished doctoral dissertation, Northwestern University, 1975.

True, J. *Relational Analysis of the Implementation of Change in a Public Elementary School.* Unpublished doctoral dissertation, University of Florida, 1974.

Tushingham, G. *A Study of Some Factors Affecting Implementation of Organizational Innovations in Ontario Public Secondary Schools.* Unpublished doctoral dissertation, Wayne State University, 1974.

Vance, P. L. *Factors Related to Successful Educational Innovation in Selected Middle Schools: Philadelphia, Pennsylvania, 1968-1973.* Unpublished doctoral dissertation, University of Pennsylvania, 1974.

Vold, L. A. *Inter-Institutional Planning: A Study of a Cooperative Teacher Education Program between the University of Wisconsin-Madison, Madison Social Studies Teachers and the Madison Public Schools.* Unpublished doctoral dissertation, University of Wisconsin-Madison, 1975.

Wacaster, C. T. *The Life and Death of Differentiated Staffing at Columbia High School: A Field Study of an Educational Innovation's Discontinuance.* Unpublished doctoral dissertation, University of Oregon, 1973.

Walker, H. G. *The Adoption of Educational Innovations by School Districts and the Selected Strategies Influencing Adoption When Federal Funding is Terminated.* Unpublished doctoral dissertation, Claremont Graduate School, 1973.

Washington, A. *Differences between Innovative and Traditional Elementary School Teachers in their Perceptions of Semantic Differential Concepts Reflecting Receptivity to Change.* Unpublished doctoral dissertation, University of Southern California, 1974.

Watson, G. *Concepts for Social Change.* Washington, D. C.: National Training Labs, 1967.

Weigle, B. C. *The Diffusion of Certain Instructional Innovation in the Public School Districts of Florida: 1965-1974.* Unpublished doctoral dissertation, University of Mississippi, 1975.

Whiting, R. H. *A Study of Change Processes as Investigated through Case Studies Conducted in Selected Colorado Secondary Schools.* Unpublished doctoral dissertation, University of Colorado, 1972.

Winkelpleck, J. M. *Organizational and Individual Variables as Predictors of Interorganizational Relations.* Unpublished doctoral dissertation, Iowa State University, 1974.

Wyner, N. *A Study of Diffusion of Innovation: Measuring Perceived Attributes of an Innovation that Determine the Rate of Adoption.* Unpublished doctoral dissertation, Columbia University, 1974.

2

Linking Agents and the Sources and Uses of Knowledge

Jack Culbertson

Linking agents and agencies have as one of their central concerns the sources and uses of knowledge. This chapter delineates the wide range of resources drawn upon by linkers, describes important knowledge uses, and shows their complementarity.

Based on a national perspective of the complex American educational system, the chapter focuses on the sources and uses of knowledge within that system. Through an examination of these variables, perhaps some of the excesses of faddism in the area of change processes and of the inadequacies in linking roles which are not knowledge-based will be made more evident. In a period when there is a growing press for dissemination and application, a focus upon multiple knowledge uses can also remind us that differing knowledge users, both in the short-term and long-term, are highly dependent upon one another and, in turn, upon the continuing generation and flow of new concepts, generalizations and findings.

Varied uses of knowledge imply varied forms; consequently, no formal or encompassing definition of knowledge will be offered at this point. Rather, the strategy will be to clarify these various forms within the context of the different uses of knowledge described below.

At this point some of the limitations inherent in the categories of knowledge utilization elaborated need to be identified. First, the categories are not presumed to be totally comprehensive; rather, they constitute knowledge uses which the writer deems as highly critical. Undoubtedly, additional uses could be postulated, and certainly other sub-uses could be formulated. Secondly, as with other categories of human behavior, the different uses are not totally discrete. A reading of the descriptions will show not only their close interrelatedness and interdependency but also some overlapping features in the categories developed. A third limitation stems from the relatively small amount of research available on knowledge uses in education. Since studies which are available on the general subject of knowledge utilization come largely from the more established sciences, there is no guarantee that the results of these studies apply precisely to the field of education.[1] Fourth, since education is a developing rather than a developed field, the division of labor implied in the description of different users is probably more marked than actually exists in practice. Stated in another way, the number of individuals specializing in a single use of knowledge is extremely limited. Finally, some of the dimensions of knowledge use are described and illustrated from the perspective of educational administration. As the categories of knowledge use are assumed to be generic ones, one could have used a different field for illustrations — curriculum or educational psychology, for example.

While the categories have limitations, they also can be used beneficially. First, they can provide concepts for use in the design of training and support systems for various knowledge users, including linking agents directly concerned with improving educational practice. Second, they can provide a basis for assessing current knowledge utilization efforts and for identifying priorities deserving special funding. Lastly, they can stimulate study directed at the attainment of a more refined system for classifying knowledge uses.

Knowledge uses will be discussed from various perspectives: the outcomes produced by the uses, the distinctive features of uses and outcomes, illustrative types and sources of knowledge used to produce different outcomes, key characteristics of different users of knowledge, and the settings in which users work.

---

[1] For a pioneering review and synthesis of knowledge utilization from the perspective of different fields, see Ronald Havelock, *Planning for Innovations Through the Dissemination and Utilization of Knowledge.* Ann Arbor, Michigan: Institute for Social Research, Center for Research on Utilization of Scientific Knowledge, 1969.

Schema I pinpoints the shorter and longer range outcomes of the differing uses of knowledge.

Using Knowledge to Create New Knowledge

Research is the process used to create new knowledge.[2] Two major classes of research are postulated: conclusion-oriented and policy-oriented,[3] each of which has significance for linking agents.

Conclusion-Oriented or Basic Research[4]

Conclusion-oriented research is designed to advance frontiers of knowledge, and inquiry of this type is represented in valid descriptions and explanations of the interrelationships between and among variables inherent in or impinging upon a given field of study. In the 1960s for example, those studying the economics of education highlighted in new ways relationships between investments in education and returns to society. Psychologists, during the same period, shed new light on the relationships between early childhood learnings and future educational achievements.

Basic researchers who are likely to reside in research and development centers, university departments, or institutes are motivated largely by curiosity and by the challenge of discovering new relationships through data-based inquiry. The results of their work can stimulate new inquiry by other basic researchers and can lead to more highly developed or even new theories. Over time, results also can have a major influence on the directions of policy, practice, or new developments. Findings on

---

[2]The discussion immediately following draws upon concepts presented in Jack Culbertson, "Specialized Career Patterns and Content Selection." See Jack Culbertson, et al., *Social Science Content for Preparing Educational Leaders*. Columbus, Ohio: Charles E. Merrill Publishing Company, 1973, pp. 327-355.

[3]Among the scholars who have proposed two distinct types of research are Lee J. Cronbach and Patrick Suppes. See their book, *Research for Tomorrow's Schools*. New York: McMillan Company, 1969.

[4]The terms "basic research" and "conclusion-oriented research" are used interchangeably in this chapter.

SCHEMA I
KNOWLEDGE USES AND CONSEQUENCES IN EDUCATION

General Uses of Knowledge	Sub-Uses of Knowledge	Short-Term Outcomes	Longer Range Outcomes
To Create New Knowledge	Conclusion Research	Valid descriptions and explanations of education and leadership-related phenomena.	Modification in bodies of knowledge.
	Policy Research	Generalizations about how and why educational programs work and the degree to which they are effective.	Modifications in educational policies and/or programs.
To Develop New Syntheses	Concept-Oriented Syntheses	Newly organized bodies of knowledge within or across disciplines.	Rational bases for advancing conclusion research and for preparing scholars.
	Practice-Related Synthesis	Research findings and generalizations organized in relation to leadership objectives, functions, problems, issues or other aspects of practice.	Rational decision-making and training bases for leaders.
To Attain New Developments	Product Development	New materials, technologies, systems or processes of specific use to leaders.	New options for leaders interested in improving existing programs.
	Idea Development	Future-oriented and untested alternatives for improving education or its leadership or both of them.	New options for leaders interested in instituting new policies or programs.
To Achieve New or Improved Practice	Improved Policies and Programs	An increase in the quality or quantity of program outcomes or a relative decrease in the resources used to produce similar outcomes.	Improved or more efficiently delivered education to the clients of schools.
	Newly Instituted Policies or Programs	Changed objectives or new programs.	More promising bases for improving or delivering education to the clients of schools.
To Improve Training Programs	In-Service Programs	New job-related learnings for currently functioning leaders.	More effective and competent behavior on the part of selected leaders currently serving in administrative posts.
	Pre-Service Programs	New learnings for personnel aspiring to initial or more advanced leadership positions.	More effective and competent behavior among those aspiring to leadership posts.

the relationships between early learnings and later academic achievements in the 1960s provided one source of support for early childhood programs. However, the most immediate and direct impact of basic research tends to be on the discipline or body of concepts from which the research evolved.

Major sources of knowledge used by basic researchers studying educational administration are the modes of inquiry and concepts of social science disciplines: History, social psychology, sociology, economics, anthropology and political science all have tested concepts and methods which can be used to study educational administration. Thus, pertinent basic research has been done by scholars trained in disciplines. Theories of human motivation, leadership, conflict, informal organization or other leadership-related phenomena, in other words, have evolved from this basis. More-recently-prepared professors in education have had better opportunities to acquire and use knowledge from one or more social science disciplines, and an increasing number of those professors are producing basic research.

With the very substantial ambiguity confronted by basic researchers, the procedures outlined for dealing with problem definition, hypothesis or question development, research design, and data acquisition and analysis in textbooks on research tend to be oversimplified. In most instances the discovery of new knowledge, in other words, involves extended search, many false starts, and long periods of conscious thinking. Basic research is typically the product of individual effort, and fellow researchers are the major sources both of psychological support and of quality assurance.

Instead of encompassing a wide range of variables as leaders do in decision-making situations, basic researchers commonly focus their inquiry on a limited number of carefully defined variables. Even a few variables such as leadership or power structure can guide a lifetime of search for knowledge, and basic researchers, as a rule, are not concerned about how their findings will impact on practice.[5]

The key linking agencies for basic researchers in the social sciences are such national professional associations as the American Sociological Association and the American Political Science Association, both of which contain sub-groups interested in the sociology of education and the poli-

---

[5]There is evidence from the scientific community more generally that the most important discoveries are made by researchers when they are in their twenties and thirties (Lehman, 1953). The capacity to identify and pursue new questions in highly fruitful ways, in other words, likely resides in those with fresh and flexible perspectives. Thus, seasoning and experience, which seem to be a requirement for effective administration, do not necessarily enhance the basic researcher's capability. Long seasoning within a context of practice is likely in fact to be antithetical to the achievement of major discoveries.

tics of education. The officers, staff and informal leaders of these associations play important roles in the diffusion of knowledge by sponsoring annual conferences and professional journals which report basic research. Some universities have taken the lead in disseminating basic research as witness, for example, *The American Journal of Sociology,* published at the University of Chicago.

Professors of educational administration engaged in discipline-based research frequently join relevant social science associations. Other important and relevant linking agencies are The University Council for Educational Administration (UCEA) which sponsors the *Educational Administration Quarterly,* the National Conference of Professors of Educational Administration (NCPEA), and Division A of the American Educational Research Association.

Basic researchers, then, link with fellow researchers through national associations and their systems for disseminating knowledge. However, at times they may be called upon to present their knowledge to policy makers at the state, local or federal levels, and in addition, they may be asked to present their research findings at meetings sponsored by other local or regional professional associations. In the main, the major task of translating basic knowledge into practice is left to knowledge users other than basic researchers.

Policy Research

Policy research focuses upon the results of chosen courses of organizational action[6]: Courses of action can reflect either changes in policy or efforts to implement established policy efficiently and effectively. By providing a better understanding of the degree to which and manner in which given courses of action work, policy research can provide useful feedback to policy makers. Ideally, this form of research should provide policy makers continuing bases for changing and adapting policies as the latter are studied and expressed in courses of action.

Philosophers, for a long time, have maintained that the political process from which policy is developed should be conceived and conducted as an experiment.[7] John Dewey argued that the scientific method could be

---

[6]For an insightful discussion of policy research see James Coleman, *Policy Research in the Social Sciences.* Morristown, N. J.: General Learning Press, 1972.

[7]For a comparison of the views of two philosophers on the subject, see Lawrence Haworth, "The Experimental Society: Dewey and Jordan." *Ethics,* Vol. LXXI, No. 1, October, 1960, pp. 27-40.

brought to bear on "experimentation" in policy and improve the process. In addition, he believed that the approach could help resolve, over time, a fundamental problem: Through the use of research on social experiments, Dewey believed the extremes of regimentation and license could be avoided.

While the concept of policy studies has been established for some time, it has not been easy to implement.[8] During the last decade there has been growing interest on the part of the public and its elected representatives in the idea. Legislation has emphasized the role of policy studies in assessing the efficacy of newly initiated programs. For example, there is a range of current studies to evaluate Title I programs of the Elementary and Secondary Education Act and, in turn, to help legislators make decisions concerning the continuance, expansion, curtailment, or change in Title I programs. Policy studies are also encouraged more generally by the so-called accountability movement which presses school leaders and scholars to depict more clearly what the schools are doing and how well they are doing it.

At this point, some general contrasts between basic and policy research may be helpful in further defining the latter concept.[9] Basic research is concerned more with the development and testing of theories, while policy research is oriented more to action. Therefore, the major immediate audience for policy research is decision makers; the major immediate audience for basic research is scholars. Basic research tends to originate in disciplines and to be fed back into disciplines. On the other hand, policy research has its origins in action, and its results are fed back into action. Thus, basic research seeks principally to modify bodies of knowledge; policy research seeks principally to modify policy.

Coleman has identified a number of "world-of-action" properties which help to define and clarify policy research (1972:3-4). First, since decisions must be taken at fixed time points, policy research must be keyed to these points. More comprehensive or new findings developed *after* decision points are reached are not helpful. Generalizations, even when limited in scope, can be helpful when provided on time. Second, language and concepts used in the world of action are different from those used in disciplines (Coleman, 1972:5). The language of the practitioner, for example, differs from the language of the researcher: The former tends to

---

[8]For a discussion of the reasons why the concept is difficult to implement, see Donald T. Campbell, "Reforms as Experiments." *American Psychologist*, Vol. 24, No. 4, April 1969, pp. 411-12.

[9]The discussion to follow will focus largely upon research directed at new programs rather than on the more effective or efficient administration of existing programs. The same concepts, however, can be applied, it is assumed, to the study of existing programs.

be popular in tone, and the latter to be technical. The language of basic researchers is oriented toward inquiry and has no concern for action, but for educational leaders the converse is more often true.

A third property identified by Coleman is that the world of action involves "interests, control of resources, and conflict." Conflict and control reflect differing values which impact upon groups differently. Certain findings may add to the power of certain groups and simultaneously diminish the power of others. This property has implications for the commissioning of policy studies, the definition of policy problems, the design of policy research, and the translation of findings into the world of action.

The concepts and methods of inquiry available to policy researchers are neither as well developed nor as tested as those available to basic researchers, for not only is policy research a much more recent phenomenon than basic research but also the rewards for university professors continue to favor basic research. It is also true that in such areas as school finance, policy studies have been conducted for a number of decades. For example, the studies of the impact of state foundation support programs at various periods in the last four decades have led to changes in state financing patterns.

Since evaluation research focuses upon studying the outcomes of new programs or courses of action, it represents one approach to policy research. Stimulated by the growth in federally funded education programs, a variety of conceptualizations for guiding evaluation research has emerged. Different approaches are found in the objectives-based, the instructional research, composite, goal-free, management-decision, transactional and adversary models of evaluation.[10]

During the last decade there also has been considerable growth in university centers concerned with policy studies in education. Although these centers have not focused on studying the outcomes of programs as consistently as have evaluation centers, they have added to the number of policy studies available.[11] It is also significant that several departments of educational administration have conducted useful and systematic studies

---

[10]For a brief description of these models plus references describing their original formulations, see Derek Taylor, "Eeeny, Meeny, Miney, Meaux: Alternative Evaluation Models," *The North Central Association Quarterly*, Vol. 50, No. 4, Spring, 1976, pp. 353-58. For a more thorough treatment of evaluation see Marcia Guttentag and Elmer Struening (Eds.), *Handbook of Evaluation Research*. Beverly Hills, California: Sage Publication, 1975.

[11]Many of the centers encompass under policy studies inquiry directed at generating and assessing alternative courses of action not yet implemented. This type of inquiry, which contrasts sharply with research directed at studying the impact of programs already implemented, is discussed later in this paper under "Using Knowledge to Attain New Developments."

of management policies by using operations research models to simulate defined courses of action.

Embedded in approaches to policy studies just noted are varying assumptions about the concepts and methodologies which should shape inquiry. Discipline-based concepts and modes of inquiry, with the exception of economics, have had limited use — at least in their original expressions. In addition those in social science or other departments who would perform policy studies must deal with conflicts between the values of sciences and the values of decision makers. For example, a value held by those in universities is that all research findings should be public; however, this value can easily clash with those held in decision arenas where timing and control of information are important. For this and other reasons, Coleman argues that independent research organizations are better equipped than are universities to carry out policy research (1972:15).

The motivation of policy researchers is to understand what works and why, given specified policies and defined courses of action. These researchers have special links both to responsible policy makers and to other groups affected by policy. The results of this type of research not only can help modify policy but also can provide content for training. Thus, policy researchers play a unique role in bridging the world of ideas and the world of action, and in the process, they must confront difficult scientific as well as complex-political issues.

Although many national professional associations provide forums for the dissemination of policy research, currently there are no formally established linking agencies which specialize in disseminating such studies. Since a growing amount of policy research is performed by non-profit organizations, there is considerable informal and individually initiated communication between and among personnel in these agencies.

The written results of policy studies generally are disseminated in the form of technical reports. Because the studies are frequently done for governmental agencies, the latter often play an important role in distributing them. In some cases the major findings of reports are disseminated in media especially designed to serve practitioners in school systems such as in such journals as the *Phi Delta Kappan* or in more specialized publications like *Integration*.

In summary, policy researchers link closely with decision makers in defining research, conducting research, and interpreting the results. They are more likely to link with other policy researchers than with those pursuing basic research. The products they produce, if effective, are useful to decision makers interested in changing policy or practice or both.

Data on selected features of basic and policy research are summarized in Schema II.

SCHEMA II
SOME DIFFERENCES IN BASIC AND POLICY RESEARCH

Sub-Uses of Knowledge	Short-Term Outcomes	Longer-Range Outcomes	Illustrative Knowledge Used	Key Artifacts	Significant Quality Assurance Agents
Basic Research	Valid descriptions and explanations of education and leadership-related phenomena	Modifications in bodies of knowledge	Modes of inquiry in anthropology	Journal articles	Other conclusion-oriented researchers
Policy Research	Generalization about how and why educational programs work and the degree to which they are effective	Modifications in educational policies and programs	Evaluation models featuring decision concepts	Technical reports	The clients served

USING KNOWLEDGE TO ACHIEVE NEW SYNTHESES

As research studies accumulate, their findings and conclusions tend to be used for purposes of consolidation or synthesis. Two general classes of synthesis are postulated: concept-oriented and practice-related. Further clarification of these two types follows.

Concept-Oriented Synthesis

Those pursuing concept-oriented synthesis seek to produce newly organized bodies of knowledge which reflect a re-ordering of concepts and research findings about selected aspects of education organizations or leadership. Ralph Stogdill's publication on leadership is one example of such a synthesis (1948:35-71). In contrast to the basic researcher who gathers data through new studies and engages in the primary or secondary analyses of the data, the synthesizer uses existing studies as major data bases.[12] Synthesizers may use existing studies to conduct "meta-analysis," a form of inquiry which Gene Glass has described as "the statistical analysis of a large collection of analysis results from individual studies for the purposes of integrating the findings" (1976:3).

When effective, concept-oriented synthesis amasses and gives new meanings to existing knowledge, and such synthesis may be within the framework of a discipline, for example, the politics of education, or it may transcend disciplines as in the case of Stogdill's work on leadership referred to above.

The concept-oriented synthesizer is much more concerned with advancing knowledge and understanding than with advancing practice; consequently, concept-oriented synthesizers tend to serve more the needs of scholars in universities than leaders in practice settings. Their products can raise new research questions or point new directions for inquiry. At best, they can achieve new paradigms which will markedly reshape inquiry in a field.[13] They also can provide content for training future re-

---

[12]Basic researchers also engage in a kind of synthesis. However, their purpose is more to identify the "edge" of knowledge and to formulate hypotheses to guide research rather than to cumulate more comprehensive bodies of knowledge.

[13]For details see Thomas S. Kuhn, *The Structure of Scientific Revolution*. Chicago: The University of Chicago Press, 1970.

searchers and scholar practitioners, and occasionally syntheses can be used by developers, practice-oriented synthesizers, and others concerned with the use of knowledge in practice.

Major resources used by concept-oriented synthesizers are theories, concepts, and research findings produced by basic researchers or by other concept-oriented synthesizers. The first task is one of collection:

> The written work of others (whether or not formally published) constitutes "raw" data for the integrator. In compiling the initial list of materials to be read, the integrator makes use of other bibliographies, reviews integrations in the specific areas of his [her] concern, as well as the variety of more general sources of information . . . . Further, as any given report is read, the conscientious integrator will make it a point to track down any references given in it that seem relevant to his [her] topic. After a given period — it may be a long one — little in the way of "new" references will be found. (Feldman, 1971:87).

After pertinent studies are collected, inquiry is concerned with the definition, classification and re-ordering of findings to achieve generalizations. A major challenge, as Glass has demonstrated, is that of devising ways of comparing diverse findings (1976:3-5); another is the treatment of studies with conflicting findings.[14]

While synthesis entails integration, the process also requires the ordering of knowledge within the components which comprise the whole. An early step in ordering knowledge is the discovery and mastery of scholarly works and fragmented bodies of knowledge, a process which must precede that of integrating concepts and findings. In the process of achieving integration there is the challenge of identifying and elaborating those organizing principles which can give order to the knowledge mastered. In contrast to the basic researchers who tend to concentrate intensively upon a limited number of variables, the synthesizer may concentrate upon a wide range of variables.

Although there are other agencies where they function, the typical work setting of the concept-oriented synthesizer is the university. Concept-oriented synthesis tends to require individual activity, but group effort through some division of labor is not uncommon. Scholars in social

---

[14] For one treatment of this subject see Richard Light and Paul Smith, "Accumulating Evidence: Procedures for Resolving Contradictions Among Different Research Studies." *Harvard Educational Review*, Vol. 41, No. 4, pp. 429-471.

science departments play leading roles in synthesizing knowledge as do selected professors of education.

Concept-oriented synthesizers have a high degree of autonomy. As with basic researchers, they typically do not require public legitimation for specific objectives they pursue. They require extended periods to produce, especially when the target is comprehensive synthesis, and their work may go through many revisions and may be subject to varied critiques from other scholars who help to control the quality of their work.

Linking agencies which serve basic researchers also serve concept-oriented synthesizers. Included would be national professional associations serving social scientists and professors of education, the national meetings of which promote exchange as do pertinent journals — the *Journal of Personality and Social Psychology*, the *Administrative Science Quarterly* and the *Educational Administration Quarterly*, among others. Major syntheses, of course, make their way into monographs and books.

Since concept-oriented synthesizers are not concerned immediately or primarily with practice, their linkage is much more to fellow scholars and graduate students. However, some synthesizers may present new consolidations of concepts to practicing educators; in addition, other knowledge users will use the consolidations developed by synthesizers to influence education and leadership.

Practice-Related Synthesis

The major goal of practice-related synthesizers is to organize existing knowledge in ways which will help educational leaders in their decision-making roles. This goal is achieved by ordering or reordering knowledge in relation to criteria outside "academic" disciplines as, for example, goals or objectives pursued by leaders, functions they perform, programs they seek to implement, problems or policy issues they confront. The typical textbook in education represents a practice-oriented synthesis and is designed to produce meanings for practicing and prospective educational leaders. Knowledge in a textbook on educational administration, for example, might be organized around such functions as staff personnel administration, evaluation, resource management, school-community relations, educational program improvement, and so forth. Less comprehensive syntheses can be organized around such specific topics as school insurance, staff recruitment, implementing open schools, among others. In other words, the topics and the concepts which illuminate them have clear links with practice. In contrast to concept-oriented synthesizers who use criteria internal to disciplines to cumulate knowledge, practice-oriented synthesizers use categories designed to help administrators and other professional personnel link knowledge directly to decisions and actions. Their goal is much more to improve practice through the use of concepts and information than it is to point new directions for inquiry.

The sources used in practice-oriented synthesis are varied. As already noted, ideas and information from concept-oriented syntheses can be used even though a new framework for ordering these concepts is required. The findings and generalizations developed by policy-oriented researchers are especially pertinent because the latter are concerned with demonstrating how programs for which administrators are responsible work. Certainly, the results of both product-oriented and idea-oriented development (see below) are pertinent, and specific studies conducted by basic researchers may at times be grist for practice-oriented syntheses.

Modes of inquiry are perhaps not substantially different from those used by concept-oriented synthesizers as definition, classification and generalization are required. A key difference, however, is that value judgments enter much more clearly into practice-oriented synthesis. Since generalizations seek to describe or explain things as they are in concept-oriented synthesis, scholars can stay within the "is" framework, but in practice-oriented synthesis, on the other hand, relationships between actual and ideal conditions are involved. In other words, the generalizations developed are designed to help leaders and organizations make decisions which will move education toward more idealized states. Choices made about objectives, problems and other rubrics used in producing practice-oriented syntheses are shaped inevitably by the ideas or values of synthesizers and/or their clients. The practice-oriented synthesizer, then, has an important role in identifying and clarifying values.

An early step in practice-oriented synthesis is the definition of elements which will serve as organizing links to practice and which will require value clarification. These elements will vary depending upon whether educational or leadership objectives, functions, programs, processes, issues, problems, or other phenomena are chosen for organizing frameworks. The number of organizing elements will increase and value questions will become more complex as more comprehensive syntheses are sought.

A range of organizations perform linking agent roles bearing upon practice-related synthesis; especially important are national professional associations. Serving administrators, for example, are the American Association for School Administrators (AASA), the National Association for Elementary School Principals (NAESP), and the National Association for Secondary School Principals (NASSP). Other organizations with large numbers of administrators as members also perform effective roles as, for example, Phi Delta Kappa. Regional and state educational associations also disseminate practice-related findings.

Many practice-related syntheses are published in periodicals sponsored by national associations serving particular groups of administrators as, for example, the *National Elementary School Principal*. The ERIC Clearinghouse on Education Management at the University of Oregon, to take another example, publishes syntheses for educational leaders under such titles as *The Bussing Controversy, Vandalism Prevention,* and *Accountability and Testing*. Practice-related syntheses also make their way into monographs, occasional papers, and more recently, into audio-cassettes.

The major or controlling judgments about the quality of syntheses are rendered by practitioners and, in some cases, by prospective practitioners. Consequently, presumed measures of effectiveness are often reflected in the number of readers of given syntheses or the number of subscribers to a specific journal which specializes in synthesis.

Practice-related synthesizers tend to be boundary-spanners much more than concept-oriented synthesizers. Many of them make oral presentations to practitioners and write for practice-oriented journals; they also have links into literature published in the research community where they obtain concepts and findings to give meaning and shape to their generalizations. If they are in a university community, they link with prospective administrators in training situations.

As already implied, synthesizers may be found in a variety of settings. Scholar-practitioners in school districts or other education agencies, may effectively serve as practice-oriented synthesizers; graduate students in training may also perform this role, as may developers in educational laboratories or research and development centers. Others performing the role would include leaders in school study councils, leagues of schools, ERIC clearinghouses, and divisions of research in large school systems.

Schema III presents summary information on practice-related and concept-oriented syntheses.

USING KNOWLEDGE TO ATTAIN NEW DEVELOPMENTS

New developments in education depend upon the inventive use of knowledge. Two kinds of development are postulated in this part of the

Sources and Uses of Knowledge 89

SCHEMA III
DIFFERENCES IN CONCEPT-ORIENTED AND PRACTICE-RELATED SYNTHESIS

Sub-Uses of Knowledge	Short-Term Outcomes	Longer-Range Outcomes	Illustrative Knowledge Used	Key Artifacts	Significant Quality Assurance Agents
Concept-Oriented Synthesis	Newly organized bodies of knowledge within or across disciplines	More rational bases for advancing conclusion research and for preparing scholars	Clusters of studies relevant to given educational or leadership-related phenomena	Monograph	Other concept-oriented synthesizers
Practice-Related Synthesis	Research findings and generalizations organized in relation to administrative objectives, functions, problems, issues or other aspects of practice	More rational decision making and training bases for leaders	Clusters of studies which shed light on decision variables	An article in a practitioners' journal	Educational leaders

chapter: product development, through which specific tools of general use to educators are created, and idea development, through which projections of new educational or leadership states are attained. Examples of product development are instruments for assessing teacher performance, computer programs to facilitate decision-making, guidelines for implementing educational innovations, programs and materials for use in training. Examples of idea development would include projections of alternative educational futures, delineations of new or untested organizational arrangements, descriptions of untried means for dealing with racial integration, and the like. Both product and idea development provide significant content for linkage networks.

Product Development

Most experience with product development has been gained in the industrial sector where knowledge from the physical and biological sciences has had major developmental uses. However, during the last few decades experience with product development in education has increased as federal funds for the first time have been allocated to educational laboratories, research and development centers, and other organizations to support developmental activities.

Product development involves the utilization of knowledge to design and create useful materials, technologies, systems, or processes of general use to educational administrators.[15] Illustrations of products would be, among others, *Ernstspiel*, a game designed to teach communication skills and understanding to school personnel, developed by Frank Thiemann at the University of Oregon Research and Development Center; computer-based simulations of various types, including one developed through the National Education Finance Project which was designed to assess the impact on state school finance of different allocation formulae; and guidelines for innovations such as those developed at the University of Wisconsin Research and Development Center which are directed at implementing the multi-unit school.

As used in this paper, product development is designed to be of use not just to one school system but to many. Effective product development

---

[15]For one discussion of development see Richard Schutz, "The Nature of Educational Development" in the *Journal of Research and Development in Education*. Vol. 3, Winter, 1971, pp. 39-62. Also see John K. Hemphill and Fred S. Rosenau, *Educational Development: A New Discipline for Self-Renewal*. Eugene, Oregon: Center for the Advanced Study of Educational Administration, 1972.

involves a process of invention where effective problem defining and problem solving are required. Problem defining often entails the use of data from a range of school situations and may require both needs assessment information and feasibility studies. However, data from real situations are not always sufficient in and of themselves for effective product development. In addition, the results of pertinent basic and decision research often need to be utilized as do relevant syntheses of knowledge. Put differently, product development involves the bringing together of problem definitions and basic or applied knowledge in new ways. When product development is effective, it is a means *par excellence* for bridging the so-called "theory-practice" gap.

In contrast to basic research, product development often requires team efforts, and dozens of individuals may be involved in product development projects. For example, more than 185 professors from more than 45 universities were involved in the development of the several UCEA Monroe City School System simulations, and scores of administrators and teachers provided data and suggestions during the developmental process.[16]

There are widely recognized problems of quality control in product development and use. Although a process of objective evaluation of products under conditions of use is highly desirable before distribution, the informed judgments of actual or potential users tend to be the major controllers of quality. These informed judgments can be rendered at various points—at the time when a prototype is completed, during the initial dissemination stages, or after distribution and use. The substantial expense required by systematic evaluation and the difficulties often encountered in obtaining valid data about product impact have led to the increasing reliance on informed judgments.

Nationally recognized linking agents specializing in transmitting educational products to administrators are limited in number. Publishers and other companies in the private sector have traditionally performed key distribution roles through mass production and marketing techniques, especially in terms of books and other written materials. More recently, non-profit organizations, including federally supported labs and centers, have played an increasingly important role in distribution. For products not handled by published companies there are many decentralized efforts; consequently, product developers themselves often play key linking roles as the outcomes of their work represent very specific uses of knowledge which can be more easily communicated than abstract

---

[16] See the *UCEA Instructional Resources Catalog*. Columbus, Ohio: The University Council for Educational Administration, 1976.

ideas. Because those who create products are more familiar with them and their purposes than anyone else, they inevitably play important linking agent roles. They may choose to limit their roles by helping those in the publishing companies or others serving in special dissemination roles to assume the task. On the other hand, they may elect to become directly and heavily involved in helping leaders acquire, use, and evaluate the products. In either case, product developers can have a major impact on the improvement of education and its management.

Idea Development

Idea development, as defined here, is designed to produce new perspectives on problems and/or new decision options. Such perspectives or options are usually projected within intermediate or longer range time frames. In contrast to product development which results in specific tools with relatively rapid implementation, idea development requires more change in the educational systems than does product adoption and more time to implement change. By definition, the ideas developed are untested in practice; thus, while they can be assessed from a logical viewpoint and sometimes through simulation for their efficacy, they cannot be assessed empirically until after they are disseminated. One advantage, then, that idea developers have is that their imagination can be unconstrained by the status quo. Their major functions are to describe and assess alternatives which transcend current societal, educational or leadership states, to delineate untried strategies for realizing identified alternatives, or to describe new or different tactics for implementing alternatives.

Imaginative or inventive thought is critical to idea development. There are various approaches and many potential sources of knowledge and of information which can undergird such thought and which can lead to idealized future states or implementation strategies for moving toward such states. Comprehensive surveys of educational practice in given systems have frequently been used to identify discrepancies between goals and accomplishments, and the identified discrepancies can be used, in turn, as a basis for generating goals for new action alternatives for decision makers. Another strategy is to use trend data about past and present conditions in order to project future goals or programs. Since the last strategy noted is based upon trend data, it assumes a continuation of past and present tendencies with minor variations. A third strategy involves projections of the future in which discontinuities in present educational trends are deliberately assumed and in which quite different options from

Sources and Uses of Knowledge   93

present and past ones are projected. In recent decades there has been an increasing number of studies projecting future states or alternatives that depart from present trends. Illich's "de-schooling" idea, for example, represented development which broke sharply with the status quo.

While imaginative thought is a critical ingredient of idea development, various methods in recent decades have been developed for projecting or delineating future states.[17] As education and its purposes are linked inevitably to societal conditions, knowledge about the future of such conditions is important to idea developers. Many aspects of education in the coming decades will be affected, for example, by changes in the family, in population distributions, in the rate of energy depletion, in economic developments, in changing governmental structures, in new legislation, in international events and in many other variables. Effective idea development is a complex undertaking requiring the use of many concepts and much information.

Although comparative studies of product and idea developers are not available, one may hypothesize that the idea developer, much more than the product developer, proceeds through individual effort. A perusal of "futures" publications will show that individual effort and perspective predominate, while the evidence is clear that products developed in education are frequently realized through team effort.

Idea developers generally tend to reside in specially created institutions such as, for example, the Futuribles in Paris, the Hudson Institute, the Rand Corporation and other "think tanks." In education, two federally supported research and development centers were established in the late 1960s to study educational futures, one at Syracuse University and the other at the Stanford Research Institute. A wide range of disciplines in universities now offer courses on futurology and such universities as Wisconsin, British Columbia, Wayne, New York, Ontario Institute for Studies in Education (Toronto), State University of New York at Buffalo, Texas, Tennessee, Texas A&M, Utah, the University of California at Los Angeles, and Illinois State offer courses on educational futures for prospective leaders in education.

There are severe problems of quality control on idea development. Because the ideas produced deal with future states, there is no scientific way to establish their validity immediately. However, these ideas tend to receive critical examination when made public, perhaps more so than does knowledge about the present and past. The major quality assurance is found in the judgments of other idea developers. Since future-oriented

---

[17]For a description of a range of methods for studying the future see Stephen Hencley and James Yates, *Educational Futurism: Methodologies.* Berkeley: John A. McCutchan Corp., 1974.

ideas often have more popular appeal than present or past-oriented ones, one may surmise that they come under the purview and judgment of a greater number of citizens than do the latter.

Currently there are no specialized linking agencies for transmitting future-oriented ideas to educators. However, the World Future Society disseminates ideas on education to interested members through a special newsletter. On the other hand, national organizations with purposes specific to education and leadership are much more concerned with transmitting practice-related syntheses or policy research studies than future-oriented ideas.[18]

The outcomes of idea development are disseminated through journals, monographs and books in a manner similar to the results of research and synthesis. *The Futurist,* for example, is a periodical which publishes an array of ideas about future aspects of society, including those related to education. There are no journals in education devoted specifically to the dissemination of future-oriented ideas. There are occasional books which depict educational futures such as *The Future: Create or Inherit* by Charles W. Case and Paul A. Olson and *Learning for Tomorrow: Role of the Future in Education* by Alvin Toffler.

Schema IV summarizes selected information on idea and product development.

USING KNOWLEDGE TO ACHIEVE IMPROVED OR NEW EDUCATIONAL PRACTICE

The use of knowledge in decision-making by educational leaders and policy makers is a key instrument for altering practice, and one of the more significant tests of all knowledge use is whether in fact it alters educational practice. To what extent, in other words, does relevant knowledge or do knowledge-related products and services exist *vis-à-vis* given decisions, and do administrators and policy makers use available knowledge, products, or services in decision-making to change practice?

Two general, if somewhat related, categories of knowledge uses in

---

[18]For one example of futures thinking sponsored by the University of Minnesota and The University Council for Educational Administration see Sam Popper (Ed.), *Imaging Alternative Future School Organizations.* Minneapolis, Minnesota: Department of Educational Administration, College of Education, University of Minnesota, 1972. Also see Louis J. Rubin, *The Future of Education: Perspectives on Tomorrow's Schooling.* Boston: Allyn and Bacon, 1975.

SCHEMA IV
DIFFERENCES IN PRODUCT AND IDEA DEVELOPMENT

Sub-Uses of Knowledge	Short-Term Outcomes	Longer Range Outcomes	Illustrative Knowledge Used	Key Artifacts	Significant Quality Assurance Agents
Product Development	New materials, technologies, systems, or processes of use to leaders	New options for leaders interested in improving programs	Needs assessment data	Prototype products	Users of products
Idea Development	Future-oriented and untested alternatives for improving education or its leadership	New options for leaders interested in instituting new policies or programs	Forecasting studies bearing upon education	Published scenarios	Potential users and other idea developers

decision-making can be postulated: the improvement of effectiveness or efficiency of existing programs or policies; and the institution of new programs or policies.[19] Each of these uses will now be illustrated and elaborated.

Improving Existing Policies or Programs

In this leadership category, policy and program objectives are already established. Effectiveness is improved as the quality or quantity of relevant outcomes is increased. To improve efficiency is to decrease energy, time or other resources required to produce given outcomes or to use the same resources to achieve improved outcomes. Since there are countless variables bearing upon the attainment of effectiveness and efficiency, many illustrations of knowledge use could be offered,[20] but only a few will be set forth at this point.

Given established objectives, what planning will ensure their effective achievement? Using knowledge through management planning is one important strategy for increasing efficiency.

One body of knowledge related to management planning and decision-making is Operations Research (OR). OR methods, developed within the last three decades, have their origins in mathematics and economics; their rigorous application through the use of computers can illuminate the consequences of given decisions. For example, linear programming techniques in cafeteria management can be used to help leaders ensure greater economy, better food value, and more choices for students.[21] The basic concepts of the methods can be applied usefully without the use of mathematical formulae, as in the Program Evaluation and Review Technique (PERT) which can be used to ensure the efficient

---

[19]It is recognized that a great deal of the behavior of even the most effective leaders is directed at maintaining the organization rather than at changing or improving programs or policies. School principals, for example, spend much time on such matters as responding to central office information requests, handling parents' complaints, or administering grievance procedures. Since the thrust of this paper is toward change rather than maintenance, the use of knowledge in maintenance decisions will not be treated here.

[20]Schwab has theorized that there are 50,000 potential variables to be considered in any important decision made by an educational administrator. See Joseph J. Schwab, "The Professorship in Educational Administration: Theory-Art-Practice." In Donald Willower and Jack Culbertson (Eds.), *The Professorship in Educational Administration.* Columbus, Ohio: UCEA, 1964 pp. 47-70.

[21]For a review of different OR methods, see Russell L. Ackoff and Patrick Rivett, *A Manager's Guide to Operations Research.* New York: John Wiley and Son, 1963.

scheduling and monitoring of work.

Efficiency can also be sought through the adoption of instructional or management technologies. Using knowledge to implement management information systems or data processing systems can make management more efficient. Computer-assisted instruction (CAI) or language laboratories are two illustrations from a range of instructional technologies; efficiencies are achieved when tasks are performed through technology as well as, but less expensively than, by school personnel.

Available knowledge bearing upon organizational effectiveness is also varied. For example, school principals represent a key management support system for facilitating effective teaching and learning in schools. Management support may involve such functions as recruiting and placing competent personnel, providing these personnel needed means to achieve objectives, maintaining fruitful links with parents, giving personnel needed reinforcement and feedback, and so on. In making decisions to implement these and related functions, one can draw upon knowledge about many subjects — knowledge of communication processes, group psychology, the politics of education, among others.

Effectiveness can also be pursued through special management strategies. One approach is found in management-by-objectives (MBO), an essential feature of which is its capacity to monitor progress toward objectives. Through the use of knowledge about this method one can continuously target efforts toward more effective attainment of goals.[22] Knowledge-based approaches to effectiveness and efficiency are always applied in a social context; consequently, organizational climate becomes an important consideration. The degree to which leaders motivate and reinforce personnel and the extent to which they contribute to widespread understanding and commitment to school objectives are among the factors which shape organizational climate. By using knowledge about morale, productivity, organizational communication and motivation, leaders can achieve greater effectiveness and efficiency.

Among those using knowledge to improve the efficiency and effectiveness of programs are principals, superintendents and other leaders in school systems. They may choose to play an important internal linking role by providing a bridge between external linking agents and agencies and those seeking improvements in school systems. They may, for example, contact product developers for instructional or management technologies or practice-related synthesizers for pertinent knowledge. Publications which provide product descriptions and practice-related

---

[22]For one treatment of management-by-objectives, see Terrel Bell, *A Performance Accountability System for School Administrators.* New York: Parker Publishing Company, 1974.

syntheses are major sources of knowledge bearing upon efficiency and effectiveness. Leaders in networks, leagues, intermediate service agencies, and universities who are specialists in external linking all can offer resources to leaders desiring to make programs more effective or efficient.

Instituting New Policies or Programs

The goal of new policies or programs is educational change. Again, decision-making by administrators and other school leaders is an important instrument for change, and knowledge is a servant of the decision process.

Leaders concerned with the establishment of new objectives or policies can use knowledge from many sources including references on strategic planning. Strategic planning, for example, involves the establishment of new goals and objectives, and therefore, an analysis of conditions requiring the establishment of new directions and the kinds of policies needed to achieve new directions. A wide range of knowledge is also available about societal needs which education might serve and to which its policies and objectives should be related. For instance, there is a growing amount of knowledge about the depletion of energy resources by society, and such knowledge has important implications for the setting of objectives having to do with conservation education in schools, as well as objectives for managing the schools themselves.

Any effort directed at new policies or programs involves change processes. Knowledge about these processes has been growing in recent years, and there are many sources of knowledge which can be drawn upon. There is knowledge, for example, about adoption of innovations and about the problem-solving approach to change. Such knowledge is very relevant to educational leaders committed to the attainment of alterations in practice.

Decision-makers concerned with change occupy posts in school systems, institutions of higher education, and other educational agencies. They often perform change agent roles themselves as they link school leaders and knowledgeable experts. If decision-makers are interested in establishing new programs to achieve established objectives, especially pertinent is the work of policy researchers whose function is to evaluate programs. Also pertinent is the work of idea developers whose major function is to project new decision alternatives for leaders. If decision-makers are concerned about the establishment of new objectives and policies, synthesizers who treat such topics as strategic planning offer useful knowledge, as do those concerned with analyzing societal and educational futures.

Educational leaders concerned either with program or purposive change or with greater effectiveness of efficiency do not produce outcomes as visible or as specific as those of other knowledge users already discussed. There may be tangible results of the decision process in the form of minutes or reported actions. More intangible residues are available in the memories or actions of those comprising the informal network of the organization where change is implemented. The artifacts produced by leaders in their work, then, are different from those produced by researchers, synthesizers, and developers.

Those in leadership posts, more than other knowledge users, are severely time-constrained in decision-making situations and are continually pressed to take action. The decision-making arena is much more complex and attended by more uncertainty than are the arenas of other knowledge users.

Other leaders may have a role in evaluating the quality of the leaders' performance; this performance, however, is evaluated ultimately by the public, more specifically, by its designated representatives. School board members play an important role in decisions about the current or continued performance of school superintendents.

Many factors other than explicit knowledge shape decisions of leaders. They inevitably must be concerned with the differing interests of the various groups affected by decision outcomes. In addition, the critical values both shaping and transcending decisions which form the public interests of education are highly significant variables in decision making. So it is understandable that experts with various types of knowledge are seen by decision makers as only one of many referent groups in the decision process.

The same linking agencies provide support for leaders whether they are engaged in improving existing policies or programs or are instituting new policies and programs. National administrator associations are the major linking agencies, and staff in these organizations, leading members and others play key linking roles through a variety of dissemination activities.

During the last decade especially, there has been marked growth in external linking agents who facilitate change processes through knowledge utilization. They facilitate change through a variety of tactics as, for example, performing studies and developing recommendations for change in programs or policy; facilitating group problem solving directed at change; providing informational or human resource linkages related to program change; offering needed training programs; and so forth.

SCHEMA V
DIFFERENCES IN THE USE OF KNOWLEDGE FOR IMPROVED IN CONTRAST
TO NEW PROGRAMS OR POLICIES

Sub-Uses of Knowledge	Short-Term Outcomes	Longer Range Outcomes	Illustrative Knowledge Used	Key Artifacts	Significant Quality Assurance Agents
Improved Policies and Programs	Increased efficiency or effectiveness in existing programs	Improved or more efficient educational practice	Operations research methods	Recorded decisions of school staff	Parents
Newly Instituted Policies or Programs	Changed objectives or new programs	Newly tested educational practice	Policy studies of desegregation programs	Minutes of school board meetings	School boards

Selected information on knowledge uses in improving existing policies or programs and in instituting new policies and programs is summarized in Schema V.

USING KNOWLEDGE TO IMPROVE TRAINING PROGRAMS

Even though there are many ways of classifying programs, only two categories will be discussed in this paper: pre-service and in-service. It is widely recognized that these two classes of training in fact are often interrelated in practice, but the two approaches can usefully be distinguished for heuristic purposes. Given the author's background, the approaches will be discussed and illustrated within the context of administrator preparation.

In-service Programs

In-service training, defined in terms of client population, is oriented to those already in leadership posts. Its major purpose is to produce job-related learnings of immediate use to those in leadership posts. Desired outcomes, then, are understandings, skills, or attitudes which have identifiable uses on the job. Leaders might acquire, for example, new skills in the resolution of conflict or more positive attitudes toward affirmative action programs.

In-service programs differ from pre-service programs on several counts. Typically, these programs, as compared to pre-service programs, are:
- shorter in duration even though they may be more intensive;
- focused more upon immediate problems (or crises);
- shaped more by the immediate desires of the clients served;
- more flexible in format, methods and staffing;
- less likely to carry academic credit;
- less controlled by certification or university requirements;

- less likely to require formal reading and study;
- oriented more to present than to future career positions;
- available from a greater variety and number of sponsors.

Effective in-service programs result in new learnings which in turn, can be used to improve decision making. At their best these programs can provide personnel better bases for leadership. In today's complex environment, in other words, those who would lead in change efforts are very dependent on new learnings. More and more leaders in school districts see in-service education as a major mechanism for organizational renewal.

Trainers, as special users of knowledge, play a key role in designing and conducting in-service education programs. They must pay careful attention to client interests by using needs assessment procedures or other feedback mechanisms for determining training objectives, and since in-service programs are not mandated, their continuance is more dependent than that of pre-service programs on the perceptions clients have about their value. In-service programs enable leaders to acquire and use new knowledge about administration.

Three client systems to be served through in-service programs can be conceptualized: individual, group, and organization. The Kettering Foundation has helped stimulate the development of individually oriented learning opportunities for school personnel (Brainard, 1973). In this approach, principals (or other leaders) establish learning objectives specifically for themselves, and in addition, they define indicators to denote when objectives will be achieved. While they may rely upon groups for support at certain stages or help with certain objectives (e.g., group skills), both the targets and the processes of learning are their own responsibility. As a result, there can be much flexibility both in objectives and in processes. This approach assumes that individuals differ in learning objectives they value, as well as the learning styles they prefer. It is significant, however, that a recent study showed that a relatively small percentage of principals (five per cent) in a national sample of 500 responding expressed a preference for individualized in-service programs (Davis, 1976).

The group is another client system. Small-group theory and research have long influenced in-service education. A variety of knowledge about methods and content for facilitating group learning is available. If the group's learning objectives are of an affective nature (e.g., interpersonal understandings), for example, sensitivity methods might be used. In this case members of the group would generate their own content largely from their own experiences, perceptions, and interactions. If the objectives stem from shared perceptions about an organizational or societal problem, a problem-solving strategy might well be used.[23] The group, under these circumstances, would likely seek content or knowledge beyond that available from its own membership. Whatever approach is chosen by a small group, a fundamental assumption holds—namely, that the learning process is a social process, and the dynamics of learning are best expressed through group interaction.

There are contrasts between small-group and large-group client systems. Group interaction is not so much the mode of learning in large groups; rather, it is typically based upon one-way communication by lecturers or speakers. Participants often come from many systems rather than one. A result is that large groups are usually an aggregate of individuals rather than a cohesive social system. Learning objectives, particularly at large conferences, tend to be associated more with awareness development and understanding than with skills or attitudes. Large-group instruction operates on the assumption that the diffusion of ideas to individuals will lead to new understandings and that these understandings will be applied by participants in contexts of practice.

A client system of more recent vintage is the organization, and organizational development (OD) is the approach customarily used by those focusing upon this client system (Argyris and Schon, 1974). The approach does not deny that learning can result through individual and group efforts; however, students of OD argue that the transfer of individual or group learning to organizational systems is likely to be nil or very limited. Rather, for organizations to grow and develop, the learnings of their members must be intimately related to the problems and processes of their working environment. It follows, then, that learning needs to involve teams of leaders from specific organizations. In general, the learning objectives of teams are stated in relation to increased organization health, planning capability, problem-solving ability or some similar goal.[24]

The types of knowledge and information used in in-service programs are varied. Needs assessment information and concepts for arriving at training objectives constitute one type which can come from multiple

---

[23]For an early discussion of group learning based upon problem-solving strategies see Patrick Lynch, "Inter-Institutional Model for In-Service Training and Changes in School Systems." In Patrick Lynch and Peggy Blackstone (Eds.), *Continuing Education of School Administrators*. Albuquerque, New Mexico: Department of Educational Administration and Foundations, University of New Mexico and the University Council for Educational Administration, 1966.

[24]For a succinct and useful description of organizational health criteria see Matthew B. Miles, "Planned Change in Organizational Health: Figure and Ground" in Richard Carlson (Ed.), *Change Processes in the Public Schools*. Eugene, Oregon: CASEA, 1964.

sources. Perceptions of trainees (and/or their superiors and subordinates) about their training needs, as gathered through instruments or interviews, are one source; generalizations about needs deduced from identified discrepancies between actual and desired performance in schools or school systems are another. Third, needs can be derived from theories dealing with aspects of organizational life such as Hertzberg's theory of motivation. In still another approach, emergent training needs are deduced from trend extrapolations designed to identify projected leadership problems or challenges. Finally, training needs can be inferred from normative forecasts — ideal programs, ideal organizations, ideal leadership, and so forth.

Another illustrative type of knowledge involves concepts, research findings and generalizations about aspects of administration. Knowledge inherent in practice-related syntheses and policy research is especially pertinent. For in-service programs focusing upon the adoption of administrative or instructional technologies, knowledge-based products designed by developers are relevant. Idea developers, on the other hand, can offer content for programs in which the objectives encompass future-oriented but untested alternatives for improving education or its leadership.

The sources to which trainers can go for knowledge and information are many: journals, books, multi-media systems, films, filmstrips, videotapes, and audio cassettes. Increasingly, there is the use of the concept of "human resources" in staff development. Such resources might include individuals who have developed products or promising practices which are not yet widely disseminated; individuals who have special content to supplement or reinforce that already disseminated; individuals who themselves are familiar with a wide range of in-service resources; and individuals who are skillful not just in communicating content but in seeing that it is applied.

As already noted, those engaged in in-service programs reside in various agencies. A growing number of the 11,560 school systems with minimum enrollments of 300, for example, are adding new staff development directors or are assigning in-service responsibilities to existing staff. These individuals serve as important knowledge users as they draw upon concepts, findings and experiences in school systems and as they involve external linkers or trainers in in-service programs for personnel.

During the seventies especially, professional associations serving educational administrators have expanded markedly their role in in-service education. The American Association of School Administrators, with a membership of most of the country's school superintendents, has pioneered the National Academy for School Executives (NASE). This new organization has a full-time staff and offers approximately 70 seminars annually. Other associations have developed similar but not as extensive in-service systems.

Professional associations also perform a major role in getting ideas to administrators through national, regional, and state conferences and a wide range of publications. The numbers served by associations reach into the tens of thousands. The National Association for Secondary School Principals, for example, has in its membership most of the 23,585 high school principals in the United States plus thousands of vice-principals. The National Association of Elementary School Principals, to take another example, diffuses ideas and information to most of the nation's 62,750 elementary principals plus a substantial number of vice-principals. Thus, the role of national (and state) professional associations in in-service education is both an important and a growing one.

Since the new federally supported labs and research and development centers came into being in the 1960s, they not only have developed training materials but also have become involved in using the materials in in-service programs for administrators. Assisted by the National Institute of Education, nine labs and centers have formed in recent years a cooperative designed to enhance staff support for administrators and others involved in improving educational processes.[25] Linkers in these agencies, then, have expertise both in the content and format of training materials and in their use.

In recent years intermediate service agencies have also played a growing role in staff development activities for administrators. The Board of Cooperative Services (BOCES) in New York would be an example of agencies which offer planning, administrative staff development and other support services to the districts to which they are linked.[26] Most states have intermediate agencies and the number of states now creating or strengthening intermediate service agencies is growing. The probability that there will be an enhanced role for these agencies offering in-service education to leaders is also increasing. This is only one expression of the growing role of states in advancing in-service training.

In more recent years, new emphases in in-service education are beginning to emerge in some higher education institutions as selected professors are assigned full-time to in-service education programs, as more

---

[25] For a catalog of materials produced by the group see *Educational Dissemination and Linking Agent Source Book*. Washington, D.C.: National Institute of Education, 1976, (First Draft).

[26] See Troy McKelvey and William B. Harris, "The Board of Cooperative Educational Services Models" in Troy McKelvey (Ed.), *Metropolitan School Organization: Basic Problems and Patterns*. Berkeley, California: McCutchan Publishing Corporation, Vol. 1, 1970.

workshops or short courses for the practitioners are designed and offered, and as the mission of campus-based school study councils is changed to encompass more in-service activities. There also seems to be a trend toward in-service education based upon special types of interchange between and among school systems and universities. Witness, for example, the Danforth Foundation-supported program involving cross-system exchange, the Kettering-supported educational development management centers, the Rockefeller-supported urban internship and the USOE-supported and UCEA-sponsored, university-school system-state education partnership program.

During the mid-sixties the number of profit-making agencies offering staff development programs for educational personnel increased as federal funds became available and the so-called "business-education interface" was encouraged.[27] However, as federal funds for training have decreased and as the complexities involved in effectively joining the private and education sectors have become more evident, the staff development role of profit-making organizations in education has apparently declined.

Linking agencies advancing in-service education programs, then, tend to be varied and decentralized operations. However, it is significant that a new national organization (The National Staff Development Council) has recently emerged to serve directors of staff development in school districts. An emergent national network of professors and administrators interested in staff development is also being sponsored by UCEA.

Pre-Service Programs

Pre-service programs are designed for those who are aspiring to initial administrative posts or, if they already have one, a higher or more attractive post. In other words, a teacher may aspire to be a principal, or a principal may aspire to be a superintendent. The major goal of a pre-service program, then, is to produce learnings of use to individuals in future administrative posts.[25] These learnings may be based on general knowledge (e.g., organizational theory), or they may be based on content

---

[27]See Jack Culbertson, "Business-Education Interface," in Jack Culbertson, et al., (Eds.), *Preparing Educational Leaders for the Seventies*. Columbus, Ohio: UCEA, 1969, pp. 30-76.

[28]The distinction is a relative one. A principal, for example, who is seeking to meet state credential requirements for the superintendency through a pre-service program can acquire knowledge of use in his or her current post.

specific to a given position such as superintendent-board relationships.

Pre-service requirements are commonly stated in terms of state certification or degree requirements. In some cases they may coincide, as in the case of the two-year specialist degree and certification requirements in some states. Doctoral degrees are for those interested in preparing for positions which require more training than certification standards require. Pre-service programs differ from in-service programs in several ways. They are:

- Longer in duration, especially for students meeting degree requirements[29]
- More conceptual in content
- More likely to involve on-campus residence experience
- Less flexible in staffing, format and method
- More likely to carry graduate credit
- More the province of institutions of higher education institutions than other agencies
- Directed at preparation more for future than for present positions
- More controlled by state and/or university requirements
- More likely to involve the study of social science and related disciplines

Not only do effective pre-service programs produce new learnings of use to those desiring to enter a new administrative post, but also they serve as a screening mechanism for administrative and leadership talent, as well as facilitating the flow of talent into administrative posts.

Key knowledge users in pre-service programs are professors of educational administration who concentrate either upon the use of formal knowledge in the university or upon the use of tacit knowledge in school systems or associated agencies. In the former case, a part of their role is to link with professors beyond departments of educational administration in order to see that the base of preparation is broadened and the number of learning options available to students is increased. In providing linkage between universities and administrative practice the professor can play various roles, but an important one is to see that the knowledge used in preparatory programs has relevance to positions and environments in which administrators serve.

Rationale for pre-service programs and, in turn, the criteria for selecting and using knowledge are diverse. This diversity in rationales is inevi-

---

[29]Differences between pre-service and in-service programs are more marked in advanced degree than in certification offerings.

table: There are differing assumptions about and definitions of administration and leadership. There is the assumption, for example, that administration is very similar even in such differing organizations as hospitals, business organizations, school systems, and government agencies. Under this assumption one can argue that graduate schools of administration should be created to prepare personnel for positions in quite diverse organizations utilizing a curriculum which incorporates a general core of knowledge and concepts about organizations, leadership and administration generally.[30]

Others would assume that the role of the administrator is to lead in the improvement of instruction, an assumption which differs markedly from the previous one that administration is similar in all organizations, in that it implies that instruction is a primary and unique function of schools. Knowledge used in building upon this rationale would differ from knowledge selected for use in graduate schools of administration.

Even though assumptions about what administration is may differ, it has been widely accepted for some time that three agencies have important roles in pre-service programs: institutions of higher education, school systems (or other contexts of practice for which administrators are prepared) and professional associations.[31] Institutions of higher education have a major responsibility for developing, organizing and presenting the theoretical or conceptual bases of administration; school systems make a substantial contribution by providing field settings in which prospective administrators can apply knowledge as well as acquire clinical or tacit knowledge about administration; and professional administrator associations and agencies can monitor and study preparatory programs generally and, in the process, use the knowledge gained to articulate standards and identify ends and means for improving programs.

In more recent years the old debate about the relative value of clinical or tacit knowledge available in practice settings and the more theoretical knowledge offered in universities has been reactivated. From the mid-fifties to the mid-sixties the role of theoretical knowledge in preparation was clearly in ascendance, but more recently, the proponents of clinical knowledge have grown in number and theoretical knowledge has been called into question. Thus, the latter group supports field-based prepara-

---

[30] See Erwin Miklos, *Training-in-Common for Educational, Business and Public Administrators.* Columbus, Ohio: UCEA, 1972.

[31] See Dan C. Lortie, "Complexities, Specializations and Professional Knowledge: Overall Strategies in the Preparation of School Administrators." In Jack Culbertson and Stephen Hencley (Eds.), *Preparing Administrators: New Perspectives.* Columbus, Ohio: UCEA, 1962.

tion and a much greater role for school system leaders in training.[32] They are very critical of traditional training programs and tend to support competency-based preparation, since they believe it helps ensure that the knowledge used in preparation will be relevant to practice.

Three general types of knowledge of use in pre-service programs can be identified. There is knowledge which can be used in the design or updating of programs, in the implementation of programs, and in the evaluation of programs. Especially during the last two decades, the number of studies related to design has grown substantially. For example, a recent publication which reviewed the 1962-72 period contained 91 references on administrator preparation, and the large majority of these dealt with pre-service programs and such topics as program content, program structure, recruitment and selection, instructional approaches, and field-related experience (Farquhar and Piele, 1972).

Knowledge which has been and can be selected and used in preparation is many-faceted. One reference, for example, has identified four types: practice-based content, social and behavioral science content, discipline-based content and content from the humanities (Farquhar and Piele, 1972:4-14). These categories, in turn, can be broken into more specific sub-categories. Practice based content can include knowledge about functions performed by administrators, processes or technologies used, problems addressed and so forth. In other words, a problem faced by program implementers, is that administration, however defined, is a very broad concept; there are many categories of knowledge which can be used. This knowledge is found in hundreds of different journals, books and monographs as well as in practice settings.

Finally, there is knowledge which can be used in evaluating programs. This knowledge illuminates how programs work and the degree to which or manner in which they have impact. In this sense one can speak about policy research on pre-service programs. Because most of the studies involve generalizations based upon perceptions about effectiveness, policy research on pre-service programs is limited. A small number of studies has involved criteria of actual learnings and other objective measures of effectiveness.

As noted above, pre-service preparation takes place almost totally under the auspices of institutions of higher education. A 1972 study found that there were 362 institutions offering programs for educational administrators; further, that the growth in programs between 1940-70 was

---

[32]For a treatment of how concepts can be used in field experiences see Joseph M. Cronin and Peter T. Horoschak, *Innovative Strategies in Fields Experiences for Preparing Educational Administrators*. Columbus, Ohio: UCEA, 1972.

very rapid (Culbertson, 1972). For example, the two year specialist program, which increased twenty-fold between 1940-70, grew much more rapidly than did MA, EdD, and PhD programs.

In the United States there are approximately 2100 professors of educational administration. Others in colleges of education and other university colleges or departments also participate in pre-service programs. These professors pursue many specializations and offer diverse sets of knowledge.[33]

For programs directed at certification requirements the state serves as a major quality assurance agent. It draws together representatives of school systems, professional associations, institutions of higher education, and other agencies to establish or revise certification standards.[34] It also approves institutions judged capable of offering pre-service programs and in some cases also monitors actual courses or programs to determine if they meet specified standards.

With regard to doctoral, specialist, and masters programs, institutions of higher education have a major role to play in quality control. They establish criteria which programs must meet and processes which are used for reviewing both new and existing programs. They also control the staffing of programs and establish admission criteria for students.

There are also others involved in quality control. National and regional accrediting associations seek to establish and maintain minimum standards of quality. University and administrator associations perform studies as noted above and seek to identify ways to improve program quality. The reactions of clients to programs over time also affects quality.

A major linking agency for those involved in pre-service preparation is The University Council for Educational Administration, the mission of which is the improvement of preparatory programs for educational administrators. Concentrating principally upon the development and dissemination of knowledge related to program design and quality, it also facilitates the conduct of evaluation studies of preparation and the dissemination of these studies.

The National Conference of Professors of Educational Administration (NCPEA) is another important linking agency which disseminates pertinent knowledge at its annual meetings. Professional administrator associations serve important linking agent roles especially related to standards

---

[33] For a description of professors of educational administration see Roald F. Campbell and L. Jackson Newell, *A Study of Professors of Educational Administration*. Columbus, Ohio: UCEA, 1973.

[34] For a recent study of certification see UCEA Commission Report, *The Preparation and Certification of Educational Administrators*. Columbus, Ohio: UCEA, 1973.

Sources and Uses of Knowledge 111

SCHEMA VI
SELECTED FEATURES OF KNOWLEDGE AS USED IN TRAINING

Sub-Uses of Knowledge	Short-Term Outcomes	Longer Range Outcomes	Illustrative Knowledge Used	Key Artifacts	Significant Quality Assurance Agents
In-Service Programs	New job-related learnings for currently functioning leaders	More effective and competent behavior by those already in leadership posts	Research on inter-personal relations	Evidence training requirements met	Clients of training programs
Pre-Service Programs	New learnings for personnel aspiring to initial or more advanced administration positions	Better bases for effective and competent behavior among those aspiring to leadership posts	Models of decision-making	State administrator certificate	State certification and accrediting agencies

of preparation. The Committee for the Advancement of School Administrators of the American Association of School Administrators, for example, has been active in formulating standards for preparatory programs and in disseminating the results.

Schema VI summarizes selected information on the pre-service and in-service programs.

SUMMARY

Some of the major underlying assumptions of this paper are that there are differing types of knowledge users; that they make differing uses of knowledge; that if the linkage agent concept is to be understood and defined within education as a macro-system, the uses of knowledge and the conditions affecting knowledge utilization need clarification.

Toward this end, five major uses and ten sub-uses of knowledge have been set forth, as have been some of the conditions affecting knowledge use. The chapter, written largely from the perspective of educational administration, has sought to document that the objectives sought and the outcomes produced by different users differ; that knowledge users draw upon differing types of knowledge and link with different groups as they seek outcomes; and that different settings encourage differing uses which, in turn, are influenced by diverse quality assurance agents. Thus, the environment of knowledge sources and uses is a diverse one which can influence and abet linking agents in many ways.

KNOWLEDGE SOURCES AND USES: SOME GENERALIZATIONS

With the wide-ranging knowledge sources and uses outlined in the previous discussion, what are some of the major implications for linking agents and agencies? This paper will conclude with selected generalizations bearing upon this question.

Effective linking agents will need some understanding of the larger environment of knowledge sources and uses, because the major bases of their authority reside in their ability to tap relevant knowledge sources and in their skill to help others acquire and use these sources. Since they are dependent on help from others in order to help those directly involved in linking activities, they need many use options. The fact that they pursue improvement through rational persuasion rather than through the exercise of power highlights further the critical role of knowledge in their performance. It is true that linkers may have adequate sources of knowledge and still fail because appropriate commitments to improvement, needed interpersonal or process skills, or required planning capacities are lacking. However, they cannot succeed without an adequate grasp of available knowledge sources and uses. Nor can they, without an understanding of their larger environment, maximally influence policy decisions affecting this environment. Finally, by understanding key dimensions of knowledge use, linkers can influence the products achieved and the processes used by researchers, synthesizers, developers and trainers.

This volume focuses principally upon primary linking agents, namely, internal and external linkers who are directly involved in educational improvement activities. However, implicit in the previous discussion is the generalization that all knowledge users are linkers; and that linkers differ to the degree that they specialize in distinct knowledge uses. Thus, distinct uses of knowledge make for different linkages, different groups spanned, different strategies of improvement, different knowledge used and different outcomes achieved. The basic researcher, for example, uses knowledge from disciplines while internal linkers concerned with educational improvement can draw knowledge from disciplines, from practice and from practice-related synthesis. In the process, the internal linker would span school organizations and organizations external to schools while the basic researcher would link with researchers in settings other than his or her own. Improvement would be pursued by the basic researcher through the attainment of new knowledge; the internal linker would pursue improvement through the implementation of new practice. Such differences not only show that there is a close relationship between linkage and specialized knowledge use but also help to explain why so many differing concepts of linking agents are found in the scholarly literature.

The information on knowledge sources and uses suggests why there is a growing need for support systems to help internal and external linking agents. The growth in recent decades both in specialized knowledge and in specialized uses of knowledge is one of the critical factors shaping the need. As knowledge grows, the options for its use increase, and this creates a special problem for those involved in finding, selecting and using knowledge to improve practice in varied settings. A basic researcher concerned with using knowledge to study power structure can master all of the pertinent sources. Internal and external linkers using knowledge to improve various facets of education cannot begin to master all of the pertinent sources. Because they must draw upon an expanding universe of sources and uses, they need special support.

With different sources and uses of knowledge of potential use to linking agents, where might investments best be made? Conclusion researchers and, to a lesser degree, concept-oriented synthesizers, have the capacity for providing major bases for providing long-range support to internal and external linkers, but they have limited capacities for providing short-range or immediate support. Policy researchers, practice-related synthesizers, product developers, idea developers, in-service program designers and trainers all have the potential for providing linking agents immediate support; in the long range, however, linking agents are dependent upon researchers and concept-oriented synthesizers for a continuing source of "conceptual capital."

Immediate investments to strengthen linker support for those desiring to achieve new or improved practice, then, might best be made in knowledge users producing in-service programs; intermediate investments might best be made in practice-related syntheses, development products and development ideas; and longer range investments might best be made in basic research, policy research and pre-service programs.

References

Ackoff, R. L., and Rivett, P. *A Manager's Guide to Operations Research.* New York: John Wiley and Son, 1963.

Argyris, C. and Schon, D. *Theory in Practice: Increasing Professional Effectiveness.* San Francisco: Jossey-Bass, 1974.

Bell, T. *A Performance Accountability System for School Administrators.* New York: Parker Publishing Company, 1974.

Brainard, E. *Individualizing Administrator Continuing Education.* Englewood, Colorado: CFK, Ltd., Fall, 1973.

Campbell, D. Reforms as Experiments. *American Psychologist,* Vol. 24, No. 4, April 1969, p. 411-12.

Campbell, R. F., and Newell, L. J. *A Study of Professors of Educational Administration.* Columbus, Ohio: UCEA, 1973.

Coleman, J. *Policy Research in the Social Sciences.* Morristown, N.J.: General Learning Press, 1972.

Cronbach, L. J. and Suppes, P. *Research for Tomorrow's Schools.* New York: McMillan Company, 1969.

Cronin, J. M., and Horoschak, P. T. *Innovative Strategies in Field Experience for Preparing Educational Administrators.* Columbus, Ohio: UCEA, 1972.

Culbertson, J. Business-Education Interface. In J. Culbertson, *et al.,* (Eds.), *Preparing Educational Leaders for the Seventies.* Columbus, Ohio: UCEA, 1969, 30-76.

Culbertson, J. Specialized Career Patterns and Content Selection. In J. Culbertson, *et al., Social Science Content for Preparing Educational Leaders.* Columbus, Ohio: Charles E. Merrill Publishing Company, 1973, pp. 327-355.

Davis, W. *Staff Development Preferences of School Principals.* Columbus, Ohio: University Council for Educational Administration, 1976.

Feldman, K. Using the Work of Others: Some Observations on Reviewing and Integrating. *Sociology of Education Review,* 1971 (44).

Glass, G. Primary, Secondary, and Meta Analysis of Research. *Educational Researcher.* Vol. 5, No. 10, November, 1976, p. 3.

Guttentag, M. and Struening, E. (Eds.) *Handbook of Evaluation Research.* Beverly Hills, California: Sage Publication, 1975.

Havelock, R. *Planning for Innovations through the Dissemination and Utilization of Knowledge.* Ann Arbor, Michigan: Institute for Social Research, Center for Research on Utilization of Scientific Knowledge, 1969.

Haworth, L. The Experimental Society: Dewey and Jordan, *Ethics.* Vol. LXXI, No. 1, October, 1960, p. 27-40.

Hemphill, J. K., and Rosenau, F. S. *Educational Development: A New Discipline for Renewal.* Eugene, Oregon: Center for the Advanced Study of Educational Administration, 1972.

Hencley, S. and Yates, J. *Educational Futurism: Methodologies.* Berkeley: John A. McCutchan Corp., 1974.

Kuhn, T. S. *The Structure of Scientific Revolutions.* Chicago: The University of Chicago Press, 1970.

Lehman, H. C. *Age and Achievement.* Princeton: Princeton University Press, 1953.

Light, R., and Smith, P. Accumulating Evidence: Procedures for Resolving Contradictions Among Different Research Studies. *Harvard Educational Review.* Vol. 41, No. 4, p. 429-471.

Lortie, D. C. Complexities, Specializations and Professional Knowledge: Overall Strategies in the Preparation of School Administrators. In J. Culbertson and S. Hencley, (Eds.), *Preparing Administrators: New Perspectives.* Columbus, Ohio: UCEA, 1962.

Lynch, P. Inter-Institutional Model for In-Service Training and Changes in School Systems. In P. Lynch, and P. Blackstone, (Eds.), *Continuing Education of School Administrators.* Albuquerque, New Mexico: Department of Educational Administration and Foundations, University of New Mexico and the University Council for Educational Administration, 1966.

McKelvey, T., and Harris, W. B. The Board of Cooperative Educational Services Models. In T. McKelvey (Ed.), *Metropolitan School Organization: Basic Problems and Patterns.* Berkeley, California: McCutchan Publishing Corporation, Vol. 1, 1970.

Miklos, E. *Training-in-Common for Educational, Business and Public Administrators.* Columbus, Ohio: UCEA, 1972.

Miles, M. B. Planned Change in Organizational Health: Figure and Ground. In R. Carlson, (Ed.), *Change Processes in the Public Schools.* Eugene, Oregon: CASEA, 1964.

National Institute of Education, *Educational Dissemination and Linking Agent Source Book.* Washington, D.C.: NIE, 1976 (first draft).

Popper, S. *Imaging Alternative Future School Organizations.* Minneapolis, Minnesota Department of Educational Administration, College of Education, University of Minnesota, 1972.

Rubin, L. J. *The Future of Education: Perspectives on Tomorrow's Schooling.* Boston: Allyn and Bacon, 1975.

Schutz, R. The Nature of Educational Development, *Journal of Research and Development in Education.* Vol. 3, Winter, 1971, 39-62.

Schwab, J. J. The Professorship in Educational Administration: Theory-Art-Practice. In D. Willower, and J. Culbertson, (Eds.), *The Professorship in Educational Administration.* Columbus, Ohio: UCEA, 1964 p. 47-70.

Stogdill, R. Personal Factors Associated with Leadership: A Survey of the Literature. *Journal of Psychology,* 1948 (25), pp. 35-71.

Taylor, D. Eeeny, Meeny, Miney, Meaux: Alternative Evaluation Models. *The North Central Association Quarterly.* Vol. 50, No. 4, Spring 1976, p. 353-58.

UCEA Commission Report. *The Preparation and Certification of Educational Administrators.* Columbus, Ohio: UCEA, 1973.

UCEA Instructional Resources Catalog. Columbus, Ohio: The University Council for Educational Administration, 1976.

3

The Administrator's Role in Educational Linkage

James M. Lipham

INTRODUCTION

The school administrator, particularly the principal, performs a key boundary-spanning role in bringing human and material resources from the larger environment to bear upon improvement of the ultimate client system to be served — the local school. As an educational linkage agent, the administrator is positioned at the critical confluence of the intraorganizational and extraorganizational forces which either foster or impede educational change and improvement. Although much has been written to date regarding the routine managerial aspects of the administrator's role, less has been said about the role of the administrator in fostering educational improvement; and still less is known about the unique linking functions of the local school administrator.

Since concern with educational linkage is relatively recent, the term connotes a variety of meanings. In this paper educational linkage is defined as a mutual process which makes available the conceptual, technical, human, and material resources required for improving individual and institutional performance. These resources may come from inside as well as outside the school organization. All educators sometime serve as linking agents; administrators frequently do so in providing leadership to the process of implementing educational improvement in the local school.

In examining the linkage aspects of the administrator's role, one must seek answers to three basic questions: What leadership functions must be performed by the administrator? What supports are needed by the administrator? What training is required of the administrator? Answers to these questions should serve two purposes: (1) to enhance the understandings, skills, and attitudes of practicing administrators who, as internal change agents, provide leadership in educational improvement, and (2) to improve and strengthen relationships with external linking agents who provide assistance to the local schools. Increasing the degree of congruence between the expectations held by internal linkage agents (e.g., administrators) and external linkage agents (e.g., consultants) for their mutual roles should facilitate the implementation of programs and practices which may lead to educational improvement (Ferneau, 1954; Litwak and Meyer, 1966).

One assumption in this paper is that increasing the quantity and quality of linkage relationships in the field of education has great potential for improving educational theory and practice, now and in the future (Walter, et al., 1977). To implement educational improvement, one must develop needed and appropriate linkages both within the school and between the school and the established and emerging institutions, agencies, and groups which support educational innovation — the school district, intermediate educational agencies, regional leagues and teacher centers, private educational enterprises, state departments of education, teacher education institutions, multi-state consortia and compacts, and national and international agencies and professional organizations.

In implementing educational improvement, many persons in addition to the administrator — coordinators, specialists, teachers, among others — also serve effectively as educational linkers. Research has shown, however, that administrators are crucial authority figures, particularly in the introduction of innovations, and can handle system problems associated with change more effectively than can other staff members (Carlson, 1965; Griffiths, 1964; Miles, 1964). Since it is likely that no major program of educational improvement can succeed without the understanding, support, and involvement of the administrator of the local school, this paper deals only with the role of the administrator. Future efforts should also be directed toward examining the linkage aspects of other major roles within the school.

The opening section of this paper treats the first basic question: What are the essential functions of the administrator in implementing educational change and improvement? Here the focus is on the substantive content of a programmatic change — the task or functional approach to educational leadership. Attention is then directed to the leadership functions—the means by which the administrative processes are utilized. This section concludes with a consideration of the interaction of the functions with the processes in implementing any minor or major program of educational improvement.

The second part of the paper addresses the next basic question: What kinds of support are needed by the administrator? Discussed here are the personnel, financial, informational, institutional, and political supports needed in the various stages of implementing an educational innovation. Some implications for the local administrator's role are then drawn from examining the interactions of the supports with the major phases of the implementation process.

In the third section, the following question is considered: What training is required of the administrator? Here, attention is given first to the competencies required of the administrator who would be a leader in educational improvement. Then, the required competencies and some procedures utilized to develop them are discussed. In the final part of the paper, the interrelationships of the functions of the administrator, the supports needed, and the agencies involved are presented in terms of an interactive model which is used to pinpoint issues needing further attention if linkage in the field of education is to be improved.

THE LEADERSHIP FUNCTIONS OF THE ADMINISTRATOR

The administrator engaged in educational improvement must provide leadership in each of the basic functions of the school. In the functional approach to administration the concern is with the activities to be performed — "what" tasks are to be done by each role incumbent in the school. Literally thousands of normative studies have been conducted regarding the tasks that *actually* are performed by administrators and other role incumbents in the school, and even a greater number of prescriptive articles have been written concerning the tasks that *ideally* should be performed if the school is to be improved. In fact, the functional approach to education was for several years disparaged in educational administration as being unduly prescriptive, technique-oriented, and recipe-centered (Halpin, 1958). If programs of educational improvement are to be implemented appropriately, however, one must give attention to "what" should be done, or the improvement program is without substance.

In addition to considering "what" is to be done, the administrator is also continuously concerned with "how" the functions are performed — the administrative process. Because improvement programs inevitably involve change (although the converse may not hold), it is also helpful to note that both the change process and the administrative process involve similar types of activities and behaviors central to the performance of each administrative function. Those who would provide leadership in the improvement of the school, therefore, must understand both the administrative functions and the administrative processes, as well as their interactions.

The Administrative Functions

Typically, any major program of educational improvement focuses upon the objectives to be achieved by the schools. Whether in terms of the classical cardinal principles of education or the traditional tasks of education, this approach considers both actual and idealized instructional outcomes and includes such objectives as the following (Downey, Seager and Slagle, 1960):

1. Gain a foundation of facts as a basis for knowledge.

2. Develop skills in reading, writing, and arithmetic.

3. Learn how to weigh facts as the basis for conclusions.

4. Develop a desire for learning, now and in the future.

5. Learn how to respect and get along with people with whom we work and live.

6. Understand and practice democratic ideas and ideals.

7. Understand and respect people from different cultural and religious backgrounds.

8. Learn about the relationship between humans and their environment.

9. Practice and understand the ideas of health and safety.

10. Develop a feeling of self-respect and self-worth.

11. Develop moral character and a sense of right and wrong.

12. Appreciate culture and beauty in the world.

13. Develop an awareness of careers and the world of work.

14. Understand and develop the skills required for homemaking and home maintenance.

15. Learn how to be a good manager of money, property, and resources.

16. Learn how to use leisure time.

Most existing or proposed programs designed to achieve the objectives of education can be related to the following functional categories (Lipham and Hoeh, 1974):

1. Curriculum and instruction — assessing the community context for education, determining educational needs, stating educational objectives, implementing curricular programs, and evaluating educational outcomes.

2. Staff personnel — recruiting, selecting, assigning, developing, and evaluating certified and non-certified staff.

3. Pupil personnel — counseling, testing, placing, evaluating, and governing students.

4. Finance and business management — acquiring, planning, programming, budgeting, accounting, purchasing, and inventorying resources.

5. Educational facilities — planning, constructing, maintaining, and operating school plant and equipment.

6. School-community relations — analyzing, communicating with, and involving the community, and resolving actual or potential conflicts between the school and the community.

Current educational innovations are directed at improvements in each of the above functional categories, hence the administrator must be skilled in managing each function. In addition to concern with "what" is to be done, however, the administrator must also give attention to "how" the functions are performed.

The Administrative Processes

Scholars have long been concerned with identifying and describing those processes considered crucial to effective administration. As early as 1916, Fayol described the life processes of an organization to include planning, organizing, commanding, coordinating, and controlling (POCCC). Utilizing the framework of Fayol, Gulick (1937) formulated POSDCoRB which included: planning, organizing, staffing, directing, coordinating, reporting, and budgeting. Subsequently, Sears (1950) saw the central processes as planning, organizing, directing, coordinating, and controlling. As applied to education, Gregg (1957) synthesized the administrative process in terms of the following stages: decision making, planning, organizing, communicating, influencing, coordinating, and evaluating. In this paper, the view is taken that the administrator engaged in educational linkage must be skilled in the following processes: purposing, planning, organizing, training, implementing, and evaluating.

Purposing. The first stage in the administrative process is that of purposing, often called goal setting. This stage involves identifying, clarifying, and defining goals and objectives. Needs assessment, issue analysis, and value clarification are typical relevant techniques for reaching agreement on proposed programs.

Although it may seem superfluous to ask what our purposes are, this obvious question unfortunately is often ignored. Yet misperceptions and misunderstandings about the objectives of an innovative program often contribute significantly to program failure. Administrators engaged in implementing improvements are well advised, therefore, to utilize appropriate goal-clarification and goal-setting techniques as a basis for program planning.

Planning. Despite sustained attention to authorities in educational administration to planning, there is widespread disagreement over operational definitions of the term. Some view planning as a highly personalistic process and tend to equate planning with the "mental effort" from which a plan evolves (Drucker, 1966). Others define planning as "forecasting the future" (Gregg, 1957), and still others take to a much broader view and make planning almost synonymous with the total administrative process including such stages as determining goals, specifying objectives, developing strategies, and making long-range decisions (Simon, 1957). In effect, planning involves investigating conditions and operations related to purposes and objectives, considering possible alternatives, and recommending changes to be made. Thus while planning may precede a major decision, it may also follow a decision and be concerned with its implementation.

Organizing. As with the concept of planning, different viewpoints exist concerning the concept of organizing. Again, there are those who view this stage of the administrative process in highly personalistic terms, in the sense of an ability to organize (Dale, 1960). In other definitions, organizing is seen in terms of the entire structural-hierarchical view of formal and informal organization (Barnard, 1938). Other conceptualizations use the term "coordinating" to include the processes utilized to make a plan operational (AASA, 1955). The stage of organizing includes the following: selecting specific rational processes to implement a plan, assigning primary role responsibilities, and relating people and tasks. In effect, organizing includes activities designed to increase the degree of congruence between organizational and individual goals, roles, behaviors, and outcomes so that organizational effectiveness and individual efficiency may be enhanced (Getzels and Guba, 1957).

Training. The fourth stage of the administrative process includes providing pre-service and in-service training for those engaged in the improvement effort. An adequate program of staff development is absolutely essential if a major educational change is to be implemented effectively. Since the field of education involves an intensive, interpersonal technology, the quality of most attempted innovations depends directly upon the knowledge, skills, and attitudes of each member of the staff. Staff development also includes recruiting, selecting, assigning, orienting, and evaluating the staff, as well as motivating them to implement a program of educational improvement.

Implementing. The fifth administrative process is that of implementing the program as planned. At this stage, even the best laid plans may go astray. To implement programmatic change, one not only must define tasks and assign roles but also must set timelines and provide the necessary facilities, equipment, and materials to accomplish each responsibility.

Several management tools have been designed to assist with program implementation. One is flow charting which permits a synthesis of both the elements of the system and the operations that the system performs. It is particularly useful in relating functions to decisions. Another is network analysis, which includes program evaluation review technique (PERT) and critical path method (CPM) (Cook, 1967; Evarts, 1964). Such methods are particularly valuable in that they show not only what is happening in an overall effort but also how each part affects all the other parts of a system.

In implementing a change one must determine whether the program is making gains toward achieving its objectives. A program may be implemented exactly as planned but still not reach its intended objectives. Obviously, it would be wasteful to install a program in the Fall and to wait until Spring to learn that it had failed or that it might have been effective had corrective action been taken earlier. Administrators need information about progress during the course of a program so that as problems develop they can be identified and corrected quickly. Thus, process evaluation provides information on how a program is being implemented relative to short- and long-range objectives.

Evaluating. The final stage of the administrative process is that of determining the worth of the implemented program. Such judgments, typically called program certification, are based upon outcome evaluations (Alkin, 1969). These evaluations are concerned with examining the extent to which the objectives have been achieved, as well as with assessing the impact of the outcomes on subsequent decisions. Outcome evaluation deals with questions such as the following: Shall the program be tried in different subject fields? Should we continue the program next year?

Evaluating includes: reviewing plans and objectives; obtaining data regarding inputs, processes, and outputs; interpreting the data obtained; drawing implications for future planning; and reporting results. Evaluating, therefore, may be defined as the process of defining, obtaining, and providing useful information for judging decision alternatives. Because local school personnel tend to ignore evaluative processes, greater attention to systematic evaluation is now mandated for participation in many educational improvement programs — particularly, those that are federally funded.

The foregoing stages in the administrative process closely parallel the steps in the problem-solving model of change (Jung and Lippitt, 1966) which by now are familiar to most educational administrators. Those engaged in educational improvement, however, immediately recognize that the implementation of change is not always a sequential, logical, rational process. Instead, the several steps and stages are "nested within each other" and are continuously recycled as a major educational improvement is being implemented. Moreover, there is a continuous dynamic interaction between the administrative processes and the administrative functions.

Function-Process Relationships

Analyzing the administrative functions as interactive with the administrative processes is useful to the administrator engaged in implementing a program of educational improvement at the local level. Consider, for example, a typical, targeted curricular improvement — that of selecting a new reading text. In terms of the administrative functions, it can be seen that this "simple" curricular change either immediately or ultimately impacts upon the staff, the students, finances, school-community relations, and other functions. Clearly, it is not sufficient for the administrator simply to be proficient in managing certain of the functions or each of the functions. The administrator who would be a leader must be skilled in assessing and structuring the required functional interrelationships since the school is a dynamic, interactive social system (Getzels, et al., 1968).

In terms of the administrative processes involved in this straightforward example, the following kinds of questions must be answered: What are the reading objectives to be achieved? What alternative texts and programs are available? Who will work on the problem? What expertise from within the school or from outside sources is required? When will the adoption be made and the program be implemented? How will present and future materials be evaluated? As stated earlier, answers to each of these questions can only be found by continuously recycling the processes within each of the relevant, interrelated functions. Administrators, therefore, find the function-process relationship to be useful in discovering "how to do what next" in implementing even a minor educational improvement.

As with the previous example, many educational innovations are quite narrow in scope, including community involvement projects, curriculum development projects, in-service training programs, guidance programs, school building projects, and a host of other specific endeavors. Most of the major educational innovations today, however, are quite broad and deal with such issues as equality of educational opportunity, individualized instruction, interpersonal and intergroup relations, environmental utilization and preservation, and similar perennially perplexing social and educational issues. In fact, these broad programs typically include components which attempt to deal with all of the functional categories.

As an example of a major educational innovation we can consider not a minor improvement, such as selecting a new textbook, but a major one, such as implementing Individually Guided Education (IGE). This programmatic innovation includes components which simultaneously require changing to the multiunit school organization, utilizing compatible curricular materials, installing a system of evaluation for decision making, improving home-school-community relationships, providing a facilitative environment for learning, and enhancing continuous research and development in the school (Klausmeier, 1977). The local administrator mounting such a massive effort, of which IGE is only an example, finds consideration of functional-process relationships to provide a useful gestalt, not only for guiding his or her daily activities, but also for mobilizing the intraorganizational and extraorganizational supports needed to effect a major program of improvement.

THE SUPPORT NEEDS OF ADMINISTRATORS

Pose the following question to practicing administrators: "Suppose that you wish to implement a major educational improvement. Tell me, what support would you need?" Overwhelmingly, the immediate response is, "I need support personnel." These include teachers, consultants, specialists, parents, citizens, and others. Next in importance is financial support for facilities, equipment, books, and other instructional materials. Informational, institutional, and political supports are also needed to put "people" and "things" together.

The implementation of a major educational innovation requires different kinds of support at different stages in the implementation process. In the pre-decisional awareness phase, for example, the need for adequate and appropriate information is acute. During the decision-making or commitment phase, financial and political supports are paramount. During the post-decisional phases of changeover, refinement, and renewal, individual and institutional support are crucial, so it is useful to consider the kinds of support needed by the administrator in terms of the major phases of the implementation process.

Kinds of Support Needed

Depending, of course, on the nature of the program and the processes utilized, several kinds of support are necessary to mount a successful program of educational improvement. These include personnel, financial, informational, institutional, and political support.

Personnel Support. The administrator obviously needs the support of many persons to implement any educational improvement. At the local level the essential personnel may include school board members, other administrators, central office supervisors, teachers, parents, citizens, and several significant others. Major innovations may also require the help of professors, practitioners, consultants, and other specialists in national, state, intermediate, and other educational agencies, institutions, and associations.

The administrator must exert leadership not only in the appropriate utilization of each individual's skills and abilities but also in obtaining psychological (if not moral) support for program improvement. As Hall (1974) has demonstrated, the concerns, attitudes, involvement, and commitment of participants are the essential ingredients of educational change. To obtain the support of personnel, the administrator must be able to demonstrate the rationality of the effort in terms of both organizational and individual goals so that personal identification, belongingness, satisfaction, effectiveness, efficiency, motivation, and morale may be enhanced (Getzels, et al., 1968).

Financial Support. In education, considerable resources typically are allocated to ongoing operational programs, yet scant monies are available for the improvement of educational theory and practice. Since most major innovations require time, money, and materials, the administrator who is a leader must either "scrounge" for new resources or "juggle" existing ones to accommodate the demands of the program. Moreover, increasing demands for accountability coupled with declining enrollments, inflation, and other constraints, have reduced resources still further. In fact, the administrator often is placed in the incongruous position of having to demonstrate that an educational innovation is cost-effective even before it has been attempted. Even so, it is obvious that in addition to personnel, provisions must be made for obtaining the requisite facilities, equipment, books, supplies, audiovisual and other materials required to implement the improvement program.

Informational Support. In any program effort, participants must be adequately informed about the nature of the change. To establish adequate two-way communication, the administrator must pay attention to the amount, form, and flow of information (Lipham, 1974). Regarding amount of information, those involved in educational improvement frequently err by engaging in "information overload," that is, providing information on the basis of comprehensiveness, rather than selectivity. Another common tendency is to utilize one-way, formal communication channels, such as newsletters, questionnaires, bulletins, and report cards, to the neglect of informal, two-way communication techniques, such as conferences, interviews, and visits.

Concerning form, information must be more than a mere collection of random data; it must be organized, and often reduced. Thus, considerable attention is directed within organizations to the importance of exchanging information. Recently, powerful management information tools and techniques have been developed which use computers to reduce and present data according to relevant parameters.

Finally, concerning flow, information must be made available at the time that it is needed; otherwise, it is useless. The administrator, therefore, must provide leadership in structuring responsive communication channels which foster the flow of information downward, parallel, and upward within the school organization, as well as outward to the larger environment.

Institutional Support. Since education is a hierarchically structured enterprise, at the least the local administrator must obtain institutional approval and at the best must receive institutional support for the innovative efforts being attempted. Depending upon their size, location, and a host of other environmental contextual variables, school districts and schools differ widely in terms of their structural-functional processes (Hage, 1965). Most school systems are quite centralized in their decision-making processes. Some are quite formalized in terms of the policies, rules, and regulations to be followed, to the extent that the informal organizational climate is often neglected. Many are quite stratified according to differences in status relationships between and among role incumbents. In terms of desired educational outcomes, some schools stress productivity more than they do flexibility; others stress cognitive achievement more than affective development. Therefore, the administrator who would lead must both understand the institutional context for an innovation and exert leadership in changing the school from a mechanistic, ritualistic institution to one that is dynamic and organic (Schmuck, et al., 1972).

Political Support. Whether conceived in terms of formal power or informal influence, political support for a change program is absolutely essential in a democratic society. It is not enough for the administrator to be supportive of a change effort; significant other opinion leaders and policy makers must lend their support. Governmental bodies, teachers' organizations, parent and community groups, and others must become involved.

To marshal appropriate political support, the administrator must be skilled in analyzing the values, expectations, and behaviors of many groups and individuals. Effective two-way channels of communication must be established and maintained. Latent and manifest conflicts must be resolved and coalitions built. Then it is possible to engage in collaborative effort to implement the program.

The Phases of Implementation

When any major complex educational innovation is being attempted, it appears to proceed through several broad phases which may take several years. Implementation incorporates elements of the various views of change, including the problem-solving model (Jung and Lippitt, 1966), the social interaction model (Rogers, 1962; Rogers and Shoemaker, 1971), the concerns-based adoption model (Hall, 1974), the research-development-diffusion model (Guba, 1968, Guba and Clark, 1974), and the linkage model (Havelock, 1969, Havelock and Lingwood, 1973) of educational change.

The major phases of implementation have been conceptualized as follows (Lipham and Fruth, 1976):

> 1) *Awareness Phase.* Local educators become sensitive to the need for change and become informed about programmatic alternatives. Decision makers are given an overview of a program in order to stimulate them to consider it and information regarding the required commitments to adopt it.
>
> 2) *Commitment Phase.* Local decision makers compile the necessary information and secure the necessary commitments, approvals, and cooperation of people — staff, parents, community groups, and the school board. At the end of this phase, the decision to adopt or not to adopt the program improvement is made. In making the decision to adopt, local educators are provided with information describing the change, cost fac-

tors, evaluation results, and the requirements for implementing the change.

3) *Changeover Phase.* The school staff becomes prepared to make the changeover. First, leaders are identified, receive instruction regarding the change, and develop plans for implementation. Specific plans are operationalized during the changeover period, and throughout, the school staff participates in ongoing staff development.

4) *Refinement Phase.* After school staffs have begun implementing the change program, they find that new understandings and skills are required to refine their implementation efforts. The need for refinement emerges out of the fact that the staff members are expected to perform their responsibilities in new ways. On the basis of systematic feedback, the change program itself may also be refined.

5) *Renewal Phase.* This stage includes activities designed to identify and resolve unanticipated problems to develop improved ways of implementing the change, and to prepare successive generations of professional personnel to fill new and expanded roles.

Most theorists of change processes and many educational practitioners have been quite concerned with numbers two and three above, the commitment and changeover phases of implementing an educational innovation. Considerably less attention has been paid to the awareness phase — how local educators find out about and become interested in an innovation — or to the refinement and renewal phases in which an innovation becomes institutionalized. It is useful, therefore, to consider the interaction of the needed supports and the implementation phases.

Support-Implementation Relationships

As with the function-process relationship, there is a continual recycling and interaction of the needed supports and the implementation phases. In a succeeding chapter by Crandall, for example, the functions, processes, and relationships are shown to differ substantially between the pre-decisional and the post-decisional stages of the several phases of implementation.

How do local administrators become aware of an innovation? Through reading, attendance at conferences and seminars, contact with other practitioners, visits to other schools, and many other means. In fact, most of the dissemination efforts in education are probably more informal, if not haphazard, than they are formal and systematically planned. Greater attention must be given in the future to providing accurate and adequate informational support to local administrators to increase their awareness and understanding of educational innovations.

During the commitment phase, political and financial supports become paramount, because it is here that the decision is made to adopt an educational innovation. Frequently, policies, rules, and regulations must be changed, permissions granted, and financial and other commitments made in order to attempt the improvement program.

During the changeover phase, personnel support is most critical. The needs and concerns of the staff must be identified and met. Adequate in-service training must be provided, and specific plans developed for making the changeover.

During the refinement and renewal phases, institutional support is paramount. Role relationships must be restructured and provisions made for involving others in making decisions which affect them. Through continuous and systematic feedback, both the school as an institution and the innovative program itself become modified, dynamic, and self-renewing. Likewise, the individuals within the institution become better prepared to engage in future implementation efforts.

THE TRAINING REQUIRED OF ADMINISTRATORS

What competencies are required of the administrator engaged in implementing a program of educational improvement? What programs are needed to develop the competencies? Which training procedures are useful? If innovations are to be implemented in the local schools, appropriate answers to these questions must be sought.

Competencies Required

During this decade enormous effort has been expended in developing the competency/performance based approach to teacher and administrator education. Basically, this approach assumes that persons can be professionally prepared to be leaders because systematic attention in their training has been given to (1) identifying requisite programmatic inputs; (2) specifying the desired behaviors and assigning priorities to them; (3) developing measures of competent performance; (4) providing individualized, reality-centered learning experiences; (5) evaluating the acquisition of understandings, skills and attitudes; and (6) certifying competency to perform as educational leaders (Lipham, 1975).

As alluded to in previous parts of this paper, the administrator must be competent in several domains including educational change, program knowledge, decision involvement, instructional leadership, and facilitative environments.

Educational Change. It is likely that many administrators have been so heavily engaged in maintaining the educational organization that knowledge of educational change has largely passed them by. Even so, it seems apparent that in order to implement a major educational innovation one must understand theories of educational change, must possess positive attitudes toward change, and must be skilled in the processes of change.

As indicated in the earlier chapter by Paul, educators should be thoroughly knowledgeable about the following descriptive and prescriptive models of change: the social interaction model; the concerns-based adoption model; the research-development-dissemination model; the rational process model, and the linkage model of change. Each of these perspectives is helpful to practitioners engaged in implementing major educational improvements.

Knowledge about "macro" and "micro" theories of educational change, however, serves only as the cognitive basis upon which specific skills may be developed and exercised. Research (Howes, 1974; Goodridge, 1975) has shown that the successful adoption and institutionalization of a major educational change is directly and systematically related to the extent to which local leaders are informed about the nature of the change, are able to communicate effectively with others engaged in making the change, and are able to receive and provide support during implementation of the change program. Thus, administrators must develop the understandings, skills, and attitudes required to initiate, manage, and sustain the educational change process.

Program Knowledge. Perhaps the greatest impediment to educational innovation is the lack of awareness about — much less understanding of — innovative programs and practices already available. Although recent effort has been devoted to abstracting and disseminating at least the products of the educational laboratories and research and development centers (Far West Laboratory for Educational Research and Development, 1976), additional attention must be given to dissemination efforts — particularly in programs which prepare administrators. Systematic dissemination is critical since most of the extant educational change programs are quite complex and require specific technical and interpersonal skills if they are to be implemented appropriately.

Recently it has become quite popular to emphasize process skills and to downplay content knowledge. Research (Klausmeier, 1976) shows, however, that those who would implement a major educational change effectively must become thoroughly knowledgeable about the program prior to its attempted implementation. In education, there is a widespread tendency to adopt innovations without foreseeing what one is "getting into." Instead, adequate and appropriate information about the demands, constraints, and relative merits of each component of an innovative program should be communicated and understood during each of the phases of implementation: awareness, commitment, changeover, refinement, and renewal. A comprehensive nationwide dissemination network is needed in the field of education in order to enhance program knowledge.

Decision Involvement. The appropriate involvement of others in decision making is a crucial domain of competence for administrators engaged in educational improvement. Although school-wide decisions were once the prerogative of the principal, and instructional decisions were those of the teacher, today most of the major decisions are shared. Knowledge of decision theory should provide the practitioner with appropriate answers to the following questions: What is the real and ideal decision-making structure of the school as an organization? Which decision content items are perceived as potent? What are the actual and desired levels of involvement? What structures and mechanisms may be utilized to enhance involvement? How satisfied are participants with their involvement in the decision-making process?

Recent research reveals that organizational participants desire increased involvement in making potent instructional decisions (Holmquist, 1976; Wright, 1976) and that appropriate involvement in decision making is significantly related to teacher satisfaction (Feldman, 1976; Mendenhall, 1977) and instructional effectiveness (Nerlinger, 1976). Until now, administrator preparation programs have largely emphasized individual decision-making skills, but in the future they should stress shared decision-making skills and competencies.

Instructional Leadership. Instructional leadership is universally prescribed for those engaged in educational improvement. Although variously defined, it includes those behaviors which initiate and maintain structures and procedures for accomplishing instructional goals and objectives or for changing those goals and objectives (Lipham, 1973). Preparation programs should help the administrator in developing and exhibiting the following kinds of leadership behavior (Stogdill, 1963):

1) Representation — the leader speaks and acts as the representative of the group.

2) Demand Reconciliation — the leader reconciles conflicting demands and reduces disorder to the system.

3) Tolerance of Uncertainty — the leader is able to tolerate uncertainty and postponement without anxiety or upset.

4) Persuasiveness — the leader uses persuasion and arguments effectively and exhibits strong convictions.

5) Initiation of Structure — the leader clearly defines his or her own role and lets followers know what is expected of them.

6) Tolerance of Freedom — the leader allows followers scope for initiative, decision, and action.

7) Role Assumption — the leader actively exercises the leadership role rather than surrendering leadership to others.

8) Consideration — the leader regards the comfort, well-being status, and contributions of followers.

9) Productive Emphasis — the leader applies pressure for productive output.

10) Predictive Accuracy — the leader exhibits foresight and ability to predict outcomes accurately.

11) Integration — the leader maintains a closely knit organization and resolves intermember conflicts.

12) Superior Orientation — the leader maintains cordial relations with superiors, has influence with them, and strives for higher performance.

Recent research (Gramenz, 1974) on educational leadership has shown that the behavior of the principal bears a significant and systematic relationship to the effectiveness of the instructional program of the school. Hence, the administrator must provide instrumental and supportive leadership both within the organization and between the organization and its larger environment if the instructional program is to be improved.

Facilitative Environments. As an agent of change, the administrator must be competent in strengthening the facilitative environment for innovation and improvement. This supportive environment includes not only intraorganizational functions, processes, structures, and relationships, but also extraorganizational linkages with institutions, agencies, groups, and individuals concerned with educational improvement. These extraorganizational resources are numerous, but for analysis they may be grouped as follows:

1) National educational agencies, including such governmental groups as the National Institute of Education and the U.S. Office of Education; professional organizations and associations of administrators, teachers and others; private consulting firms; and commercial publishers of educational materials.

2) Colleges and universities, particularly those engaged in administrator and teacher education.

3) Educational laboratories and centers, including university-based research and development centers and regional educational laboratories.

4) State educational agencies, including state departments of education and state professional associations in education.

5) Intermediate educational agencies, in some of the states, including general and specialized cooperative

service agencies, teacher centers, and regional leagues and consortia.

6) District agencies, including central office personnel and local professional organizations and associations.

Although the above agencies appear neatly arrayed from the broad national level to that of the local school, the implementation of a major educational innovation may require simultaneous assistance and support from several of the sources.

In establishing facilitative environments for educational improvement, the administrator must be competent in clarifying the roles of resources personnel in terms of what will be done, how it will be done, and when it will be done, since ambiguous or assumed roles will result in frustration, dissatisfaction, and conflict. Identifying consultative resources, orienting consultants and participants, ensuring that interaction is direct and personal, establishing the nature and frequency of interaction, and evaluating the quality of relationships are central responsibilities of the administrator in the area of facilitative environments (Walter, et al., 1977).

Recent studies (Ironside, 1973; Paul, 1974; Turnbull, Thorn, and Hutchins, 1974) have found that the frequency of interaction, structures for collaboration, and resource capability between and among local schools, colleges of education, state departments of education, and research and development centers contribute significantly to the successful implementation of innovations. To structure appropriate facilitative environments, administrators must be professionally prepared to perform effectively as educational linking agents.

Preparation Programs. A wide variety of undergraduate and graduate, pre-service and in-service programs is currently utilized to develop the leadership competencies required of the administrator. These include courses and seminars, workshops, conventions, academies, leagues, and independent study.

Courses and seminars continue to constitute the basis for most programs of professional preparation in educational administration. Many colleges and universities, however, are reexamining their programs in terms of the objectives to be included, the competencies to be mastered, and the sequence of prerequisites required. Some are experimenting with restructuring their programs into block-of-time arrangements, instructional modules, common and unique learnings, and other creative approaches to professional preparation.

Workshops, whether conducted on campus or in local school districts, provide opportunities for informal as well as formal knowledge acquisition and skill development. Particularly potent are workshops devoted both to individual and organizational development. Values clarification, interpersonal communication, interpersonal influence, and group process skills (Northwest Regional Educational Laboratory, 1976) are among emerging areas of emphasis for those engaged in implementing educational change.

Although conventions and conferences of state and national professional organizations and associations appear to be attended as much for their recreational as for their educational benefits, such meetings continue to serve an important training function — particularly in linking commercial publishers with local educators. The substantive programs at such conventions, however, are now characterized by the following promising practices: a focus on thematic issues, an emphasis on small group meetings, and the scheduling of meaningful presessions and postsessions.

Academies and topical institutes offered by private and professional organizations have proliferated in education during this decade. Usually of short duration, they permit the examination of an issue in depth and provide opportunities for developing skills and changing attitudes. Especially exemplary in this regard is the National Academy for School Executives (AASA, 1976) which might well be emulated by other associations and organizations as a productive mechanism for stimulating educational improvement.

Leagues and consortia of cooperating schools also provide useful training for those who are implementing educational improvement. Research (Goodridge, 1975) has demonstrated that classes, books, films, conferences, consultants, and other means are quite helpful in stimulating awareness of an innovation, but visits by educators to other schools utilizing an innovative program are the most powerful stimuli in making the adoption decision. Leagues of cooperating schools engaged in innovation provide the means by which practitioners can test theory, exchange ideas, observe practices, share opinions, and otherwise grow professionally.

Independent study includes those formal and informal activities in which one participates to enhance professional competence. Reading, reflecting, observing (even other linking agents), travel, independent research, and a multitude of other training procedures are available to those motivated to improve.

Training Procedures

A wide variety of procedures can be utilized to develop the desired competencies, including lecture-discussion, case analysis, simulation, observation, and internship. Some suggestions are offered here for improving each of these training procedures.

Perhaps the greatest impediment to the effectiveness of the commonly used lecture-discussion method is the lack of awareness on the part of professors of innovative practices in education. Commonly, several years elapse before the products of educational research and development find their way into refereed journals and standard textbooks. Means must be found, perhaps by federal subventions, to incorporate new knowledge into the substance of college and university lectures and seminars in education.

The case study method not only permits the application of cognitive knowledge but also lends vitality to the teaching-learning process. Videotapes and problem films are particularly productive for the exercise of specific skills. Here again, numerous instructional resources deserve dissemination.

Simulation represents a significant improvement over the case study method in that both the background situation and the problems to be solved are held constant for all participants, leaving role performance as the critical variable to be analyzed. In administration, the University Council for Educational Administration (UCEA, 1976) has pioneered in the development and dissemination of several substantive sets of simulation materials. Recent research (Myren, 1976) reveals that computer based simulation is particularly promising in that it provides instantaneous feedback regarding the achievement of specific leadership and decision-making skills.

Participant and non-participant observation, although time consuming, are well worth the effort — particularly when augmented with records analysis and individual interviews. Multiple schemes for observing, categorizing, and analyzing administrative behavior have been developed, and their use, even by novices, undoubtedly improves subsequent role performance.

Internships, apprenticeships, and other clinical experiences have long been recognized as perhaps the most viable component of teacher education programs, but for administrators these programs are not as prevalent as they should be. For persons without previous administrative experience the administrative internship is particularly valuable for developing the conceptual, technical, and human skills required if linkage in the field of education is to be improved.

THE IMPROVEMENT OF EDUCATIONAL LINKAGE

To improve linkage relationships in the field of education one must consider the functions performed, the supports needed, and the agencies providing the services as three interactive dimensions. In the first part of this chapter, the functional dimension was shown to include programs and activities in curriculum and instruction, staff personnel, pupil personnel, finance and business management, educational facilities, and school-community relations. The second dimension includes the following supports needed: personnel support, financial support, institutional support, and political support. The third dimension encompasses the following kinds of educational agencies: national agencies, colleges and universities, laboratories and centers, state agencies, intermediate agencies, and district agencies.

A model for the improvement of educational linkage which depicts the interactive relationships among the three dimensions — educational functions, educational supports, and educational agencies — is shown in Figure 1. Consideration of some of the cells of this taxonomy is helpful both in describing current educational improvement efforts and in targeting certain cells needing additional attention if linkage in the field of education is to be improved.

Before considering specific interactive cells, however, one should remember that the basic dimensions as defined are more exemplary than they are exhaustive. Each of the function, support, and agency dimensions could be expanded indefinitely. Moreover, the interactions of the dimensions are shown as neat, symmetrical structures, when, in fact they probably are more like "bulgy boxes." Even so, it may be instructive to examine certain of them.

Consider, for example, cell 1 in the top left corner which contains the function of curriculum and instruction, the support need for personnel, and the agencies involved as being national in scope. During the past decade, many major nationwide efforts have been devoted to this cell. Massive curriculum development projects have been mounted in such critical fields as reading, mathematics, physics, biology, career education, and many other subjects. The Education Professions Development Act (EPDA), Title III programs of the Elementary and Secondary Education Act (ESEA), and numerous other programs have been designed and implemented to upgrade the subject matter knowledge and teaching exper-

The Administrator's Role 141

FIGURE 1
TAXONOMY FOR IMPROVING EDUCATIONAL LINKAGE

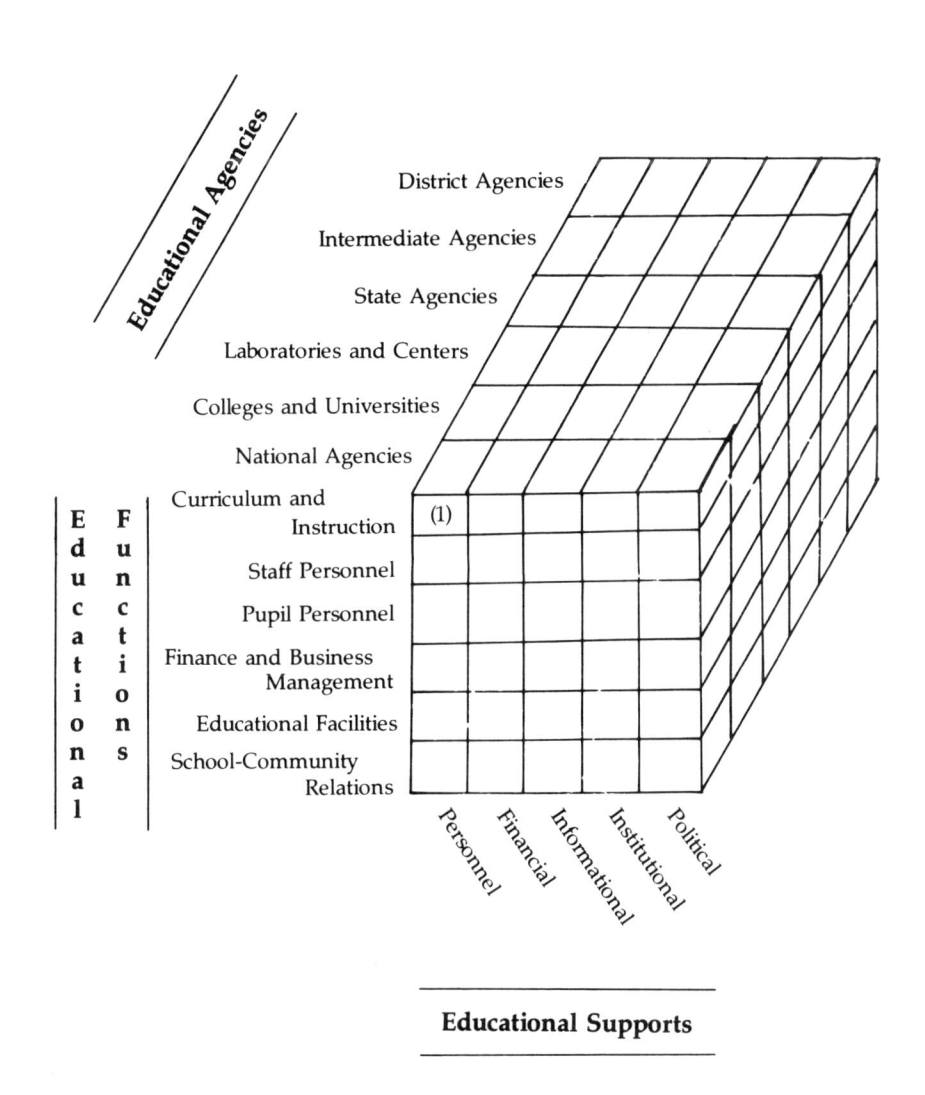

Educational Agencies:
- District Agencies
- Intermediate Agencies
- State Agencies
- Laboratories and Centers
- Colleges and Universities
- National Agencies

Educational Functions:
- Curriculum and Instruction
- Staff Personnel
- Pupil Personnel
- Finance and Business Management
- Educational Facilities
- School-Community Relations

Educational Supports:
- Personnel
- Financial
- Informational
- Institutional
- Political

tise of personnel in education. Evaluations of these efforts have led some to conclude that while certain of these efforts have been effective, other cells in the educational linkage system are weaker and should be given their share in the system of national priorities. Some, for example, would move the emphasis of national agencies from the functions of curriculum and staff development to that of student personnel and would focus upon improved guidance and other pupil personnel services. Still others would cite the need for improved school-community relations and would provide subventions for community action and similar community involvement programs.

Moving from national to other agencies, we can consider, for example, the role of colleges and universities in educational improvements. The most powerful linking relationship for improving education is that which exists between colleges and universities and local schools. They assist the schools with problems in all of the functional areas and particularly provide informational and personnel support. For example, student teaching programs, internships, and similar clinical experiences contribute substantially to the resource capability of the local school (Paul, 1974). These programs also provide feedback whereby the colleges and universities can update and upgrade their conceptual, research, teaching, and service capabilities. Even so, the relationships of colleges and universities with the local schools can continue to be strengthened.

Moving along the agency dimension, we can consider the role of the educational laboratories and centers in performing the several educational functions. Some laboratories and centers have been heavily engaged in curriculum development projects; others have been concerned primarily with staff development activities; others have been engaged in developing management systems; and still others have been concerned simultaneously with all of the educational functions. In terms of the support dimension, what kinds of support can the regional educational laboratories and the university-based research and development centers provide for the local administrator? Clearly, personnel support and financial support are circumscribed, as are institutional and political support. What the laboratories and centers can do, and perhaps better than others, is to provide informational support — knowledge of the research and development programs and projects which the local administrator can use effectively. The dissemination effort of which this chapter is a part is only a modest beginning of this domain.

Moving from a consideration of the role of laboratories and centers, we can examine the role of state education agencies in fostering educational improvement. Except for a very few strong state departments, most are not structured to provide assistance to the local administrator, except perhaps in the functions of finance and business management and educational facilities. Substantive programs in curriculum and instruction, staff personnel (except for teacher certification), pupil personnel, and school-community relations are notably lacking in most state education departments — with the possible exceptions in the fields of special and vocational education. So, programs to strengthen state departments of education in all of the functional areas and in providing each kind of support are a particularly pressing need.

The responsibilities of intermediate educational agencies are even less clear than those of state departments of education. As the "Johnny-come-lately" to the field of education, many intermediate educational agencies are torn asunder regarding both the supports they should provide and the functions they should perform. In terms of personnel support, their staffs are woefully inadequate in comparison with, for example, extension agents in the field of agriculture. In terms of financial support most intermediate educational agencies cannot give it; they must receive it in order to survive. Their informational and institutional support systems are also ambiguous. In some situations, however, their political support has been productive. Therefore, the entire functional-support relationship of intermediate educational agencies should be re-examined so that these agencies can help the local school.

Without continuing to consider specific cells, we can move to the final ones in the taxonomy — the functions performed and support provided by school district agencies *vis-à-vis* the individual school. Included here are central office personnel and local professional organizations and associations. Here again, one may encounter more impediments than assistance — at least as viewed by the local school administrator. Recent research (Benka, 1972) has shown, for example, that central office coordinators and consultants are not in the vanguard of change, and that the activities of many local unions and associations seem more directed toward forbidding than fostering educational innovation and improvement. Despite this somewhat pessimistic circumstance, some schools do continue to improve owing to the efforts of concerned administrators and others.

Each of the remaining cells in the taxonomic model shown in Figure 1 could be examined in detail in terms of the policy decisions to be made to improve education. Suffice it to state simply that this framework is proposed and presented for future analysis.

SUMMARY

In this paper educational linkage has been defined as a mutual process which makes available the conceptual, technical, human, and material resources required for improving individual and institutional performance. Three dimensions, one dealing with the educational functions, another with the support needs, and the last with educational agencies, were used for considering the issues involved in training administrators and others to engage in implementing educational change and improvement in the local schools.

The educational functions include curriculum and instruction, staff personnel, pupil personnel, finance and business management, educational facilities, and school-community relations. The administrative processes are purposing, planning, organizing, training, implementing, and evaluating. The functions and processes interact continually in the implementation of an educational innovation.

The supports needed by the administrator are comprised of personnel, financial, informational, institutional, and political support during each phase of implementing an educational innovation (awareness, commitment, changeover, refinement, and renewal). Again, the needed supports and the implementation phases are interactive.

Programs that prepare administrators should be designed to develop competence in the following domains: educational change, program knowledge, decision involvement, instructional leadership, and facilitative environments. Programs needed to develop these competencies involve courses and seminars, workshops, conventions and conferences, academies, leagues, and independent study. Helpful training procedures include lecture-discussion, case analysis, simulation, observation, and internship. The programs and procedures are provided by numerous educational agencies.

A model for the improvement of educational linkage encompasses consideration of three dimensions: the educational functions performed, the supports needed, and the agencies responsible. From a multitude of educational issues, a few examples have been cited to illustrate the utility of this model for enhancing educational improvement in the local school, both immediately and in the years ahead.

REFERENCES

Alkin, M. C. Evaluation Theory Development. *UCLA Evaluation Comment.* 1969, 2, 4-6.

American Association of School Administrators. *Staff Relations in School Administration.* Washington: AASA, 1955.

American Association of School Administrators. *Program of the National Academy for School Executives, 1976-77.* Washington: AASA, 1976.

Barnard, C. I. *The Functions of the Executive.* Cambridge, Mass.: Harvard, 1938.

Benka, J. T. *The Director of Instruction as an Agent in Organizational Change – Individually Guided Education in the Multiunit School.* Doctoral dissertation, University of Wisconsin, Madison, 1972.

Carlson, R. O. *Adoption of Educational Innovations.* Eugene, Oregon: The Center for the Advanced Study of Educational Administration, 1965.

Clark, D. L., and Guba, E. G. A Re-examination of a Test of the Research and Development Model of Change. *Educational Administration Quarterly,* 1972, 8, (3), 93-103.

Cook, D. L. *Better Project Management through Control and Use of System Analysis and Management Techniques.* Columbus: Ohio State University, 1967.

Dale, E. *The Great Organizers,* New York: McGraw-Hill, 1960.

Downey, L. W., Seager, R. C., and Slagle, A. T., *The Task of Public Education.* Chicago: Midwest Administration Center, University of Chicago, 1960.

Drucker, P. F. *The Effective Executive.* New York: Harper & Row, 1966.

Evarts, H. F. *Introduction to PERT.* Boston: Allyn and Bacon, 1964.

Far West Laboratory for Educational Research and Development. *Educational Dissemination and Linking Agent Sourcebook.* San Francisco: Far West Laboratory, 1976.

Fayol, H. *Administration Industrielle et Generale,* (C. Storrs trans.), London: Pitman, 1916.

Feldman, R. H. *Involvement in and Satisfaction with Decision Making Related to Staff and Student Behavior in IGE Schools.* Technical Report, No. 408. Madison, Wisconsin: Wisconsin Research and Development Center for Cognitive Learning, 1976.

Ferneau, E. G., 1954. Which Consultant? *Administrator's Notebook,* 1954, 4, 1-4.

Getzels, J. W. and Guba, E. G., Social Behavior and the Administrative Process. *School Review,* 1957, 65, 423-441.

Getzels, J. W., Lipham, J. M., and Campbell, R. F., *Educational Administration as a Social Process.* New York: Harper & Row, 1968.

Goodridge, C. G. *Factors That Influence the Decision to Adopt an Educational Innovation: IGE.* Technical Report No. 376. Madison, Wisconsin: Wisconsin Research and Development Center for Cognitive Learning, 1975.

Gramenz, G. W. *Relationship of Principal Leader Behavior and Organizational Structure of the IGE/MUS-E to I and R Unit Effectiveness.* Technical Report No. 320. Madison, Wisconsin: Wisconsin Research and Development Center for Cognitive Learning, 1974.

Gregg, R. T. The Administrative Process. In R. F. Campbell and R. T. Gregg, (Eds.), *Administrative Behavior in Education.* New York: Harper & Row, 1957.

Griffiths, D. E. Administrative Theory and Change in Organizations. In M. B. Miles, (Ed.), *Innovation in Education.* New York: Teachers College, Columbia University, 1964.

Guba, E. G. Development, Diffusion and Evaluation. In T. Eidell and J. Kitchel, (Eds.), *Knowledge Production and Utilization in Educational Administration.* Eugene, Oregon: Center for the Advanced Study of Educational Administration, 1968.

Guba, E. and Clark, D. *The Configurational Prespective: A Challenge to the Systems Field of Educational Knowledge Production and Utilization.* Washington, D.C.: Council for Educational Development and Research, 1974.

Gulick, L. and Urwick, L. F. *Papers on the Science of Administration.* New York: Institute of Public Administration, 1937.

Hage, J., An Axiomatic Theory of Organizations. *Administrative Science Quarterly,* 1965, 10, (December)).

Hall, G. E. *The Concerns-Based Adoption Model: A Developmental Conceptualization.* Austin, Texas: Research and Development Center for Teacher Education, University of Texas at Austin, 1974.

Halpin, A. W. The Development of Theory in Educational Administration, in A. W. Halpin, (Ed.), *Administrative Theory in Education.* Chicago: Midwest Administration Center, University of Chicago, 1958.

Havelock, R. G., et al. *Planning for Innovation through the Dissemination and Utilization of Knowledge.* Ann Arbor, Michigan: Institute for Social Research, Center for Research on Utilization of Scientific Knowledge, 1969.

Havelock, F. G., and Lingwood, D. *R & D Utilization Strategies and Functions: An Analytical Comparison of Four Systems.* Ann Arbor, Michigan: Institute for Social Research, Center for Research on Utilization of Scientific Knowledge, 1973.

Holmquist, A. M. *A Definitional Field Study of Decision Making in IGE/MUS-E Schools.* Technical Report No. 385. Madison, Wisconsin: Wisconsin Research and Development Center for Cognitive Learning, 1976.

Howes, N. J. *Change Factors Related to the Institutionalization of the Multiunit Elementary School.* Technical Report No. 319. Madison, Wisconsin: Wisconsin Research and Development Center for Cognitive Learning, 1974.

Ironside, R. A. *The 1971-72 Nationwide Installation of the Multiunit/IGE Model for Elementary Schools: A Process Evaluation.* Durham, N.C.: Educational Testing Service, 1973.

Jung, C. and Lippitt, R. The Study of Change as a Concept in Research Utilization. *Theory into Practice,* 1966, 5, 25-29.

Klausmeier, H. J. *Leadership Series in Individually Guided Education.* Reaching, Massachusetts: Addison-Wesley, 1976.

Klausmeier, H. J. Origin and Overview of IGE. In H. J. Klausmeier, R. A. Rossmiller, and M. Saily, (Eds.), *Individually Guided Elementary Education: Concepts and Practices.* New York: Academic Press, 1977.

Lipham, J. M. Content Selection in Organizational Theory and Behavior. In J. A. Culbertson, et al. (Eds.), *Social Science Content for Preparing Educational Leaders.* Columbus, Ohio: Merrill, 1973.

Lipham, J. M. Improving the Decision-making Skills of the Principal. In J. A. Culbertson, C. Henson and R. Morrison, (Eds.), *Performance Objectives for School Principals.* Berkeley, California: McCutchan, 1974.

Lipham, J. M. Competency/Performance-Based Administrator Education (C/PBAE): Recent Developments in the United States. In M. Hughes, (Ed.), *Administering Education, International Challenge.* London, England: Athlone Press, University of London, 1975.

Lipham, J. M. and Hoeh, J. A., Jr. *The Principalship: Foundations and Functions.* New York: Harper & Row, 1974.

Lipham, J. M., and Fruth, M. J. *The Principal and Individually Guided Education.* Reading, Massachusetts: Addison-Wesley, 1976.

Litwak, E., and Meyer, H. J. A Balance Theory of Coordination between Bureaucratic Organizations and Community Primary Groups. *Administrative Science Quarterly,* 1966, 2, 31-58.

Mendenhall, D. R. *The Relationship of Organizational Structure and Leadership Behavior to Teacher Satisfaction.* Technical Report, Forthcoming. Madison, Wisconsin: Wisconsin Research and Development Center for Cognitive Learning, 1977.

Miles, M. B. Innovations in Education: Some Generalizations. In M. B. Miles, (Ed.), *Innovation in Education.* New York: Teachers College, Columbia University, 1964.

Myren, R. W. *Design for Implementing Simulation Projects to Investigative Decision Making Utilizing Computerized Random Access Video Equipment (CRAVE).* Unpublished doctoral dissertation. University of Wisconsin-Madison, 1976.

Nerlinger, C. M. *Participative Decision Making in IGE/MUS-E Schools,* Technical Report No. 356. Madison, Wisconsin: Wisconsin Research and Development Center for Cognitive Learning, 1975.

Northwest Regional Educational Laboratory. *Linker Competency Skills Assessment.* Portland, Oregon: Northwest Laboratory, 1976.

Paul, D. A. *The Diffusion of an Innovation through Interorganizational Linkages: A Comparative Case Study.* Technical Report No. 308. Madison, Wisconsin Research and Development Center for Cognitive Learning, 1974.

Rogers, E. M. *Diffusion of Innovations.* New York: Free Press, 1962.

Rogers, E. M., and Shoemaker, F. F., *Communication of Innovations: A Cross-Cultural Approach.* New York: Free Press, 1971.

Schmuck, R. A., et al. *Handbook of Organization Development in Schools*. Palo Alto, California: National Press, 1972.

Sears, J. B. *The Nature of the Administrative Process*. New York: McGraw-Hill, 1950.

Simon, H. A. *Administrative Behavior*, (2nd ed.). New York: Macmillan, 1957.

Stogdill, R. M. *Manual for the Leader Behavior Description Questionnaire*. Columbus, Ohio: Bureau of Business Research, Ohio State University, 1963.

Turnbill, B. J., Thorn, L. T., and Hutchins, C. L. *Promoting Change in Schools: A Casebook*. San Francisco, California: Far West Laboratory for Education Research and Development, 1974.

University Council for Educational Administration. *Instructional Resource Catalog*. Columbus, Ohio: UCEA, 1976.

Walter, J. E., Lipham, J. M. and Klausmeier, H. J. Facilitative Environments for IGE. In H. J. Klausmeier, R. A. Rossmiller, and M. Saily, (Eds.), *Individually Guided Elementary Education: Concepts and Practices*. New York: Academic Press, 1977.

Wright, K. W. *Real and Ideal Decision Structure and Involvement in IGE Schools*. Technical Report No. 374. Madison, Wisconsin: Wisconsin Research and Development Center for Cognitive Learning, 1976.

4

Linking Processes In Educational Change

Ann Lieberman

> There is a great need for
> the synthesis and integration
> of existing information as there
> is for the generation of the new.
>
> *Research in the Service of Mental Health.* Report of the Research Task Force of the National Institute of Mental Health, J. Segal, (Ed.), Rockville, Maryland (page 398)

In the last fifteen years there has been a marked change in the view that schooling can be improved by outside agencies. In the late 1960s, many projects and the agencies which planned them developed at federal, state, and local levels and created new sets of relationships between these projects and local school districts (Bentzen, 1974; Berman and McLaughlin, 1974; Klausmeier, et al., 1977; Takanishi, 1973; Tempkin, 1974; Tye and Bentzen, 1971). The roots of creating a linkage between institutions came in the 1940s with Paul Mort's organization of the Metropolitan School

Study Council, a group of schools linked to Teachers College (Paisley and Paisley, 1975).[1]

These linkages have created new possibilities for the improvement of schools and have brought forth some complex research questions (Berman and Pauley, 1975; Corwin, 1973; Fullan, 1972). Additionally, these questions have involved a number of persons in a quest for a better understanding of what factors lead to their linkages, of what transpires between these agencies and schools, and of what work is accomplished (Goodlad, 1975; Miles, 1976).

Even though there are many people involved in all kinds of agencies fulfilling these linkage functions, there has been very little systematic study of people who deliberately intervene in social systems in order to bring about change (Baldridge and Deal, 1973; Hall and Alford, 1976; Lieberman, et al., 1973; Tichy, 1972). This paper is seen as one building block in a continuing effort to understand the nature of school improvement by looking at what needs to be known by those participating in linkage efforts and what support needs to be provided for schools by linking agencies. The current state of the art includes model building, hypothesis testing, propositional thinking, case studies and the like, but we are only now at the point of being able to form an initial conception of the processes embedded in models used by linking agencies as these agencies interact with school systems.

These processes may be performed by one person or by several persons working in various organizational patterns. (More important are the processes, not the creation of a super-person to perform them.)

Agencies vary in the way tasks are assigned. It is more usual today to think of a team of people working as linking agents performing complementary functions, or at least the possibility that one person can call on other people to perform a variety of functions.[2] These linking processes occur within a given social context, that is, those performing linkages

---

[1] Linkage refers to the possibility of connecting people, institutions, agencies, and the like in such a way that they exchange information and resources (both human and material) to help solve their problems. Further illumination of this view can be found in Seymour Sarason's book, *Human Resources*, forthcoming.

[2] Crandall's chapter takes issue with this stance. He describes a "super person" with an enormous amount of conceptual knowledge and skill. At least part of the difference in viewpoints may be explained by whether we are talking about a "new role" as Crandall does, or about a broader definition of all kinds of people in all kinds of organizational arrangements performing linkage tasks. The latter view is taken by this writer. One must also note the differences in range, complexity and duration of the linkage. Some agencies are embedded in a larger social context, whereas others might perform a single job or have a specified task, and these procsses may be performed by State Education Agencies (SEA), intermediate agencies (IEA), research and development centers, projects, local education agencies (LEA), district-in-service programs, teacher centers, cooperative agencies, etc.

move back and forth between the context of their own agency and that of the social system. How one sees the job of linkage has a great deal to do with how one views his/her clients. The focus of this chapter is on the school system and the way that system affects the people in it, and consequently, the processes utilized by linking agencies. The next chapter includes a discussion of the host agency of the linking agent.

Four assumptions underlie the paper and can be used to guide the discussion:

> 1. Knowledge about the school as a social system can reveal some understandings essential to those who would seek to build and to participate in linking agencies.
>
> 2. Sufficient research evidence and experience with attempts at linkage exist so that some basic processes which these agencies perform can be identified.
>
> 3. Linkage, by definition, implies some concept of collaboration. Ways of organizing, of acknowledging this relationship, can be inferred from field experience.
>
> 4. Certain conditions which influence both linker, agency, and school system can be identified.

The paper will close with some vignettes that reveal some of these understandings, processes and conditions as they affect the linkage relationship.

THE SCHOOL AS A SOCIAL SYSTEM

A substantial number of educators and some research evidence suggest that innovations, however defined, fail to be implemented because the social system of the school is neither understood nor dealt with adequately (Baldridge and Deal, 1975; Giacquinta, 1973; Goodlad and Klein, 1970; Gross, et al., 1971; Jackson, 1968; Lieberman and Shiman, 1973; Sarason, 1971; Smith and Keith, 1971; Tye, 1975). Others have studied schools as social systems to develop a better understanding of what they are like, what behaviors occur in them (Sarason, 1974), and what pressures, contradictions and conflicting sets of expectations make up school life (Bidwell, 1965; Dreeben, 1973; Getzels, Lipham, and Campbell, 1968; Gordon and Adler, 1963; Ianni, 1974; Lortie, 1975; Miles, 1967; Waller, 1932). Based on these studies, one can divide the school system into three entities — the teacher, the principal, and the environment — in order to understand better the functioning of school and the way in which these understandings can be important to people performing linkage processes.

The Teacher

Since 1932 when Waller wrote so poignantly about the teacher numerous people have attempted to describe the role of the teacher (Jackson, 1968; Lortie, 1975, Sarason, 1974), and still others have tried to identify teacher characteristics as they affect learning (Rosenshine, 1973). But by far the most helpful understandings for our purposes are those that describe the teacher as (s)he responds in a variety of ways to involvement in a social system of contradictory pushes and pulls.[3]

Contradictory Nature of Teaching
Teachers are expected to deal with all children who come to school and with each child individually (Bidwell, 1965; Gordon and Adler, 1963; Lortie, 1975; Waller, 1967).
Understanding 1 – To deal with this contradiction, teachers develop a set of skills that work for them. These skills or methods form the basis of their "style" and, as such, are highly personalized. It is not hard to see then why so many teachers hold on tightly to what they know and resist new methods of teaching. This condition has implications for agencies or agents bringing in new packages, new programs, or what appears to be "different."

Multiple Interpretations of School Goals.
Goals of schooling are global, sometimes conflicting (Miles, 1967), and so are open to many interpretations as they are translated into practice. No one view predominates or gives direction to that translation. This discrepancy between goals and one's mode of putting those goals into

---

[3]This discussion is not meant to imply that all teachers are the same. Tremendous variation exists among teachers in terms of their behavior toward the job, toward each other, resources, ideas, etc.

practice forms the basis on which teachers learn to teach.

When "new curricula" or "better methods" are promulgated by "experts" (usually from outside the school), teachers are wary because — among other reasons — their own learning has been forged through their own struggle to link theory and practice. The assumption that one is or should be open to fresh ideas does not account for teachers' modes of learning, nor does it consider the reasonable skepticism of teachers to ideas which commonly fail to attend to the complexities of their role. Openness to new ideas is something that needs to be nurtured continuously.

Understanding 2 – Teachers are in a double bind over new ideas. On the one hand they hold on to their tried and tested ideas; on the other, they become dependent on ideas from the outside as the primary source of new knowledge (Lieberman, 1972; Smith and Keith, 1971).

Teacher Isolation

Most teachers perform their teaching functions in total isolation from other adults, and yet they are expected to cooperate and collaborate on ideas, new programs, et cetera (Sarason, 1972).

Understanding 3 – Collaboration and cooperation are only possible when isolation is broken by organizational arrangements that allow, even encourage, teachers to participate *with* one another.

Autonomy and Control

There is no real "program" in most schools in the sense that there is coordination among teachers, subject areas, and so on. Even though teachers seem to have a great deal of independence "behind the classroom door," there are norms controlling the behavior of teachers (Goodlad and Klein, 1970; Meyer, 1975).

Understanding 4 – One must learn what the norms are in a school to understand organizational behavior, individual behavior, and the different perceptions of those norms by groups and individuals within groups. The existence of group norms has implications for evaluating the situation, having perceived who volunteers, who is seen as "opinion leader," who will resist . . . .

Individual vs. Collective Activity

Much has been written describing the fact that teachers are not interdependent (Meyer, 1975; Miles, 1967; Sarason, 1971), that is, they perform their jobs without much interaction, even need of others. This condition leads to an individualistic view of what each teacher thinks teaching is. Yet when teachers are asked to engage in innovative activity, there is commonly an urgent need to support others and often a need for some people to assume leadership roles (Culver and Hoban, 1973). Provision for discussion about the complexities of the teaching role and for the construction of a set of shared definitions about teaching can provide an antidote to the isolation and "individualism" of teachers.

Understanding 5 – Engaging people in innovative activities will involve breaking two powerful norms in school life: that of teachers' thinking that all teachers do the same thing, and that being interdependent intrudes upon one's view of teaching. The breaking of these norms leads to the next understanding, intricately woven into the one above, that rewards must be consciously provided as these norms are replaced with others (Miller, 1975).

The Principal

There is substantial evidence that the principal is a key controller of what happens in a school (See Lipham in the previous chapter, Berman and Pauley, 1975; Gross, et al., 1971; Gross and Herriott, 1965; Lieberman, 1973; Smith and Keith, 1971; Williams, et al., 1974). In other words, the principal has been associated with powerful effects on teachers—the way they work with one another, the way they feel about the work, the way new ideas come into the school and, in general, with the way the staff assumes their morale. Looking at these associations leads us to consider several understandings of the role of the principal.

Involvement of the Principal

If it is evident that the principal is a crucial figure in the local school setting, through his/her active involvement with teachers, then any innovative activity must involve the principal.

Understanding 6 – Involvement of the principal can take many forms, depending upon the ideas, the innovative project, and the principal's interest, capabilities, and skills. Involvement may be only his/her understanding of what is going on, or it may be knowing enough to support the teachers, or it may be gathering community support.[4]

Principal as Learner

Most principals now in leadership positions are being asked to perform functions for which they have had little preparation (Tye, 1973). For

---

[4]Community members and students are recognized as key members of the school system, but the emphasis here is on those people who are the *initial* focus of most linkage activities.

example, negotiations with unions, initiating and maintaining innovative projects, involvement in legal decisions affecting the school, and providing for the continuing growth of a stable staff are a few areas for which principals have received little training.

Understanding 7 – Part of our understanding of the social system must include a diagnosis of his/her knowledge and ability to perform, to support and to facilitate functions for the school staff. Does the principal have access to the means to learn? To observe? To discuss? Who will support the principal as (s)he learns new behaviors? Are principals being given feedback on what is happening so they can enlarge their behavioral repertoire (Miller, 1975)? (See especially Bentzen, 1974; and Klausmeier, 1977.)

Principals in the Larger Context

Principals are enmeshed in a larger socio-political context (Tye, 1973), and there are all kinds of pressures apparent to teachers and linking agencies.

Understanding 8 – People in linking agencies must look at a principal with an understanding not only of his/her position within the school but also of the larger context within which the principal resides. For example, a principal with a great deal of skill and enthusiasm but no central office support will suffer from isolation, whereas a principal with district support and community problems, a reluctant staff, and lack of organizing skills may have plenty of external support but no means to do anything with that support. Each case compels a diagnosis that considers the source of constraints, and facilitating forces and their impact on that principal.

The Environment

Because local schools have both internal and external environments that affect the linkage relationship, our understanding of the social system of the school needs to be placed in a larger framework.

External Environmental Constraints of the School

It is naive to think that the local setting is unaffected by the external environment, that is, we must recognize the extent to which schools are creations of the world around them. Sometimes there is a tendency to be comfortable by forgetting or ignoring events beyond the school building. Districts differ in their philosophy, state support, utilization and allocation of resources, size, organizational complexity, organized constituencies, history of innovative activity, and stability of population[5] (Baldridge and Deal, 1975; Tye and Novotney, 1975).

Understanding 9 – School people respond to external conditions as these affect the local school. Small and large districts communicate differently and are connected to the outside world differently. Stable and rapidly changing communities deal differently with their schools — budget cuts, teacher lay-offs, new superintendents — all affect the local scene.

Consider the difference between a principal in a large city district who has learned how to circumvent rules and regulations and make use of a variety of linkages versus a principal in a district of four schools where decisions, people, and conversations are major topics of concern to all living within the village. Or the difference between large city districts where high level bureaucrats decide which schools to close as opposed to a small, closely knit district where plans are being discussed five years *before* a decision to close a school is made.

The Central Office Staff

Clearly, the central office helps create part of the climate of the school by the number of personnel, their availability, their relationships with school, staff, the types of activities in which they engage, their numbers and functions, and their presence in the schools.

Consider the differences between a superintendent who organizes the principals to support one another, creates problem-solving groups for teachers to work on a specific problem, and uses district staff to facilitate schools' working together on common problems, as opposed to a superintendent who provides district staff with total autonomy to run their own projects with no linking between and among the schools, versus a superintendent who involves principals in every and any project that will look favorable to the community.

Understanding 10 – Additional data from the central office provide information on general questions. How much support are the schools (principals and teachers) getting? How are decisions made in the district? What is the history of the district in terms of stability and change? How cosmopolitan is the leadership? How open to ideas are they? How cooperative will the district be? What are the motivations behind linking efforts?

---

[5]Consider the difference between a small Westchester Village in New York, where there is no growth, and a community with rapid turnover in the San Fernando Valley in California.

PROCESSES OF LINKING WITH SCHOOLS

Having looked at some selected understandings of the school as a social system, one can now expand the view of the interaction of that system with linking agencies (1) by looking at the dynamics of the change process as school people interact with it, (2) by reviewing linkage studies and propositions, and (3) by inferring linkage processes.

Dynamics Of The Change Process In Schools

The different foci of three major studies underlie the discussion of dynamics of change within the schools: the Hall, *et al.*, studies, the I/D/E/A study, and the Rand Change Agent studies. One may look at the user (the teacher) as (s)he interacts with new ideas, to the school as it looks at its problems and attempts solutions, to a cross section of schools as they implement new ideas. (See Tables 1, 2, 3.)

The Concerns Based Adoption Model (CBAM) (Hall and Rutherford, 1975) assumes that to understand how change takes place, one can look at the teacher and see that (s)he seems to go through stages of development of personal *concern* about innovation, matched with stages of actual *use* of the innovation (Hall and Loucks, 1975). Teachers move from very personal concerns, the time involved (Hall, 1975), through task concerns to concerns about the impact of the innovation on other teachers. At the same time, one can observe a developmental pattern of how teachers use new ideas (Loucks and Hall, 1976). Teachers alter their behavior along a continuum from wanting information and feeling unsure about using their innovation to trying it out, exploring its consequences, and talking about it with others. The last stage of use becomes one of asking and searching for "more universal benefits" (Hall, 1975).

These stages of concern and levels of use can be *linked* to findings of the long-term I/D/E/A study of eighteen schools in Southern California. These schools were joined together in a "league," and this group of schools engaged itself in a study of school improvement and in the documentation of the change process for a five-year period.[6] Those who

---

[6]For details of the entire study, see Culver and Hoban, 1973, Bentzen, 1974; and Goodlad, 1975.

were studying the league observed the process of Dialogue, Decision-Making, and Action (DDA). As schools began to look at their problems, a common process was observed: Teachers talked. They talked about new ideas, their ability to perform new roles, and whether support would be forthcoming. Then another stage was observed: Decisions were made — to individualize reading, to create a learning center, to team teach (usually by a few teachers). Field notes were kept to identify patterned behavior across schools, and these patterns were like those identified in CBAM. Teachers talked, engaged in an activity, then compared that activity to the rest of what they were doing. As they felt comfortable managing change in their classrooms, they sought collaboration between and among schools.

Both these studies revealed a pattern that clarified the dynamics of school improvement. Teachers, as individuals and as participants in subgroups in school social systems, appear to move from personalized concerns (after they become aware of new ideas), to more task-oriented management problems, to questions about the effectiveness of the new ideas, to concerns and strategies for involvement with more people. Questions that might involve "programs" or collaboration came after a period of trial and satisfaction with their competence in integrating new ideas.

TABLE 1
THE DYNAMICS OF CHANGE IN SCHOOLS

THE USER
Concerns Based Adoption Model (CBAM)

Stages of Concern	Level of Use
0 Awareness	0 Non-use
1 Informational	I Orientation
2 Personal	II Preparation
3 Management	III Mechanical use
4 Consequence	IV A. Routine
	B. Refinement
5 Collaboration	V Integration
6 Refocusing	VI Renewal

Adapted from Hall, G. E., Wallace, R. C., and Dossett, W. F., *A Developmental Conceptualization of the Adoption Process Within Educational Institutions.* Austin, Texas: Research and Development Center for Teacher Education, University of Texas at Austin, 1973.

TABLE 2
THE DYNAMICS OF CHANGE IN SCHOOLS

GROUP OF SCHOOLS
I/D/E/A STUDY

Dimensions of Receptivity to Change Which Were
Used for Measurement of the DDAE Process

	Dialogue	Decision	Action
Scope	How open is it?	How consensual is it?	How extensive is it?
Importance	How meaningful is it?	How substantive is it?	How significant is it?
Relevance	How sustained is it?	How consistent is it?	How patterned is it?
Flexibility	How inquiring is it?	How flexible is it?	How modifiable is it?

Stages of Change

1) Talk about new ideas.
2) Someone individualizes reading, changes the furniture . . . .
3) The innovative activity makes the rest of the program look shabby.
4) People ask questions like "How can the *school* provide for individual differences?"
5) Dialogue begins again on new set of questions.

Adapted from Lieberman A., and Shiman, D., Stages of Change in Elementary School Settings. In C. Culver and G. Hoban (Eds.), *Power To Change*. New York: McGraw-Hill, 1973; and from Bentzen, M. M., *Changing Schools: The Magic Feather Principle*. New York: McGraw-Hill, 1974.

Linking people must recognize the developmental pattern of *initial* teacher "self" concerns which demand a supportive environment in dealing with new ideas. Collaboration and questions involving large numbers of faculty appear *after* teachers are comfortable with new ideas and have learned to manage them.

A third study that added to the understanding of the dynamics of school change and serves as a link to a discussion of the processes of linking is the Rand Change Agent study (Berman and McLaughlin, 1974;

TABLE 3
THE DYNAMICS OF CHANGE IN SCHOOLS

NATIONAL SAMPLE OF SCHOOLS
Rand Change Agent Study

Summary of Major Findings

1) Effective implementation dependent on supportive setting and on a strategy that fostered mutual adaptation of staff to project demands.

2) *Within-program variations* affected implementation more significantly than did differences among federal programs.

3) Projects using similar methods varied in their implementation strategies and institutional settings. The variations were more important than the methods or technologies.

4) Elementary school principals facilitate or inhibit implementation.

5) These elements of implementation strategies promoted teacher change:
    a) Staff training
    b) Frequent and regular meetings
    c) Meetings and training
    d) Quality and amount of change required by project
    e) Local material development (in Title III projects).

6) The more concentrated the resources were (Title III), the more likely was teacher change.

Adapted from Berman, P., and Pauley, E., Factors Affecting Change Agent Projects. *Federal Programs Supporting Educational Change, Volume II.* Santa Monica, California: Rand Corporation, April, 1975.

Berman and Pauley, 1975). The researchers looked at 293 federally funded change agent projects across the country and focused on implementation of innovations through agencies of in-depth case studies. Their major findings corroborated earlier findings about the effectiveness of involving people in decision-making (Lewin, 1947) and the importance of building group morale as an important factor facilitating changes in behavior (Cartwright, 1968).

The Rand study, like the Hall and I/D/E/A studies, documented once again that the local setting influences the course of innovation. Their focus on the local setting revealed that the principal could facilitate or block innovation and that there were certain strategies that appeared to be linked to successful implementation. These strategies, using different terminology, were also to be found in the Hall research on individual teachers and the I/D/E/A in-depth study. These strategies include:

1. Active participation

2. Face-to-face interactions

3. Opportunities to learn new behaviors

4. Local materials development

5. Support from the principal

These three major studies give us a more comprehensive picture of four factors which are crucial to the processes of linkage. They are:

1. The nature of participation

2. The substance of educational change

3. The mechanisms used

4. The rewards of the system (Lieberman, 1976)

Organizing for Participation, Process 1 – Organizing for participation appears to require the principal, some initial volunteers, and eventually a "critical mass" of people who will create innovative norms. However, interesting questions are still being raised about the nature of participation. Gross, *et al.*, (1971) found that initial volunteers became resisters when they were not adequately supported. The Rand study concluded that volunteers did not necessarily lead to more volunteers. And the

League study found that although initial voluntarism appeared to be a legitimate way to organize for participation, there was a continuing problem of socializing the new volunteers. Sharing experience often was unconvincing. New recruits needed their own experiences to provide for their own learning. Considerable care, then, needs to be taken as one organizes for involvement.

Developmental Substance, Process 2 – Regardless of the substance of an educational change that might eventually be implemented (team teaching, individualized reading, alternative teaching strategies), initial substance should revolve around questions of personal concern and local problems, as well as new information. For example, if faculty in a school are discussing individualized reading, it is common for someone to talk about organizing the classroom, the number of books to have, and recordkeeping, among other topics. It is less common, but essential, to have as part of the discussion such questions as: Can all teachers handle this type of organization? What skills, abilities and attitudes does a teacher need to do it? What emotional tensions does such a program initially create? How does one deal with the initial uneasiness of learning to do something new and unfamiliar?

Developmental Mechanisms, Process 3 – Mechanisms (meetings, groups, workshops) can be organized around a developmental cycle which appears to be, first, acquiring information related to personal and local concerns, then, trying out the new idea with a focus on management problems, and ultimately, making provision for sharing, collaborating and integrating the ideas into a larger context.

Planning New Rewards, Process 4 – Rewards for learning new skills or becoming more competent must be planned for both the short-term and the long-term. What is being called for includes timing, meeting new people, creating new relationships, being involved in a larger world and a larger network of ideas (Goodlad, 1975). For a long time we have been attached to extrinsic rewards; these studies provide evidence for the greater power of intrinsic rewards.

Linking Studies

There have been numerous people studying and describing models of linking (See Appendix 1), roles of various types of linking agents* (See Appendix 2), and the processes by which people organize for and interact with linking agencies (See Appendix 3). From an analysis of these works

---

*Linking agents are also described as change agents, adoption agents, innovative or personnel consultants.

and the understandings of the school as a social system, the remainder of the processes used by linking agencies can be suggested.

Problem Solving Orientation, Process 5 – Whether one looks holistically at the models proposed for linkage or the roles proposed for linking agents, every model refers to the process of problem solving. Havelock (1971) discussed the linking agent's aid in problem identification as a significant function (See Table 4).[7] Lingwood and Morris (1974) found that the federal agencies they studied provided for the "users [sic] ability to solve their own problems" (See Table 5[7]). Jung (1967), Miles (1976), Tichy (1972) and Wallace (1974) began to flesh out the process of problem solving orientation when they referred to "diagnosing of the situation" (Wallace), "earning the right to help" (Miles), and "relating to staff in identifying needs and training" (Jung). There seems to be no doubt in all these studies and descriptions that in order for people to be open to new ideas, to adapt to changing conditions, or to deliberately make changes in their own system, they must develop the capacity to solve their own problems.

If one refers back to the previous description of the school social system and its complexity, it is clear that professing an ideal model of problem-solving capabilities involves a linking agent in a complex array of learnings — especially when linking schools to other agencies is included. Again, there is the possibility that it is more reasonable, with our state of knowledge, to think developmentally about problem solving. People need to learn to talk about their needs, and they may require help defining their needs and putting them in a form to be acted upon. (Some may be unaware that they have problems or needs at all.) The capacity to solve problems involves one in the sensitivity to the work-life of school people and the ability to engage them in activities in which they have a vested interest (their competence and self-betterment as teachers and principals). This situation creates a tension for a research and development center with a specific program or product to be diffused, or a state department mandating a special program. When there is a specific product to sell, it is hard to be sensitive to the work life of clients.

A problem solving *orientation* must guide the activities of the linking agency. And orientation means developing activities that will increase individual capacity to identify and clarify problems, to identify alternatives, to develop criteria with which to judge alternatives, to try out solutions, to evaluate their utility, and to start again — regardless of the substance that is being offered. Here a person-oriented approach is linked to a task-oriented approach.

---

[7]See Appendix 1, Tables 4 and 5

[8]See Appendix 2, Tables 6, 9, 8, and 11

Diagnosis, Process 6 – The importance of diagnosis as a process for those engaged in linkage is closely linked to a problem solving orientation. Diagnosis can be described as a process on a continuum, ranging from informal procedures in assessing a situation (Tichy, 1972) to a set of more substantive questions such as, "What beliefs and knowledge are held by various persons to be affected by innovation?"

Miles'[9] focus on linking planners and environment, as well as on looking at power strategies, cognitive clarity (does everyone share at least part of the same reality?), affective support and reflexivity are part of the substance involved in the diagnosis of a situation. Havelock (1971)[10] and Griffin/Lieberman[11] view diagnosis as one function of the linking role. The current phrase "needs assessment," we suspect, makes a mechanical process out of a well developed skill in deciding how to enter a system, with whom to work, what the state of the field is, how fast or slow to move, what activities are most relevant, and where to start building relationships. Diagnostic procedures need to take place as a continuous process; they will be informal, formal, or both, depending on the skills of whoever is making the assessment and the exigencies of the situation. What is important is that some diagnosis take place — it provides the information for present and future work — about the state of the relationship between linker and client, and that it take place on all the levels involved in the linkage relationship. Diagnosis that has as one of its outcomes leaving clients with the ability to use new information and to help solve their own problems must continually involve the construction of new support systems (Griffin/Lieberman) and the recognition that the most successful linkage will leave the school people as linkers (Havelock, 1971) and the linking agent out of a job.

Strategy Building, Process 7 – Closely associated with a problem solving orientation and a diagnosis of the social system with its complex array of variables is the ability to build strategies. Strategy building is the process of creating a plan of action, in our case, one that considers in its simplest form where one wants to end and the means to get there. Building strategies is at the heart of any intervention, for it is here that one must deal specifically with the conflicts, tensions and complexities of linking two social systems — the school and the linking agency.

The literature refers to solution-building functions (Lingwood and Morris, 1974), or linkage as described by type, mode and frequency of

---

[9] See Appendix 2, Table 11

[10] See Appendix 2, Table 7

[11] See Appendix 3, Table 10

interaction (Paul, 1976), or the manipulation of human financial and material resources (Wallace, 1974). Griffin and Lieberman refer to plans that include acting upon subsystems, whereas Jung speaks about creating the conditions for training, demonstrating and arranging access to resources. Havelock's strategy building moves from bringing new information into the system to planning linkage functions that deal with how to use the knowledge, to the clients' initiation of activities on his/her own behalf.

Sieber *et al.*, (1972) began to build a way of looking not only at the strategies one uses but also at the relationships between strategies and particular settings.

Most strategies are described in specific terms, such as:

1. Trains staff in skills (Jung)

2. Works with groups (Griffin and Lieberman)

3. Focuses on cognitive clarity (Miles)

4. Carries information (Havelock and Havelock)

5. Focuses on affective support (Miles)

We must again stress the need for a developmental approach to strategy building in schools. If one wants to build (the school) a self-sustaining problem solving approach within the local setting, then strategies need to move from involving people initially in fresh ways of thinking about their work (information giving), to building supportive structures (linkage) where *trial* testing of new ideas can take place, to engagement in problems of management (finding resources) to building cooperative structures that can be mutually supportive (networks).

Strategy building processes must act dynamically to move from dependence on outside sources to mutual sharing, from information receiving to creation of new knowledge, from immediate, concrete strategies (meetings, workshops) to long-term strategies (institutionalized structures), from involvement of two interested teachers to a "critical mass" of teachers. The essential core of this process is, again, that strategies include:

1. Knowledge of the specific social system, as well as new information.

2. Movement from concrete to more global concerns.

3. Movement on several fronts at once: personal, organizational, programmatic and inter-organization.

Organization for Linkage, Process 8 – Perhaps one of the most crucial processes, yet one known least about, is the creation of supportive structures that will facilitate improvement of schools. Although there are several long-term field studies upon which to draw (Bentzen, 1974; Corwin, 1973; Goodlad, 1975; Walter, *et al.*, 1977), scores of agencies have created linkages of all kinds, and the experience base is far larger than the written materials would indicate. (For example, research and development centers, ESEA projects, teacher corps, teacher centers, existing state, county and local agencies, to name a few.) Two large scale linkage projects have been selected here because of the author's long term involvement in one of them, because others have written about them, and because as a group they offer an initial understanding of organizing linkage purposes. One other is referred to, as it is in process of being organized (See Appendix 3).

The League. The League of Cooperating Schools, a consortium of eighteen schools, was organized and studied between 1966 and 1971 (See Table 12). The purpose of the League was to improve schools and to have schools innovate in dealing with their own problems. The nuances of dealing with individual schools, the creation of a group of schools, and the problems of linkage with one agency, I/D/E/A, will be the major focus.[12] This project highlights some of the difficult problems with which linkage agencies must deal if collaboration is to be effective. The essential problems of linking are that school people and the outside people who become involved with schools have different purposes, perspectives, interests, work styles, and time frames. These are a source of tension, but these differences must be worked through to achieve the basis upon which a collaborative relationship is built. The League study draws attention to the fact that schools tend to distrust outsiders, to see research and development products as "not helpful," and to see most outsiders as "too theoretical" and using the school for their own purposes. (These problems have been cited elsewhere — Baldridge, *et al.*, 1973; Carlisle, 1967; Miles, 1976; Takanishi, 1973).

Collaboration Orientation. It is necessary, therefore, in a collaborative effort to build an orientation toward collaboration that considers the school's time perspective and work life. Collaboration means a mutual *respect* and *understanding* for the differences which exist between schools and linking agencies, and that this respect and understanding is reflected

---

[12] The Institute for Development of Educational Activities (I/D/E/A) was the funding agency and also the name given to the office where the research staff worked.

in the expectations, activities, exchanges, and strategies that take place.[13]

Working the Collaboration. The League study suggests that a "hub" is needed, a clearinghouse to "work" the relationship between schools and agency (Goodlad, 1975). It also suggests that expertise is already in the system and that this hub can facilitate use of such experts. These realities of school life suggest that new knowledge can be institutionalized and spread by the very people within the school social system by their own involvement in solving their problems. But this collaboration is a process, and the process includes activities which move through a developmental cycle (as has been suggested above), a cycle reflecting the fact that different people will be at different places in their development at different times and that activities will be part of a strategy that reflects knowledge of this cycle.[14] Too often the assumption has been made that if a group is formed for collaborative purposes, it will collaborate. The League study extensively documents the need for understanding of and building plans for creating a *working* collaboration.

Individually Guided Education (I.G.E.). From the components of I.G.E. as institutionalized in several states, some structural requirements of the collaborative relationship can be outlined. I.G.E. uses a term, "facilitative environment," and a structure to understand what may be the most elaborate linkage that exists to date. The design includes five systems: The local school, the teacher education institution, an intermediate agency, a state education agency, and I.G.E. agencies (a research and development center, for example). The phases of building such a linking environment have been identified: awareness, commitment, changeover, refinement, and renewal. Each phase is associated with specific activities to be performed by each supportive agency.[15] From I.G.E.'s work it seems clear that the local school, in order to effectively implement new roles and relationships, needs support from within the local school and reinforcement from outside agencies. A developmental sequence of how these agencies work from phases of awareness to renewal can be delineated (See Table 14, Appendix 3).

Organizations as Complements. Linking agencies can take advantage of their differences and serve complementary roles: Research and development centers can create materials, teacher education institutions can provide skills and knowledge, and state departments can provide financial

---

[13]For an extensive discussion of the nature of collaboration and the problems of linking several institutions, see Corwin, 1973.

[14]For an extensive discussion of such activities, see Bentzen, 1974.

[15]For detailed phases and activities, see Klausmeier, H., *et al.*, 1977, especially Chapter 11, "Facilitative Environments for Individually Guided Education."

support and human resources. What has been missing from our knowledge and experience of linking organizations together has been a clearer understanding of the need for complementary functions and a developmental delineation of these functions.

Developmental Nature of Linkage Relationships. No matter how complex the linkage, it appears that the linkage relationship itself is developmental at every level. Each level of the school system appears to go through the processes described, from those at the teaching level, to the managerial level, and to the policy-making level.

The processes described do not imply any particular order; as a matter of fact, one of the prime difficulties of the linking relationship is that these processes occur and overlap in a dynamic way. We have suggested a developmental approach, rather than a linear one, because we recognize that, although one plans linking activities, organization for linkage occurs on several fronts at the same time. Consider the creation of a network involving several states: An agency must decide on who shall participate, how to begin activities, what kinds of mechanisms to create, the substances of initial meetings, who will take what responsibilities, how to create supportive conditions, and how to keep the process going. (See Louis (1975) and Sieber, Louis, and Metzger (1972).[16]

INFLUENTIAL CONDITIONS

At the outset it was recognized that given understandings of the school social system and processes describing linkage would be affected by certain conditions. We discussed these conditions to create an awareness of the delicate balance of forces involved in linking activities and to recognize that linking activities are embedded in a larger socio-historico-political context. And as such, these conditions need to be better understood as they represent a non-linear, sometimes idiosyncratic, often unexpected view of the way things are.

---

[16]Both these references refer to the Pilot State Dissemination program which involved study of, among other things, the field agent role. The discussion includes references to different contingencies that different field agents have as they work with people in varied organizational settings.

History of the School/District

We assume that different districts have a history of different types of involvement with outside agencies: Some have always had agencies such as county services in Los Angeles or cooperative services in New York, while others have been relatively isolated. This variation makes a difference in the way people view ideas, are open to them, and are ready to engage in activity. The history of previous linking and linkages would serve as part of the diagnosis of the linker. Such questions as who is involved, for how long, and with what kinds of involvement would depend on past experience. In general, the less the experience, the more time need be spent on linking activities.

Nature and Scope of the Linkage

There will be a difference between a specific project (such as Head Start) and a linkage that joins states together. In general, the larger the number of levels, the harder it will be to insure adequate communication and shared understandings. The amount of time and the *purposes* of the linkage will be an influential factor. Consider the difference between a one-year project that attempts to implement a reading program and a three-year project that attempts the building of a network to coordinate district activities. Time is a crucial factor and is seen differently by school people than by those working outside the school.

Availability of Resources

Districts differ in both the availability of human and material resources and their allocation of such resources. This condition is becoming increasingly important as districts struggle with decreasing student enrollments, fewer teachers and fewer of everything else. But *schools* are not monolithic in the way they deal with abundance or poverty. The way school districts "think about" their use may be as significant as the actual resources themselves.

Organized Constituencies

Positions on school improvement held by teacher, community, and other local organizations, and their general attitudes toward collaboration, are significant factors affecting linking agencies. Two contradictory trends seem to be a part of American life—a trend toward greater centralization and control and a trend toward decentralization and "grass roots" control—and both these trends are easily observed when various constituencies vie for power over decision making in schools.

Unanticipated Events

Tax cuts, changes in administration, strikes, national disasters all influence the local scene and, consequently, linking activities. (Consider the morale of the New York City schools as their staffs have been severely cut by the recent budget crisis. Or the closing of a four year old junior high school for lack of students. Or firing teachers under the Taylor act after the strike has been settled.)

General Ethos of the State

States differ in their support, interest and organization of education. Some states have consistently been supportive of schools and taken leadership positions in their improvement. Some have a history of conserving, while others share a history of experimentation. Elaborate organizational structures supporting schools historically have been a part of some regions, while others have been relatively isolated from schools in other parts of the country. Clearly these differences toward stability and change will affect linkages.

Having discussed understandings of the school social system, linkage processes, and conditions that may influence the linkage relationships, some vignettes will illustrate these propositions in practice.

VIGNETTES

Newspaper Ruins Strategy!

This writer was a linking agent for one of the schools in the League of Cooperating Schools. Arrangements had been made with boards of education and principals to free one school in each of eighteen selected districts in California to participate in the League. These schools were to be linked to I/D/E/A, the research division, and to the University of California at Los Angeles. Schools then would be linked to the knowledge base of a graduate school of education, and the research division of the graduate school would provide the actual linkage. Our major purpose was to gain a better understanding of the way in which schools cope with adaptation to a changing environment—their solutions to their problems. We defined this adaptation rather broadly, assuming that all kinds of changes were happening in the society and that schools would take cognizance of those changes.

Our first strategy was to go to the schools, make friends with the people, and introduce the idea that they were now a part of a new organization—the League. This was clearly our first attempt to make a linkage which we hoped would be mutually beneficial. We would have a laboratory for finding out what the process of school improvement looks like, and the schools would have access to people, ideas and an organization that focused on them. There were few, if any, precedents to guide our work. But we were all experienced school people and were excited about the possibilities of such a linkage.

One of the schools was situated a few miles from the I/D/E/A office and close to the university. The principal was working on his doctorate in education and was extremely knowledgeable about the curriculum reform movement of the 1960s. Recently the district had hired a research-oriented superintendent who had told all the principals to get their doctorates. All the teachers had master's degrees, and many of them had worked on district committees writing new curricula for district adoption. Because of its ready access to resources, and the sophistication of staff and district, the school seemed ready to assume leadership in the League. The principal had been to the League offices and was eagerly ready to participate. We agreed that a meeting should be set up where the principal and I would introduce the idea of the League and its possibilities. We would diagnose where we were at as we went along.

The day before the scheduled meeting the local newspaper announced that ——————— school was to participate in the League of Cooperating Schools, an organization interested in studying the process of change in schools. The teachers rushed into the principal's office and demanded to know the meaning of the article. The principal explained that they had been selected to participate, that the school would be connected to UCLA with a group of other schools . . . . The teachers voted *not* to participate.

The principal called the office and asked what he should do. He was upset about the newspaper story but more upset about what to do to reverse the teachers' decision.

Against this background, the first meeting was called. Before this writer or the principal could build a case for the linkage that was to take place and the school's participation in the group, the teachers lashed out about the newspaper story. "Why were we not consulted about whether we wanted to be in this organization? How did the newspaper get the story? We are professionals! We do not need this organization. Don't you know we all participate to the fullest in our school, our district and in the university?"

The decision to participate had been made by the superintendent. And the principal had gone along with the decision. No real attempt had been made initially to gain the consent of teachers in any of the schools.

For six months meetings took place in the school and a few teachers dominated the meetings. Attempts were made to get at the problems of the school; the theme which often emerged was that the neighborhood was changing and that these were different children.

One day, this writer leaped up and blurted out, "I assume there are people who might want the opportunity of being in the League and of working on solutions to their problems by seeking fresh ideas. I will be here next week. Any volunteers who want to can sign their names and we will meet and plan together." Ten people (out of 17) showed up, and over time, we began to explore the curriculum and organization of other schools to gain new ways of viewing the school. Teachers eventually decided to team teach, to break down the walls of isolation, and the school became the focus of tremendous activity, exploration and involvement.

The understandings of the school system were only vaguely a part of this writer's repertoire, and the processes of linkage were totally unknown to her. Furthermore, so involved was she in the building of a new organization that conditions which might affect her work were not seen.

This school is a good example of our need to be sensitive to and develop an understanding of the nature of schools as organizations. The teachers were furious at the newspaper story because it ignored their sense of professionalism and self-esteem. It represented an external condition which could have been spoken about by the linking agent. It could have been an opening to a discussion of decision-making *in* the school which only eventually became salient. Ignoring it had the effect of teachers not trusting both the principal and the linking agent. Neither of us realized the insularity of teachers, nor did we see that the isolation, multiplicity of goals, and contradictory nature of teaching created in teachers a strong defense against the outside world and each other.

The principal, too, had been so used to telling the teachers what the decisions were that when an opportunity presented itself for collective decision-making, he wasn't prepared.

Although these teachers had been heavily involved in district affairs and university courses, their involvement was individual; they had never been called upon to work together in their own school, and the solitary nature of the self-contained classroom was clearly not an effective socializing agent.

The process of building linkage, in this case, would have been aided by starting with a volunteer group. There were only a few resisters, but they dominated the group. Also absent was a conscious plan to move developmentally with these teachers in terms of substance and form. Both principal and linker misdiagnosed where the teachers were. We assumed that the sophisticated nature of the district and teacher involvements made them sophisticated in how to work together. We were wrong. Self-concerns were high. (What is being in this organization going to do to my autonomy? Where will my rewards come from as I work with adults?) Such questions eventually were dealt with, but should be a conscious part of the diagnostic process as described above.

Although this case could be described as a failure in the short term, it was a success in the long term because the organization for linkage proved to be a powerful force in overcoming initial resistance, and re-socializing people to deal collectively with school problems. The linking agent became a friend in the school, bringing information, arranging meetings, facilitating new relationships, and the principal and teachers participated in an organization that drew them out of isolation and put them in contact with outside resources.

Principal Left Out!

A University team had been awarded a three year grant to "collaborate" with a local school system to prepare teachers for a move to a new, flexible spaced school. The team was present in the school four days a week providing workshops and demonstrations, facilitating resources and creating opportunities for teacher growth. About one-third of the school faculty was enrolled in a special university in-service degree program. The project team had established a Teacher Resource Room in the school, and the Resource Room became a new locus for teacher planning and activity.

The project was based on a knowledge of the social system of the school and was designed to create a series of alternative programs to augment the conventional school organization of the school. From the outset, the project was perceived in different ways by different groups. The district officers saw the project as a way to make needed changes in the structure of the high school as well as a way to prepare teachers for the new building. The superintendent had set a policy of regarding each principal as "in charge" of his/her own building; as a result, he considered it inappropriate to mandate changes to any principal. The superintendent hoped the project team would "re-educate" the principal to see the importance of school change.

The principal saw the project as a way to improve instruction of individual teachers within their classrooms. He saw problems in the school as resulting from problems in teachers' classrooms and viewed the project as providing remediation for "weak" teachers and as providing new techniques for "strong" teachers.

The teachers viewed the project as both a way to improve instruction and a way to challenge the structure of the school and the authority of the principal. Teachers were divided on this last point: Some welcomed the challenge, motivations were mixed. Some teachers genuinely wanted to change structures; others wanted to change the principal. The project staff viewed the project much as did the superintendent. They realized the range of conflicting perceptions.

The project team was rather successful in its work with teachers. Almost two-thirds of the faculty took advantage of project activities. The principal viewed the project with favor when the activities were directed towards teachers, viewed the project with alarm when its activities were directed towards the school as an organization in need of change. The hope that the project would "re-educate" the principal was not fulfilled.

Key Incident

A group of teachers wrote a proposal for the creation of several alternative programs which required changes in the school's organization and behavioral regularities. The principal dismissed the proposal as impossible to implement. The project team had expected a more cooperative reaction, and the teachers stated later that they never should have expected a different reaction and regretted having taken the risk of suggesting something new.

Because the grant depended on the creation of alternative programs, the project staff felt the principal's actions threatened the grant. The team called a meeting of the contract officers, the deputy superintendent, and the site grant liaison and declared that the grant money could not continue if the principal continued to block schoolwide change. The district officer, subscribing to the notion of the principal as being "in charge," stated that he could not direct the principal to cooperate. A compromise was reached; a new advisory committee was established to facilitate the grant. The advisory committee, composed of the principal, district officer, some teachers, and project team members met periodically to review all new proposals. The advisory committee structure served to make all the principal's decisions public. In this way, the principal saw it to be to his advantage to approve some of the new proposals and reject others. Since the principal wanted to be principal of the new school, the public nature of the advisory committee made him cooperate with the grant. Public non-cooperation would have destroyed his chances of becoming principal of the new building.

Tying our previous discussion to this case, several generalizations become apparent. Diagnosis includes an understanding of, first, the differing perceptions of the participants. In this case, the views of the district office staff, of the principal, and of the teachers toward the purposes of the linkage project should have been paramount in building strategies. Diagnosis also includes a realistic sense of the location of all these people in the political structure of the school. Teachers could threaten the principal, but the principal had the power to block teachers. On the other hand, the principal needed the project staff to heighten his credibility as the possible principal of the new school. This information was known to the project staff, but they chose to work with the teachers. Rewards were forthcoming from them — they were not from the principal.

Our social system understandings undergird the view of the principal as a participant in the change process. In this case he was a gatekeeper, and this information was crucial to the linking team's work. Like a family of three, where two gang up against one, teachers and team became a mutually rewarding group, leaving the principal isolated and resistant to changes rather than cooperative.

The school social system is not just teachers and principal and children but a complex set of exchanges, rewards, activities and behaviors, as this vignette has suggested.

The external system (the district) was pushing for re-education of the principal, but that re-education could come about only as the principal became an active participant in his/her own growth.

In this case, the team took the teachers as their clients. Although this may be legitimate under certain conditions, the stakes for the principal were enormous and his capacity to block changes very effective.

This team was skillful in political negotiations and in dealing with district offices. And although the teachers and team project suffered a set-back, the compromise allowed them to continue working with a better set of understandings about teachers *and* principals and a sharply honed set of diagnostic skills which included support mechanisms for both teachers and principal. It also included a recognition that organizing for linkage must consider the different perceptions of all the actors and actresses.[17]

SUMMARY

This paper has been concerned with a set of understandings which delineate the view of the school as a social system as that system effects the people in it. Processes performed by linkage agencies in interacting with schools were discussed, and cognizance was taken of these linkage processes' being affected by certain conditions. The approach to the processes described was basically developmental and interactive. It was suggested that linkage agencies recognize a dynamic response to the functions they perform, that the process of diagnosis, strategy building and so on, all take place continuously and not in any linear order. The processes described recognize that there is a tension between leaving school people with the ability to solve their own problems and learning specific information from outsiders. For the linkage agency, this tension creates the necessity to work with *both* a people and task orientation. Content must be linked to the social system of the school and a respect for the realities of the work life of the people involved.

---

[17]This vignette considers school-wide change. Linkages taking place in individual classrooms would have to deal with providing enough support for that teacher.

APPENDIX 1
Models of Linkage

TABLE 4
MODELS OF LINKAGE

HAVELOCK

1) <u>Linkage</u>
   Degree of interrelatedness of collaborative relationships.

2) <u>Structure</u>
   Degree of organization and coordination.

3) <u>Openness</u>
   Climate favorable to change.

4) <u>Capacity</u>
   Capability to get and use diverse resources.

5) <u>Reward</u>
   Planning of positive reinforcements.

6) <u>Proximity</u>
   Nearness in time, place, and context.

7) <u>Synergy</u>
   Forces that can be mobilized to produce knowledge use.

Adapted from Havelock, 1971.

TABLE 5
MODELS OF LINKAGE

LINGWOOD AND MORRIS

1) Users' ability to solve own problems

2) Need processing function

3) Solution building functions

4) Micro-system building

5) Macro-system building

Adapted from Lingwood and Morris, 1974.

APPENDIX 2
Roles of Linking Agents

TABLE 6
ROLES OF LINKING AGENTS

TICHY'S CHANGE AGENT STAGES OF WORK

1) Initiation

2) Diagnosis

3) Strategies

4) Implementation

Adapted from Tichy, 1972.

TABLE 7
ROLES OF LINKING AGENTS

HAVELOCK'S LINKING ROLES AND FUNCTIONS

Linking Roles	Functions
1) Conveyor	carry information
2) Consultant	aid in problem identification
3) Trainer	help user understand knowledge and practices
4) Leader	effect linkage through power or influence
5) Innovator	initiate new ideas
6) Defender	sensitize user to problems
7) Knowledge builder	opening up to new ideas
8) Practitioner as linker	engaging clients as linkers
9) User as linker	initiating activities on one's own behalf

Adapted from Havelock, 1971.

TABLE 8
ROLES OF LINKING AGENTS

WALLACE'S ADOPTION AGENTS

1) Each agent was his [her] own person.

2) Diagnosis of situation.

3) Know your innovation.

4) External agents need to link to administration.

5) Manipulation of human, financial, and material resources is a major job.

6) Time commitment is great.

7) People vs. program.

Adapted from Wallace, 1974.

TABLE 9
ROLES OF LINKING AGENTS

JUNG'S "CREATIVE MARGINALS"

1) Relates to staff in identifying needs and training.

2) Provides demonstration of some skills.

3) Trains staff in skills.

4) Supports people.

5) Arranges access to other resources.

6) Works to coordinate administration, research and learning as integrated parts.

Adapted from Jung, 1967.

TABLE 10
ROLES OF LINKING AGENTS

GRIFFIN AND LIEBERMAN'S "INNOVATIVE PERSONNEL"

1) Diagnosis

2) Work with groups

3) Self-awareness

4) Knowledge of change process

5) Shared decision making

6) Gradualism

7) Construction of new support systems

8) Action upon subsystems

9) Knowledge of own social system

10) Cosmopolitanism

11) Development of core support group

Adapted from Griffin and Lieberman, 1974.

TABLE 11
ROLES OF LINKING AGENTS

MILES' EFFECTIVE CONSULTING FOR NEW SYSTEMS

1) Earn the right to help.

2) Focus on linking planners and environment.

3) Focus on power strategies.

4) Focus on cognitive clarity.

5) Focus on affective support.

6) Focus on reflexivity.

7) Focus on leadership and social structure of planners/implementers.

8) How to handle stress.

9) Willing to be expendable but not a deserter.

Adapted from Miles, 1976.

APPENDIX 3
Organizing for Linkage

TABLE 12
ORGANIZING FOR LINKAGE

LEAGUE OF COOPERATING SCHOOLS

1) Organization of a group of eighteen schools in Southern California, linked to U.C.L.A., an office (I/D/E/A), and each other.

2) Key Learnings;
    a) The individual school is the agent for change.
    b) If change is to occur, creation of a new system seen as salient may be critical.
    c) Change must be accompanied by new knowledge and skills.
    d) A "hub" must be created — a clearinghouse that works the partnership.
    e) The process the "hub" helps facilitate is Dialogue, Decision-Making, and Action (DDA).*
    f) Identification of a peer strategy would mean teachers and principals serving as experts, eventually for each other.

*See Bentzen, 1974.

Adapted from Goodlad, 1975.

TABLE 13
ORGANIZING FOR LINKAGE

INDIVIDUALLY GUIDED EDUCATION (I.G.E.)

1) Organization of facilitative environments linking:
   a) Local school district
   b) Teacher education institution
   c) Intermediate educational agency
   d) State education agency
   e) I.G.E. agencies (e.g., Wisconsin Research and Development Center)

2) Stages involved in a facilitative environment are:
   a) Awareness
   b) Commitment
   c) Changeover
   d) Refinement
   e) Renewal

Adapted from Walter, et al., 1977.

TABLE 14
ORGANIZING FOR LINKAGE

NATIONAL DIFFUSION NETWORK (IN PROCESS)

Developer

Demonstrators, state facilitators, and adopter projects linked together to find out how to create and make use of a National Diffusion Network, to encourage communication of successful ideas, materials, and practices.

Statement of intent from Hall and Alford, 1976.

REFERENCES

Baldridge, J. V., Deal, T. E., Johnson, R., and Wheeler, J. *Improving Relations Between Research and Development Organizations and Schools.* Menlo Park, California: Stanford Center for Research and Development in Teaching, Memorandum #115, November, 1973.

Baldridge, J. V. and Deal, T. E. *Managing Change in Educational Institutions.* Berkeley, California: McCutchan Publishing, 1975.

Bentzen, M. M. *Changing Schools: The Magic Feather Principle.* New York: McGraw-Hill, 1974.

Berman, P. and McLaughlin, M. A Model of Educational Change. *Federal Programs Supporting Educational Change, Volume I.* Santa Monica, California: Rand Corporation, September, 1974.

Berman, P. and Pauley, E. Factors Affecting Change Agent Projects. *Federal Programs Supporting Educational Change, Volume II.* Santa Monica, California: Rand Corporation, April 1975.

Bidwell, C. The School as a Formal Organization. In James March (Ed.), *Handbook of Organizations.* Chicago: Rand McNally and Company, 1965.

Carlisle, D. H. Organizational Arrangements and Personnel Training Programs for Effective Use of Research and Development Information in Decision Making Processes of School Systems. A paper on the *Present State of Affairs and Suggested Options for Future Action.* San Francisco: Far West Laboratory for Educational Research and Development, 4 December, 1967.

Cartwright, D. The Nature of Group Cohesiveness. In D. Cartwright and A. Zander (Eds.), *Group Dynamics: Research and Theory.* (3rd ed.). New York: Harper and Row, 1968.

Corwin, R. *Reform and Organizational Survival.* New York: John Wiley and Sons, 1973.

Culver, C. and Hoban, G. *The Power to Change: Issues for the Innovative Educator.* New York: McGraw-Hill, 1973.

Dreeben, R. The School as a Workplace. In R. Travers (Ed.), *Second Handbook of Research on Teaching.* Chicago: Rand McNally and Company, 1973.

Fullan, M. Overview of the Innovative Process and the User. *Interchange.* 1972, 3, Nos. 2-3.

Getzels, J., Lipham, J., and Campbell, R. *Educational Administration as a Social Process: Theory, Research, and Practice.* New York: Harper and Row, 1968.

Giacquinta, J. B. The Process of Organizational Change in Schools. In F. N. Kerlinger (Ed.), *Review of Research in Education.* Itasca, Ill.: Peacock, 1973.

Goodlad, J. I. and Klein, M. F. *Behind the Classroom Door.* Worthington, Ohio: Charles A. Jones Publishing Company, 1970.

Goodlad, J. I. *Dynamics of Educational Change*. New York: McGraw-Hill, 1975.

Gordon, C. W. and Adler, L. M. *Dimensions of Teacher Leadership in Classroom Social Systems*. Los Angeles: University of California Press, 1963.

Griffin, G. and Lieberman, A. *Behavior of Innovative Personnel*. ERIC Clearinghouse on Teacher Education, August 1974.

Gross, N. and Herriott, R. *Staff Leadership in Public Schools*. New York: John Wiley and Sons, 1965.

Gross, N., Giacquinta, J. B., and Bernstein, M. *Implementing Organizational Innovations*. New York: Basic Books Inc., 1971.

Hall, D. C. and Alford, S. E. *Evaluation of the National Diffusion Network: Evaluation of the Network and Overview of the Research Literature on Diffusion of Educational Innovations*. Menlo Park, California: Stanford Research Institute, January, 1976.

Hall, G. E., Loucks, S. F., et al. Levels of Use of the Innovation: A Framework for Analyzing Innovation Adoption. *Journal of Teacher Education*, 1975, 16, No. 1, Spring, 1975.

Hall, G. E. and Rutherford, W. *Concerns of Teachers About Implementing the Innovation of Team Teaching*. Research and Development Center for Teacher Education, University of Texas at Austin, Spring 1975.

Hall, G. E., Wallace, R. C., and Dossett, W. F., *A Developmental Conceptualization of the Adoption Process Within Educational Institutions*. Austin, Texas: Research and Development Center for Teacher Education, University of Texas at Austin, 1973.

Havelock, R. G. *Planning for Innovation Through Dissemination and Utilization of Knowledge*. Center for Research on Utilization of Scientific Knowledge (CRUSK), Institute for Social Research, University of Michigan, January, 1971.

Havelock, R. G. and Havelock, M. C. *Training for Change Agents*. Center for Research on Utilization of Scientific Knowledge (CRUSK), Institute for Social Research, University of Michigan, 1973.

Ianni, F. *Studying Schools as Social Systems: A Manual for Field Research in Education*. Unpublished manuscript. Horace Mann Lincoln Institute, Teacher's College, Columbia, 1974.

Jackson, *Life in Classrooms*. New York: Holt, Rinehart and Winston, 1968.

Jung, C. The Trainer Change-Agent Role Within a School System. *Change in School Systems*. Cooperative Project for Educational Development, N.T.L., 1967.

Klausmeier, H. J., Rossmiller, A., and Saily, M. *Individually Guided Elementary Education: Concepts and Practices*. New York: Academic Press, 1977.

Leifer, R. *Boundary Spanning Activity and Boundary Spanning Personnel: A Conceptual Model*. A paper prepared for the 17th Annual Midwest Academy of Management Meeting, Kent University, 1974.

Lewin, K. Group Decision and Social Change. In T. Newcomb and E. Hartley (Eds.), *Readings in Social Psychology*. New York: Holt, Rinehart and Winston, 1947.

Lieberman, A. *Tell Us What To Do, But Don't Tell Me What To Do.* An I/D/E/A monograph, Institute for Development of Educational Activities, 1972.

Lieberman, A. The Power of the Principal. In C. Culver and G. Hoban (Eds.), *Power to Change.* New York: McGraw-Hill, 1973.

Lieberman, A., Bentzen, M., and Bishop, J. League of Cooperating Schools: Us, Them, We. *Journal of Research and Development,* 1973, 6, No. 4 (Summer).

Lieberman, A. and Shiman, D. Stages of Change in Elementary School Settings. In C. Culver and G. Hoban (Eds.), *Power to Change.* New York: McGraw-Hill, 1973.

Lieberman, A. *Factors Involved in Educational Change: Implications From Two Major Research Studies for Invention.* A paper presented at the American Educational Research Association, San Francisco, California, April 1976.

Lingwood, D. and Morris, W. *Developing and Testing a Linkage Model of Dissemination and Utilization.* A paper delivered at the American Educational Research Association, Chicago, Illinois, April, 1974.

Lortie, D. *School Teacher.* Chicago: University of Chicago Press, 1975.

Loucks, S. F. and Hall, G. E. *Assessing and Facilitating the Implementation of Innovations: A New Approach.* Research and Development Center for Teacher Education, University of Texas at Austin, Spring 1976.

Louis, K. *Linking Organizations and Educational Change: The Case of the Pilot State Dissemination Project.* Unpublished doctoral dissertation, Columbia University, New York, New York, 1974.

Meyer, J. *Notes on the Structure of Educational Organizations.* Stanford Center for Research and Development in Teaching, Stanford University, June 1975.

Miles, M. Some Properties of Schools as Social Systems. In G. Watson, (Ed.), *Change in School Systems.* Cooperative Project for Educational Development by National Training Labs, 1967.

Miles, M. *Factors Involved in Educational Change: Implications From Two Research Studies.* A speech delivered at the American Educational Research Association, San Francisco, California, April 1976.

Miles, M. Effective Consulting for New Systems. *Project on Social Architecture* (in process). Center for Social Policy, New York, 1976 (unpublished).

Miller, Lynne. *Alternatives for School Organization: A Study of Decision Making in Non-Traditional Schools.* Unpublished doctoral dissertation, University of Massachusetts, Amherst, Massachusetts, 1975.

Paisley, M. B. and Paisley, W. *Communication for Change in Education: Educational Linkage Programs in the 1970s.* A paper published by Institute for Communications Research, Stanford University, 1975.

Paul, D. The Diffusion of Innovation Through Inter-Organizational Linkages. *Educational Administrative Quarterly,* 1976, 12, No. 2, 18-37.

Rosenshine, B. and Furst, N. The Use of Direct Observation to Study Teaching. In R. Travers (Ed.), *Second Handbook of Research on Teaching*. Chicago: Rand McNally and Company, 1973.

Sarason, S. *The Culture of the School and the Problem of Change*. Allyn and Bacon, 1971.

Sarason, S. *Creation of Settings and Future Societies*. San Francisco: Jossey-Bass, 1972.

Sarason, S. Competency and Job Satisfaction. In A. Lieberman (Ed.), *Humanism Competence*. Conference proceedings, Teacher's College, Columbia University, New York, October 1974.

Sieber, S. D., Louis, K., and Metzger, L. Developing a Strategy Based on Particular Clients and Their Settings. In *The Use of Educational Knowledge*. Evaluation of the Pilot State Dissemination Program. Bureau of Applied Social Research, Columbia University, New York, 1972, Vol. 2.

Smith, L. and Keith, P. M. *Anatomy of Educational Innovation*. New York: John Wiley and Sons, 1971.

Takanishi, R. *Collaboration Between Educational Researchers and School Personnel*. Some Reflections and Proposals for Reducing the Research-to-Practice Gap, Stanford Center for Research and Development in Teaching, 26 February 1973.

Tempkin, S. A School District Strategy for Interfacing With Educational Research and Development. *What Do Research Findings Say About Getting Innovations Into Schools?: A Symposium*, January 1974.

Tichy, N. *Developing an Empirically Based Framework of Change Agent Types*. Unpublished doctoral dissertation, Columbia University, 1972.

Tye, K. A. and Bentzen, M. M. *Strategies for Change*. A report to the President's Commission on School Finance, Issue #9, Report of Task Force C, 15 October 1971.

Tye, K. A. and Novotney, J. M. *Schools in Transition: The Practitioner as Change Agent*. New York: McGraw-Hill, 1975.

Tye, K. A. The Elementary School Principal: Key to Educational Change. In C. Culver and G. Hoban (Eds.), *Power to Change*. New York: McGraw-Hill, 1973.

Wallace, R. C., Jr. *Each His Own Man: The Role of Adoption Agents in the Implementation of Personalized Teacher Education*. University of Texas at Austin, 1974.

Waller, W. *Sociology of Teaching*. (2nd Ed.). New York: John Wiley and Sons, 1932.

Walter, J. E., Lipham, J., and Klausmeier, H. J. Facilitative Environments for Individually Guided Education. In W. J. Klausmeier, A. Rossmiller, and M. Saily (Eds.), *Individually Guided Elementary Education: Concepts and Practices*. New York: Academic Press, 1977.

5

Training and Supporting Linking Agents

David P. Crandall

INTRODUCTION

The last decade has seen hundreds of millions of dollars spent in attempts to improve the quality of American schooling — dollars for new openspace buildings, dollars for carefully developed R&D (Research and Development) products, dollars to establish massive computerized information banks. These investments have yet to produce widespread improvements in schools; yet despite disappointments, there are numerous examples of modest but significant improvements in many schools across the country. An assessment of this recent history leads to the realization that *things* alone — money, buildings, products, information — are insufficient to change schools. Only *people* drawing on these resources, can produce the needed improvements. Despite the centrality of technology in American culture, and the similarity of our system of schooling to an assembly line, education within individual buildings resembles more of a cottage industry, staffed by craftspeople plying their trade in idiosyncratic, non-standardized ways. Schooling thus remains a highly interpersonal enterprise, mediated by human considerations, not by the requirements of technology or considerations of the marketplace. It is not surprising that a personalized medium—the *linking agent*—has emerged as the most promising means of bridging the gap between technological advances and individual educators striving for quality education.

The purpose of this chapter is to present a view of the realities facing those playing linking roles and to give direction to renewed efforts to develop training and support mechanisms for linking agents. Several years of experience as a linking agent and in managing a linkage agency have shaped the substance of this paper; during that time, successes and failures in work with hundreds of schools have led to insights and observations which may be useful to a larger audience.

This chapter is written for several audiences and will leave something to be desired by each. First, it will introduce the problems and potentials linking agents face, an introduction which, in the second place, may be useful to those responsible for managing the efforts of linking agents. Third, the next steps for Federal planners and policy makers who are increasingly concerned with the state of dissemination and the proper role of the Federal government in providing leadership to improve American schooling will be outlined.

The literature, with few exceptions (Jackson, 1968; Lortie, 1975, Waller, 1932), tells us little of what actually goes on in the classrooms of our schools. Similarly, we know little of the dynamics of educational program improvement efforts (but see Bentzen, 1974; Goodlad, 1975; and Smith and Keith, 1971). Although this paper, by its nature, is not itself full of rich details of "life in the trenches," the observations and conclusions have been filtered through a knowledge of the practical gained from several years of first-hand experience and pain. What follows rings true for me and I hope will be received in that light.

Progress in understanding the complexities of linking will be made to the extent that interested parties are able to suspend disbelief, jump into one vision of the subject, poke around in it, push against it, test it out in their own setting, and through such experience find ways that work for them.

Assumptions

The following assumptions are intended to restrict the content of the chapter. To the extent that the assumptions are not shared by readers, they can be thought of as springboards for dialogue in other forums. This paper does not attempt to justify them in detail.

1. The "clients" of linking agents will be people in schools, primarily in public schools.

2. In general, schools are unlikely to undergo any substantial structural changes in the next decade in the ways they organize and conduct instruction and attend to organizational functioning. Furthermore, in most places the nature of teaching staffs will remain relatively stable and conservative although their mobility and numbers will be reduced by declining enrollments and unused buildings.

3. Linking agents are essentially intermediaries between the school systems they serve and the world of knowledge production and utilization; in general, their home base is external to the school system.

4. In the larger organizational environment which impinges on the school there is a complex of actors who must be consciously dealt with by linking agents.

5. When linking agents' work with a client system involves a full-fledged problem, it must account for the organization itself as well as the individuals within it.

6. Linking agents must deal consciously and competently with the issue of power distribution and its potential effects on both maintaining the status quo or supporting program improvement efforts.

7. Experienced educators new to linking agent roles will require substantial re-education, touching on cognitive and affective areas in addition to behavioral skill development.

Organization of the Chapter

This first of four sections has set the stage and presented the assumptions underlying the paper. The second section, "The Universe of the Linking Agent," consists of four principal subsections. The first presents three major perspectives on the current practice of linking agentry; the second addresses the nature of the resource system and the common sources and attributes of the innovations that are typically the nucleus of program improvement efforts. The third subsection discusses the client system as a complex social system and as an organization subject to a multitude of influences, and the final subsection deals with the host agency responsible for supporting the many needs of Linking Agents they house. The third section on "The Linking Agent — A Specialized Generalist," deals in depth with the Linking Agent proper. The many dimensions of this multi-faceted creature are articulated and illustrated, the multiple roles to be played are described, attributes and skill clusters associated with the multiple roles are presented, and the question of selection versus education versus training is touched on. The last section presents a summary and argues for a world-view emphasizing systematic problem-solving as a means of focusing future efforts.

THE UNIVERSE OF THE LINKING AGENT

Linking agents are involved in a little understood constellation — the educational and R&D community — which is itself part of a larger and more complex universe. Within this constellation, collections of individuals are in motion around the individual linking agent. These individuals, as well as individual linking agents, are affected by other influences. While the object of primary interest in this paper is the linking agent, a brief inspection of the major influences and of the other entities should help us understand the sort of nebulae the linking agent inhabits. In this section, several issues about the major influences, the resource system, the client system, and the host agency will be presented to facilitate a later full consideration of the linking agent.

Three Major Perspectives on Current Practice

The different opinions about what constitutes an effective linking agent reflect the different orientations possessed by those actively engaged in studying, recruiting, or training linking agents. From my vantage point, three major perspectives are presently intermingled in the field —those reflecting the behavioral science tradition, the information science tradition, and the curriculum theory tradition.

Historically, the notion of a linking agent role followed from an emphasis in the last decade on improved dissemination of information. The study of communication channels, how information flows from person to person and structure to structure is the basis for the work of the Far West Lab's Educational Information Consultant (EIC) program and much of Havelock's early work. The old National Center for Educational Communications, which housed the ERIC system, sponsored many important early inquiries by Paisley and others. This view is presently reflected in efforts of the Information and Communication Division of NIE to establish a capacity in each of the fifty states for more effective dissemination and utilization of information.

The influence of the information science school in the public education arena is manifest in the variety of information centers which can access a myriad of data bases via computer in response to educators' inquiries. The most prominent of the comprehensive information centers are R.I.S.E. (Research and Information Services in Education) in King of Prussia, Pennsylvania and E.R.C. (Educational Resources Center) at ACES in New Haven, Connecticut, in the East and Northern Colorado BOCES in Longmont, Colorado, and California-based SMERC (San Mateo Educational Resources Center) in the West. Our own NETWORK/NaLDAP Information Resources Center is an example of a specialized center serving a restricted clientele (i.e., Learning Disabilities Demonstration Centers) in contrast to the general service offered by the comprehensive centers.

ERIC remains a prominent, and increasingly useful, element in an information center's resource arsenal, complemented in more sophisticated centers by "fugitive" data collected from local services or not available through computer access. In their interactions with school people, specialists with an information science orientation strive to improve the quality of decisions by concentrating on what goes into them. They *hope* that the array of alternative inputs presented in response to a focused request will be carefully considered and a more rational sequence followed by the decision maker(s). However, the nature of their relationships with clients typically precludes involvement in the dynamic processes surrounding a particular decision. Rather, transactions are discrete events, i.e., the request, "I need to make a presentation to my board on alternatives to closing schools," leads to the preparation of an information package sent to the client, presumably used in some way with the board. *How* the information is considered and its effects are rarely ascertained. It is unlikely that a client would request or that a person in an information center would maintain ongoing interaction during the many cyclings of deciding, trying out, revising, deciding, et cetera, involved in instituting a significant new practice or policy.

In contrast, the concerns of the behavioral science school exemplified by OD efforts grounded in the social psychology of individuals, groups, and organizations, attend more to the process itself. Practitioners in this school emphasize human interactions and relationships, and advocate employing consensual means to make better decisions through active collaboration during implementation and by confronting and working through the inevitable difficulties that arise in the course of instituting any significant change into an otherwise stable system. Kurt Lewin is the grandfather of this tradition, with Miles, Jung (former director of Northwest Lab's Increasing Teacher Competencies Program), Lippitt and his associates in Michigan, and Schmuck and Runkel in Oregon as exemplary contemporary practitioners of this approach. Schmuck and Runkel's "Strategies of Organizational Change" program at the Center for Educational Policy and Management (CEPM) located at the University of Oregon is one of the few efforts which integrate action interventions in schools with ongoing research into the processes involved. (The program in Educational Administration at the State University of New York at Buffalo is another.) The "Strategies" program has made many solid contributions to understanding what actually goes on, and with what effects, when conscious efforts are mounted to improve schools' organizational functioning. (see Runkel and Schmuck 1974; and Runkel *et al.*, 1974, for detailed descriptions of their efforts.)

Lastly, there is a school which one might label the curriculum theorists. Their interests do not preclude attention to matters of concern to the foregoing two schools, but they pay more explicit attention to content as traditionally defined. Tyler is generally acknowledged as the elder statesman of this school, and Goodlad at the University of California at Los Angeles has done much to bring greater clarity to it. More recent studies by Fullan and others (1975) continue this emphasis. The curriculum theory school is somewhat less visible in the current arena; there continue to be difficulties in defining curriculum as a field, and few of the current federally-sponsored program improvement efforts give it focus in the context of school-based change efforts. However, our experience at The NETWORK has shown that without careful attention to the curricular dimension, the probability of success of any change intervention is drastically reduced. Schools are just not prepared to deal with process issues alone, and since most schools see curriculum — as opposed to communication/information flow or organizational processes — as their primary responsibility, it seems essential that we incorporate this orientation into our thinking.

When one attempts to change or improve schools or school districts, these three orientations need to be synthesized. A "people" focus, which acknowledges the importance of curriculum, the place of information flow and improved decision-making, and the centrality of relationships and organizational influences is indicated. Such a focus reflects the emerging mainstream in the area of educational program improvement and should influence the design of training and support mechanisms for linking agents.

It is also essential that we focus on the overall process associated with effecting significant changes in human systems, whether the change be the adoption of a new curricular program or a new way of thinking about oneself and one's work. We need not only to study the initial stages of awareness and interest-arousal but also to look more fully at the dynamics of the implementation process. Developing this broad, long-range perspective should be a priority for linking agents concerned with program and system improvement. Further, we need to deal with here-and-now problems in schools and to challenge schools to go beyond the present by developing improved capacity to cope with the anticipated and unanticipated problems that will confront them in the future.

The Resource System

Types of Resources Available to the Linking Agent. The world of knowledge production and utilization (KPU) is an exceptionally complex one, as Culbertson noted in his early chapter in this volume. It is inhabited by all sorts of individuals, agencies, ideas, programs, products of varying *tangibility, visibility,* and *utility* to the educational practitioner. Bringing this maze of potential resources into focus and relating them to a particular school's problem so that the resources can be effectively utilized is the principal challenge facing linking agents. As intermediaries between resources and clients, their skills in resource utilization are what distinguish them from other competent professionals. (This central skill of resource utilization and other required skills are discussed in greater detail subsequently.)

Our concern here then is to focus on the notion of "the resource system"—its general parameters, its principal elements, and their relative importance to linking agents. A classification scheme which has considerable heuristic utility is presented in Figure 1. Adapted from the report of the Dissemination Analysis Group (DAG) convened by the Office of the Assistant Secretary for Education, it represents the results of long deliberation by a highly qualified and diverse group.

The question they grappled with was, "What is to be disseminated?" Restated in the context of this paper, "What is the 'stuff,' that is, the resources, of the transactions between linking agents and their clients?" The following excerpt from their report, with minor editorial clarifications (in italics), explains the preceding figure:

> Figure 1 presents a schematic display of the types of "disseminates" considered by the DAG, arrayed along two dimensions: degree of tangibility, independence, and separability; and the degree of disciplined inquiry on which they are based.
>
> Beginning at the top left *(Cell 1)* are the tangible products of research and development (R&D). Progressing to the right the R&D products shade into R&D-based or -validated programs. As these programs become increasingly intangible, they shade into "synthesized" (practice oriented) research-based knowledge *(Cell 3)*, and then finally into highly intangible, abstract, and generalized knowledge *(off the chart)*. Proceeding across the next row *(Cells 4-6)*, the same kinds of content are encountered; however, the "validity" of the content at this second level is based far less on the R&D (disciplined inquiry) process and far more on pragmatism. Successful products are usually those that are marketable, profitable, and able to win and maintain consumer acceptance. Promising practices may be purely practitioner innovations that have neither an R&D base nor evaluation data to prove their claims, but that are judged to be promising or worthy by competent educators. Consensual knowledge is not produced by disciplined inquiry or scholarship, but it is accepted as valid and reliable by those who must rely on it.
>
> In the last row *(Cells 7-9)* is encountered a vast "grey" area of relatively unvalidated products, practices, and knowledge. Their validity depends primarily on the prevalence of their use and on their utility for specific users. Credibility and utility are the operating criteria that separate the useful from the useless.

FIGURE 1
A CONCEPTUAL MAPPING OF EDUCATIONAL PRODUCTS, PROGRAMS, PRACTICES, KNOWLEDGE AND INFORMATION

	Tangible		Intangible
Disciplined Inquiry	R&D Products ①	R&D Validated Programs ②	Research-based Knowledge ③
	Successful Products ④	Promising Practices ⑤	Consensual Knowledge ⑥
Conventional Activity and Experience	Other Available Products ⑦	General Practice ⑧	General Knowledge ⑨

Depending on the type of resource needed (i.e., which cell of Figure 1), linking agents will turn to individuals or agencies/organizations/systems for tangible products or artifacts (i.e., an information package) or for less tangible practices or ideas. Thus, linking agents need to be aware of; to know how to access, and to use the full array depending on a particular client situation.

Sources of Products and Programs for the Linking Agent. The traditional information linker was concerned principally, if not exclusively, with attempting to increase the use of "research-based knowledge" (Figure 1, Cell 3), primarily that available through ERIC. While undoubtedly there have been, and still are, linkers who maintain such a tight focus, the changing nature (and improved quality and utility) of the ERIC data base combined with expanded demands flowing from continued contact with school people leads inevitably to linkers taking a broader "practice" focus.

Earlier our own experience with the centrality of curriculum in our own dealing with school people was noted. The bulk of their curriculum is shaped by the consideration and use of tangible resources (programs and products) as opposed to intangible resources (research knowledge and other information). This reality suggests these resource types be treated in a bit more detail to ensure clarity.

The vast majority of curricula in use in the schools today are produced by commercial publishers (Figure 1, Cells 4 and 7). Since most linking agents will strive to create awareness and increase the use of programs developed by local and federal sources, at first it might appear irrelevant to examine the activities of those who promote commercial products, yet the success of commercial publishers demands such an examination. For the linking agent, the feature of the commercial sector to be kept in mind is its concern with the efficient, profitable distribution of a high volume of products, rather than the successful implementation of programs. Analyses of clients probe those factors that will affect the positive decision to adopt a particular product in sufficient quantity to justify the producers' investment in advertising and other marketing. This is not to say that commercial programs are of low quality. Indeed, many individuals engaged in systematic research and development also contribute to commercial products of many kinds.

Commercial publishers need enough knowledge of the marketplace and the consumer group to be sure that the products they are promoting have acceptability and credibility. They use salesmen very effectively and have led the way in utilizing modern technology for segmenting and saturating markets. Typically, their textbooks are formatted in a way that makes it easy for the salesperson to respond to questions from potential adopters by simply flipping to an appropriate chapter subheading and saying, "Here you'll see that we cover dangling participles very adequately." Experience with more complex products, such as the Far West Lab's Minicourses, has demonstrated the difficulties of educating textbook salespersons to promote products which depart radically from the norms of schools, which require considerable supplementary equipment, and which do not yield a premium commission for the salespersons. (See Turnbull et al., 1975, for a more detailed discussion of this case.)

The commercial sector cannot deal with "thin market" materials, that is, those which do not yield high enough revenues to warrant the investment in marketing. However, there is much to learn from commercial successes, and recent studies of the utility of the marketing approach are worthy of review by interested linking agents (see in particular Engel et al., 1975; Kotler, 1975; Sikorski and Hutchins, 1974).

The second source of programs, of greater concern to the linking agent, is that of "R&D outcomes." At the present time there is considerable debate as to just what constitutes an R&D outcome and enough vacillation exhibited so that a rather broad definition (i.e., incorporating Cells 1 and 2 of Figure 1) is one that would probably be useful for the linking agent to keep in mind. A recent Request for Proposal from NIE's School Practice and Service Division defined educational R&D outcomes as follows:

> Those curricula, products, skills, programs, instruments, teaching and management methods and techniques and the like that are produced by disciplined inquiry involving activities normally considered part of the R&D process such as conceptualizing, hypothesizing, model developing, field testing, data gathering and analyzing and evaluating. Evidence of effectiveness, judged according to professionally accepted standards, is also a hallmark of R&D outcomes.

This definition is useful in highlighting the importance of a systematic process ending in some demonstration of effectiveness. In some cases, programs developed by school-based educators conform to this definition and are able to offer evidence of effectiveness to a quality control panel such as the Joint Dissemination Review Panel (JDRP). The JDRP serves the Education Division as a vehicle whereby programs which individual project officers feel are worthy are reviewed by a panel of experts. Of some 250 projects which have been submitted to the panel since its inception, 60% have been approved. Despite a number of flaws now receiving attention by its members and the field, the JDRP is likely to remain the principal means of formal validation by the Federal government. It will continue to serve as a necessary hurdle for programs expecting Federal support for dissemination activities. While the vast majority of programs which have been submitted to date are those initiated by ESEA Title III, recent efforts have brought before the panel for consideration a variety of programs initially funded by Title I, Bureau of Education for the Handicapped, Bilingual Education, and NIE. This broadening base bodes well for the creation of a more widely representative pool of programs which have withstood the scrutiny of hard-nosed professionals. *Educational Programs That Work* (1976), a catalogue produced by Far West Lab for the National Diffusion Network, describes all programs approved by JDRP. The output of directly-sponsored federal R&D is currently detailed in the two volume NIE Product Catalogue (1975).

Lastly, there are locally-developed programs (Figure 1, Cell 5) created in response to idiosyncratic local needs. One serious shortcoming of most of these programs, whether sponsored by federal or state money or simply the result of local invention, appears to be the absence of a meaningful evaluation and documentation effort. Such efforts would allow objective judgment as to both the effectiveness of such programs in their original sites and their utility for other settings. Because the motivation for most of these projects is amelioration of a particular local problem, not the creation of an entity which contributes to the greater good, this shortcoming is not surprising.

Some interesting findings about the nature of such exemplary practices and the difficulties in transporting them from one site to the other are discussed by Turnbull *et al.*, (1975). One promising development is the effort by Title III through its Identification, Validation, and Dissemination (IVD) process which encourages state agencies to establish procedures whereby locally-developed projects supported by Federal money can be reviewed by an external team using a common set of guidelines (see *Sharing Educational Success: A Handbook for Validation of Educational Practices*). Though rather expensive for the project, the on-site evaluation team mode promoted by the IVD process offers an alternative to simply relying on informal evaluation procedures and generally incomplete measurements of outcomes. While the IVD approach, like virtually all on-site inspections of complex programs, suffers budget and time constraints that produce a "five-blind-men-describing-an-elephant" phenomenon, the professional judgment a panel of peers renders after comprehending the elephant offers clear—if costly—improvements over the written report of a single observer. Whether the payoffs are commensurate with the investment is a question in need of an answer. Individual states have produced various compendia of state-developed and -validated programs which may be of interest to linking agents (see "Connecticut ESEA Title III" produced by ACES in New Haven, Connecticut, as one example).

Viewing Resources as Innovations. A recent insight which has added clarity to the writer's thinking about the difficulties of mounting and managing program improvement efforts in schools is the realization that *all* potential (i.e., currently unused) resources are *innovations* from the clients' perspective and they represent something new to them. Historically innovations in education have been thought of simply as products and practices. Diffusion researchers (Miles, 1964; Rogers, 1962; Rogers and Shoemaker, 1971) have pushed and probed the phenomena relating to their introduction into an adopting unit. Recently, inquiries into the realities faced by human innovations, "information linkers" whose role was initially patterned after the agricultural extension agent, have been sponsored (Mick, Paisley, et al., 1973; Sieber, Seashore, et al., 1972). Increasing attention has been focused on the dynamics of the adopting unit and the individuals who populate it (Bennis, Benne, and Chin, 1961, 1969, 1976; Havelock, 1973; Lippitt, Watson, and Westley, 1958; Schmuck and Miles, 1971). All these inquiries have enriched our still incomplete understanding of the complex of things, people, and perceptions which can be innovations and of what it takes to bring about change, of whatever magnitude, personal, programmatic, or organizational — in human systems (e.g., schools).

For the present discussion, let us acknowledge that all the resources arrayed in Figure 1, and their many sources and potential delivery modes, are innovations for clients which range from the seemingly concrete and simple (a new textbook or product), to the exceedingly intangible (the *idea* of using someone else as a resource, and the *act* of initiating and maintaining the relationship). It's all new, it's scary, and it all happens simultaneously [at multiple points on the tangible-intangible dimension (cf. Figure 1)] when a teacher decides to risk by exploring a new product/practice/idea or by adopting one.

Now, add to this already complex equation the newest, strangest resource/innovation of all, "the linking agent." Linking agents (the *idea* of them and the *use* of them) represent an even larger innovation than the programs or ideas to which they hope to link the system. Few, if any, clients know how to use *any* kind of helper effectively (other than to advance their own image as "innovators"), and many new linking agents are sufficiently unsteady themselves that they do not acknowledge explicitly this gap with their clients.

Perceived Attributes of Innovations. Having introduced the perspective of viewing all new resources as innovations, let us turn to the innovation itself. If linking agents are to be effective, they must understand the many facets of an innovation as perceived by the potential adopter/consumer/client/user. (The reader interested in an in-depth treatment of the importance of the user's perspective on the innovative process should see Fullan, 1972). The topic shall be touched so that the individual linking agent can pursue elsewhere those facets of greatest relevance.

There is little disagreement in the field that the attributes of an innovation as perceived by the potential user interact with the user's view of the setting to affect the rate and extent of adoption. (A parallel phenomenon is the effect of the linking agent's perceptions of the innovation and the setting on adoption.) Rogers and Shoemaker (1971) identify the attributes of interest as relative advantage, compatability, complexity, trialability, and observability. All but complexity are reported as positively related to the rate of adoption by the majority of the studies reported. A somewhat more detailed consideration of attributes and their effect on the innovation process is provided by Zaltman *et al.*, (1973). Nineteen attributes of innovations are discussed including such familiar notions as cost, relative advantage, and compatibility and some unfamiliar notions such as *terminality*, the number of points in time and the space between them, beyond which the adoption of an innovation becomes less rewarding; *status quo ante*, the cost or difficulty which must be risked relative to the *reversibility* of the innovation or return to the prior status quo; and *gateway capacity*, the extent to which the adoption of an innovation opens avenues to other (desired) innovations. Further, they suggest probable interaction of these perceived attributes with different substages of the innovation process, which they see as a series of five decision stages from initial knowledge to sustained implementation. The discussion is summarized in Figure 2.

Arraying them in this fashion clearly demonstrates the juggling act required of the linking agent. Different attributes are going to affect the user's views at different times, and it may not always be clear at what point in time one is. It is unlikely that not only a given innovation process will proceed through only one series of decision stages, but also the attributes may interact across substages. The authors acknowledge this; the "x's" are intended to show their best guess as to that substage where a particular attribute is most likely to have significant interaction. Thus, they would suggest that as the dynamics of an initial (adoption) *decision* become crystallized into a public declaration of intent, the attributes of cost, scientific status, relative advantage, and commitment become dominant. It seems reasonable to believe that all those attributes which interacted with prior substages are still floating around somewhere as well, only that their power as filters or screens has diminished at this point in the process.

Further, it is likely that the language researchers use in classifying attributes will not be meaningful to users, so linking agents may need to create lists of attributes using local descriptors and definitions which would differ from site to site. To quote Zaltman, "The particular problem and proposed solution(s), the nature of the organization, and the general context in which change is to occur are all factors in determining which particular attributes are most salient at various substages. The important point is that the various attributes of innovations should be considered in light of the substages in which they are likely to be most important" (p. 165). Worthy of particular note in light of the findings reported by Rogers and Shoemaker regarding the negative relationship of complexity to rate of adoption is the distinction between the perceived complexity of the innovation on the *idea* dimension versus its complexity in *implementation*.

FIGURE 2
PROBABLE INTERACTION OF ATTRIBUTES WITH
INNOVATION PROCESS SUBSTAGES

Attributes of Innovations	Knowledge	Attitude Formation	Decision	Initial Implementation	Sustained Implementation
Cost		X	X		
Returns to investment		X			
Efficiency		X			
Risk and uncertainty		X			
Communicability	X				
Compatibility		X			
Complexity		X			
Scientific status			X		
Perceived relative advantage			X		
Point of origin	X				
Terminality				X	
Status quo ante		X			
Commitment			X		
Interpersonal relationships				X	
Public versus private				X	
Gatekeeper	X				
Susceptibility to successive modification					X
Gateway capacity					X
Gateway innovation					X

Reprinted by permission of the publisher from G. Zaltman, R. Duncan, and J. Holbek, *Innovations and Organizations*. New York: John Wiley and Sons, 1973, p. 164. © 1973 by John Wiley and Sons.

Thus, a given program may be difficult to understand but easy to use or conversely, easy to understand but extremely difficult to implement. An example of the latter are the programs described in the *Overview of Project Information Packages* (1976), whose underlying ideas, at least those related to the curriculum, are rather conventional and quite compatible with the current practice. The difficulty comes when the other features of the program required for complete implementation and their likely effect on current practices are fully understood. Full-scale, faithful implementation of one of these programs is an exceedingly complex process, calling for different decision-making modes, staffing arrangements, space reallocation, and so on—moves that are likely to bump up against the status quo in most districts.

The foregoing paragraphs deal with a single innovation and with the myriad attributes that play some unpredictable part in its acceptance and ultimate adoption by a school, whether facilitated by linking agents or not. For most of the endeavors in which linking agents will be engaged, the problems are even greater, since there is more than one innovation being introduced simultaneously. Typically this multiple-innovation phenomenon is unacknowledged in the literature; one is faced with a figure and ground problem where the curricular innovation is emphasized to the exclusion of other features of the process. Despite its centrality in the minds of clients, it is just one of the innovations with which they are confronted.

In conclusion, it should be obvious that a prime requirement for linking agents is not only greater understanding of the tangible resources which they will be called upon to bring to clients or themselves but also increased skill in comprehending and coping with the motivations, operating assumptions and preferred styles of interaction of those in the resource system. The simplistic view that an innovation is a textbook should be laid to rest. The linking agent's task as the *intermediary* playing a *translation* role relative to potential resources is vastly complicated by the multiple-innovation phenomenon. The factors noted above are but one part of the universe with which linking agents will interact, and these factors are in dynamic tension with the features of the client system itself, the subject of the following subsection.

The Client System

Moving now to the next level closer to the linking agent, we turn to a view of the client system. Lieberman, in the preceding chapter, discusses in detail the school as a social system and presents a series of understandings derived from her work in many schools. In this section, I shall illustrate the complexity of the school culture and its subcomponents; my purpose is to stress the need for linking agents to comprehend the multiple facets of their client systems. As Sarason (1971) states, "Those responsible for introducing change into the school culture tend to have no clear conception of the complexity of the process." Figure 3, "Educational Linkage of Sub-systems within the School Culture" presents one rather elementary perspective on the nature of the beast. It arrays three principal subcomponents relative to the school culture: SCHOOL, FAMILY, and COMMUNITY and their relationship to three functions provided by the formal education system: Teaching and Learning, Control and Policy-Setting, and Other Services and Influences.

The figure illustrates that members of the various subcomponents participate in determining or influencing the major functions of education in ways that need to be acknowledged by outsiders attempting to alter the status quo. Further, it suggests that the relative centrality of particular role groups in influencing certain functions varies. Only the *principal* is potentially involved in all three functions of the educational enterprise. (This analysis is predicated in large part on our own experience and is not intended to disregard the possibility that in states or districts organized differently, the superintendent might be at the crucial intersect of all the relevant functions.) The point to be underscored is that the interests of the various constituencies within the larger school culture will be affected by any change intervention regardless of its origin.

As has been noted previously, several strands must be synthesized when assessing the functioning of schools. As Miles (1964) among others has observed, and as the field agents in the Pilot State Dissemination Program quickly discovered, educators are not farmers acting as individuals with autonomy to make decisions based solely on reliable information. The decision-making process for educators is substantially more complex, given the organizational setting within which they work. In schools, once a decision to adopt an innovation has been made, complex organizational forces begin acting on that decision. These forces require the use of new knowledge and skills, lead to the alteration of communication patterns and interpersonal relationships, and generally threaten the organizational status quo. In this environment, diffusion theory is necessary but not sufficient to manage a planned effort. Knowledge or organizational dynamics is essential.

The pay-off to such an understanding is, according to Handy (1976) "to substitute a coherent set of conceptual frameworks . . . for collections

FIGURE 3
EDUCATIONAL LINKAGE OF SUBSYSTEMS WITHIN THE SCHOOL CULTURE

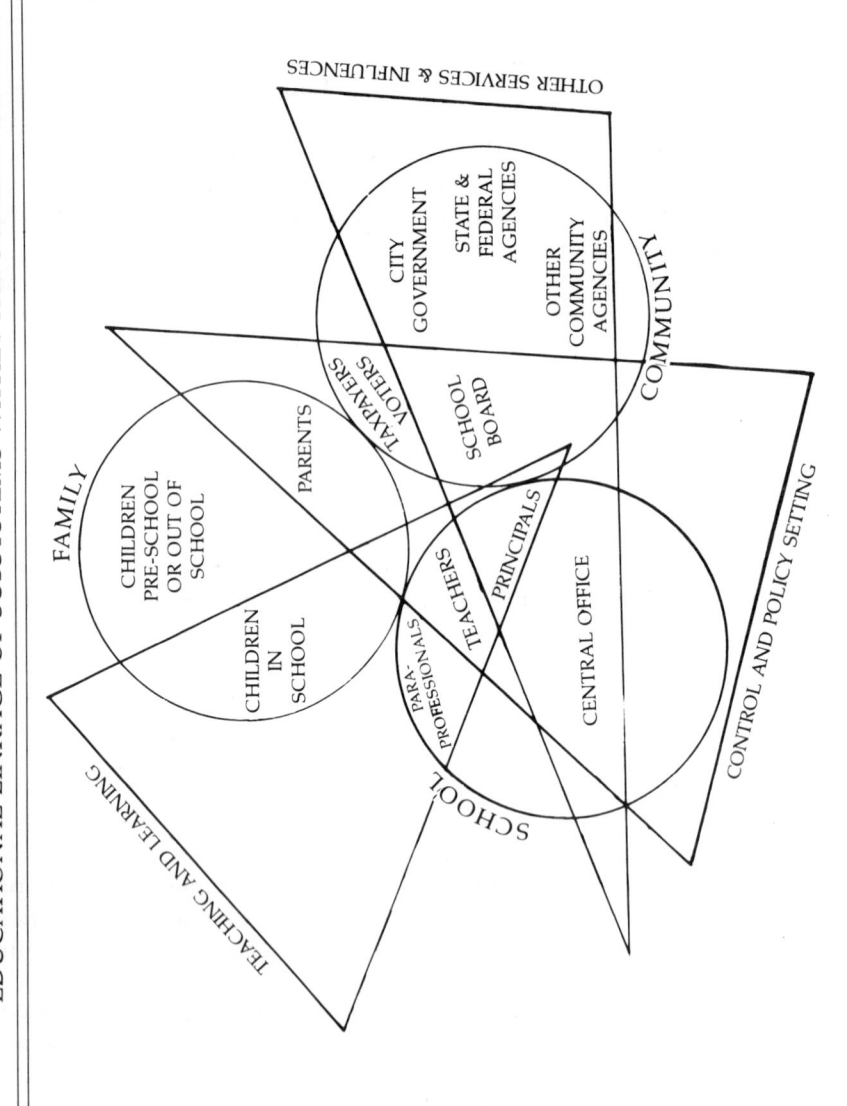

of assumptions." He states that " . . . these concepts, properly used and understood, should:

> Help one to *explain* the Past which in turn
> Helps one to *understand* the Present and thus
> to *Predict* the Future which leads to
> More *influence* over future events and
> Less *disturbance* from the Unexpected."
> (Handy, 1976, p. 14)

If one were able to reach the state of awareness suggested by the foregoing statements, one could hardly ask for more return on one's investment. Getting a bead on schools as organizations is not a simple task. The literature specifically related to schools as organizations is rather limited, although this deficit is being made up (see Baldridge and Deal, *et al.*, 1975; Corwin, 1974; Giacquinta, 1973). But if the linking agent is going to attend to more than the superficial aspects of change and to work to achieve increased organizational effectiveness with his school clients, this broader perspective must be acquired. Handy (1976) illustrates the multitude of factors that need to be taken into account (or consciously put aside) in Figure 4 on page 208.

The diagram suggests that the effectiveness of an organization is determined by factors related to the individuals within it interacting with its immediate and surrounding environment. An organization's members' motivation to work is affected by the leadership available to them and their group relations, as well as their individual roles and ability. Similarly, an organization's systems and structure are affected by the physical, economic, and technological environments within which it operates. As noted in the diagram, clusters of subfactors underlie each of these principal factors.

Using this information as a means of examining schools requires minimal translation. The factors related to individuals represent a familiar starting point; the environmental factors, especially the economic ones, have less obvious relevance in the context of the schools. Perhaps the reader can see the potential utility of such a view as a stepping-off point and can attempt the translation. Additional stepping-off points can be drawn from mainstream organizational theory, which views organizations as open systems, receiving "inputs" from the environment, affecting or processing these inputs in some ways and returning "outputs" to the environment. (One more radical perspective articulated by Pondy [1976a] in "Beyond Open System Models of Organization," may have special

FIGURE 4
SOME FACTORS AFFECTING ORGANIZATION EFFECTIVENESS

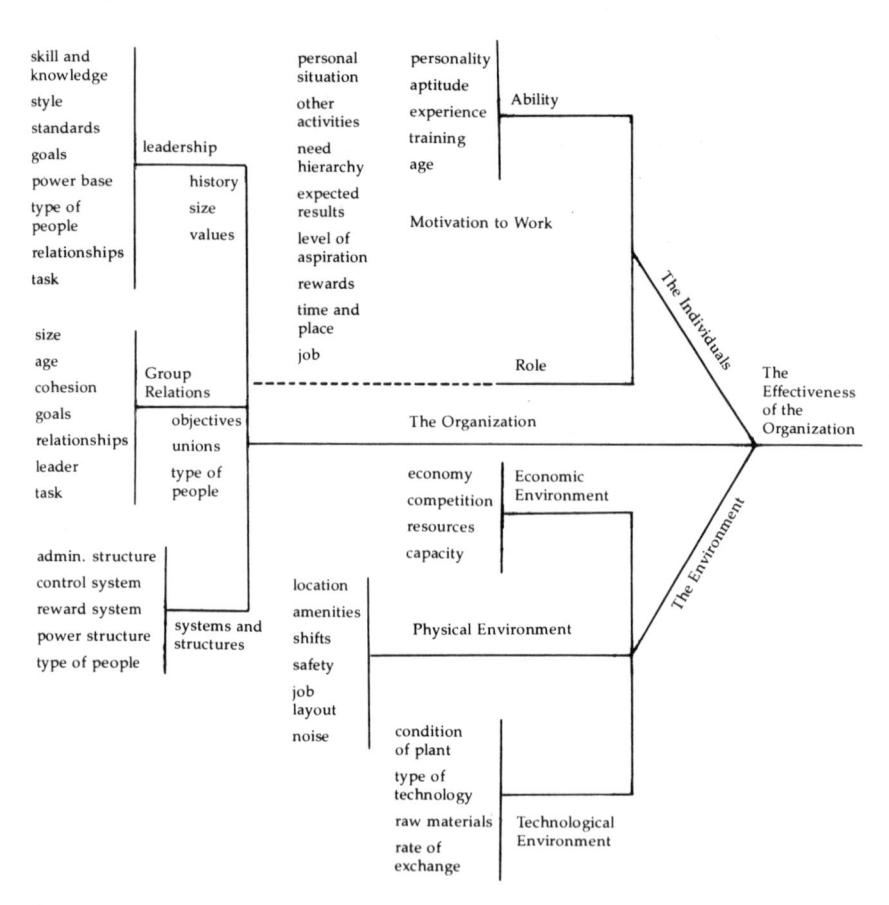

skill and knowledge style standards goals power base type of people relationships task	leadership history size values	personal situation other activities need hierarchy expected results level of aspiration rewards time and place job	personality aptitude experience training age	Ability Motivation to Work Role	The Individuals
size age cohesion goals relationships leader task	Group Relations objectives unions type of people		The Organization		The Effectiveness of the Organization
admin. structure control system reward system power structure type of people	systems and structures	location amenities shifts safety job layout noise	economy competition resources capacity	Economic Environment Physical Environment	The Environment
			condition of plant type of technology raw materials rate of exchange	Technological Environment	

Reprinted by permission of the publisher from C. Handy, *Understanding Organizations*, p. 13, Harmondsworth, England: Penguin Books, 1976. © 1976 by Penguin Books.

relevance for linking agents and others who find each school with which they must somehow establish a productive symbiotic relationship, a unique reality constructed of the perceptions of the school's inhabitants. [See also Greenfield, 1973, 1974 for more on a phenomenological perspective.]) Schools as organizations are marked by differences in their degree of openness from level to level. For example, their boundaries are relatively permeable to people who come into the schools, are affected by them, and leave them with predictable regularity.

However, most observers believe that schools do not have the same degree of openness to new ideas or practices. Zaltman et al., (1973) posited that schools typically resist innovation because of force of habit, because of primacy (it worked well the first time so we'll continue doing it this way), and because of the lack of needed peer support.

This lack of openness to new practices is understandable, given the organizational characteristics of schools. Miles (1975) noted rather strict role differentiation between teachers, a situation which resulted in their serving in specialized capacities, traditionally doing little but teaching and unable to generalize to or adapt to new functions (e.g., that of curriculum selector, program developer, or evaluator). The lack of clarity of educational goals further serves to inhibit new programs, coherent evaluation of teacher performance, and planning for the future.

According to Pincus (1974), schools have traditionally resisted change and represent self-perpetuating bureaucracies with a de facto monopoly on their constituencies. They are subject to the shifting desires of school boards whose membership and philosophy can change with frightening frequency. Schools are increasingly given the responsibility but not the wherewithal to solve social problems, i.e., the teaching of moral values, in addition to their fundamental mission of teaching basic skills. Teachers have a quasi-professional attitude, and it is virtually impossible to determine what actually constitutes good teaching (Sieber, 1975). The coordination and control mechanisms of schools seem, on the one hand, to produce ease of introduction of an innovation, but produce difficulty during the implementation phase (Sieber, 1975; Zaltman, 1973).

Despite the complexities, and this not particularly optimistic picture, change is obviously taking place although it is snail-like. If the factors of vulnerability, diffuseness, quasi-professionalism, and structural looseness cited by Sieber (1975) are acknowledged and accounted for when change programs are designed, then there is much greater promise than might appear at first glance. Further, that change agent's bugaboo, the "resistance to change" teachers supposedly display, may be a very sensible response, given their perceptions of reality.

Giacquinta (1975) views this perplexing problem as one of risking status. There is certainly a fair amount of uncertainty surrounding most innovations, and it is reasonable to expect individuals to want to minimize the uncertainty and reduce their risk. This phenomenon seems related to what Toffler (1970) sees as a need for "stability zones" in one's life and the "mutual adaptation" noted in the Rand Change Agent studies. Certainly some reshaping must occur in order for feelings of ownership to be developed, but it seems desirable to go beyond simple acceptance of this to understand *why* such adaptation might be necessary reshaping. Giacquinta's explanation is instructive:

> The change literature on school reform is committed to the notion that participation of subordinates is central to the success of an innovative effort. It is usually argued this is critical because it leads to commitment or a satisfaction of our democratic sensibilities. The status risk framework offers another explanation: participation acts as an extinguisher of uncertainty and/or a suppressor of organizational members' estimation of risk. It does this through the mechanism of communication. (pp. 112-113)

A provocative perspective on the power of language (communication) in a context parallel to that discussed by Giacquinta is presented in "Leadership as a Language Game" by Louis Pondy (1976b).

The foregoing discussion about client systems and their complexities, the multitude of factors which need to be accounted for and delimited before any manageable effort can be mounted, could be extended by analogy to the organizations within which linking agents are housed. Of course, in one's own house the linking agent is the insider, not the outsider, and thus the phenomena encountered are sometimes mirror images of those to be found in dealings with clients. Thus, while one many find one's clients responding openly and favorably to advice on increasing the amount of non-judgmental feedback between peers or principal and teachers, it may be quite a different story when one tries to offer advice on (and promote change in) similar practices with one's superior and coworkers.

The Host Agency

I turn briefly now to the function of the host agency within which the linking agent will be housed; most linkers will be found in agencies external to their client systems. The agencies will be state departments of education, intermediate units which may or may not be legally connected to state departments, R&D Labs and Centers, institutions of higher education, non-profit educational service agencies, and other school districts' R&D units, few though they may be. Most of these agencies do not or are unlikely to conceive of themselves self-consciously and primarily as "linking agencies" as we have at The NETWORK. And even if they did, the "care and feeding of linking agents" would be difficult to keep on the front burner as an organizational priority. (Our own difficulties in this regard undergird this conviction.)

Most agencies housing linking agents tend to think in terms of the agency's functions vis-à-vis their clients and do not look expressly at their expectations for the linking agents themselves. As has been illustrated, while linking agents may be primarily concerned with the client systems with which they are engaged, the reality of their host agency will affect their day-to-day functioning and ultimate effectiveness in major ways. Acknowledging that the reality of the host agency needs attention is a small but crucial first step. The importance of the host agency in developing and providing a support system for linking agents that will enhance both their short-term functioning and long-term effectiveness with clients and their personal satisfaction in their role should be understood.

Principal Problems Faced by Linking Agents Which Necessitate A Support System. The role of the linking agent, as noted by Farr (1971) and Havelock (1969), among others, is a *marginal* one. The role of the Pilot State field agents studied by Sieber *et al.*, (1972) certainly verified that characterization. Owens (1970) stated the positive aspect of marginality by noting that the external agent "will never really be a part of the power structure but is privileged to raise questions, to suggest procedures, and to generally facilitate the operations of the group more candidly and objectively than if he/she were an insider." But marginality carries with it certain disadvantages. Working externally to the organization, a linking agent's socio-emotional needs for inclusion, identity, feedback, and influence cannot be fully met within the system without jeopardizing the agent's effectiveness. External linking agents who relinquish their marginality also lose much of their potential for impact upon the system, so it is essential for the linking agent to maintain a posture of "functional neutrality" to best serve the long-term interests of the relationship.

Thus, the responsibility for meeting the linking agent's needs must fall to his/her host agency. Linking agents obviously need to be provided with the basic amenities, but with their potentially specialized jobs, they also need certain atypical resources. After adequate housing, heat, light, paper, and pencils, the linking agent needs access to a professional library of substantial proportions and the ERIC data-base—if at all possible. This last need not be through a computer, although access to a terminal is certainly desirable. Beyond these resources, the linking agent needs an array of collegial supports. Many of them can be provided within the host organization; others will require researching outside. Some of the external connections will be formal, as in professional associations such as AERA,

ASCD, The OD Network, ASTD, Phi Delta Kappa, ASIS, etc.[1]

Working in teams will often minimize some of the day-to-day difficulties experienced by linking agents, but it is usually an expensive practice not easily instituted in any but the most well-financed situations, (not a characteristic of most educational service organizations.) A less expensive method is to develop in-house support teams, the members of which need not have the same role as the linking agent. They need not be working with the same type of client or the same sort of problem to be an effective sounding board and "crying towel" for the individual member. Through our experience at The NETWORK, triads work relatively well and avoid one-to-one deadlocks. The support groups can arrange to convene on a scheduled basis or on a functional basis around critical incidents that emerge during their individual activities. In the case of geographically dispersed enterprises, it is conceivable that some (low level) support can be provided long distance, facilitated by contemporary technology, e.g., telephone, telecopier, computer terminals, and the like, once relationships are well-established.

Linking agents also need relief from *overload*. Havelock (1969) classifies the overload problems as those related to number, complexity, and difficulty. It is easy, and subsequent sections of this paper will display this in even starker detail, for linking agents to be viewed by one and all as persons capable of being all things to all people. Given the range of clients with whom they are likely to work, linking agents are confronted with the problem of wearing many hats, some of them simultaneously. Complex linking agent roles magnify overload. Even at the beginning, the merely changing one's current role to that of linking agent may produce a psychic overload.

Havelock and Havelock in *Training for Change Agents* (1973) argue for "whole role training" as opposed to an emphasis on skill sets or functions and stress the importance for extensive support within the host agency: Training for new roles is far more difficult than training for specific skills or functions . . . a whole new identity needs to be developed. Also, if whole role training is to be meaningful, it must be coupled with extensive institutional support arrangements in the back home situation. If the training is to "stick," the returning change agent must be officially *and* informally accepted in the new role by his/her superiors, peers, and subordinates. (p. 41)

---

[1] AERA (American Educational Research Association); ASCD (Association for Supervision and Curriculum Development); The OD (Organizational Development) Network; ASTD (American Society for Training and Development; ASIS (American Society for Information Science).

But it is unlikely that many linking agents will be able to take on one or more roles as their exclusive domain. The best that can be hoped for is that one or more linking agent roles will become dominant segments of an individual's conscious concept of "My Job." Individuals taking on linking agent roles need to see those roles as relatively compatible with their concept of "self" as well as with their concept of other roles that they play, be they societal roles — spouse, parent, child, or professional roles — program monitor, author, advisor. Pareek (1976) suggests mapping all the relevant roles and their distance relative to one another, thereby constructing a "role-space map."

It should be apparent that conflict of some sort is likely to emerge from such an analysis. Pareek identifies four typical role-space conflicts: self-role distance, intra-role distance, role-growth stress, and inter-role conflict. He further suggests we attend to "role-set" conflicts which emerge from the relative proximity of one's central role to the perceived roles of relevant or significant others. A role-set map can be created just as can a role-space map. Typical role-set conflicts are role ambiguity, role overload, role-role distance, and role erosion.

The relevance of these notions to a host agency's support of the linking agents it houses should be obvious. Linking agents will invariably face ongoing problems of marginality (role-role distance) with both their clients and their colleagues. They may suffer from a sizable gap between their various professional roles or their concept of self. It is the host agency's responsibility to build in support mechanisms which lead to increasing *role linkage,* defined as a relatively small perceived gap between one's own role and that of others and of self. Pareek suggests a number of coping strategies which can be employed to handle the inevitable role conflict.

He goes on to outline briefly what might be termed a "creative blend" coping strategy labeled "Inter-role Exploration." It is characterized by:

1. Mutuality versus exclusiveness

2. Creativity versus conformity

3. Confrontation versus avoidance

4. Exploration versus expectation of ready-made solutions.

Such inter-role exploration would likely benefit from process assistance by a third party and is a useful extension of the technologies for role negotiation proposed by Harrison (1972) and role renegotiation proposed by Sherwood and Glidewell (1973).

In addition to these active strategies for coping with this inevitable role strain linking agents will face, support mechanisms can acknowledge the compensating benefits of "role accumulation" for which Sieber (1974a) has put forward a theory. In commenting on an early draft of this chapter,

FIGURE 5
TWO TYPES OF COPING STRATEGIES

Role Conflict	Avoidance: Dysfunctional, Degenerating Strategies	Confrontation: Functional Regenerating Strategies
Role-Space Conflicts		
1. Self-role Distance	Self Role Rejection	Role Integration
2. Intrarole Conflict	Role Shrinkage	Role Linkage, Creativity
3. Role-Growth Stress	Role Fixation	Role Transition
4. Interrole Conflict	Role Elimination and Rationalization	Role Negotiation
Role-Set Conflicts		
1. Role Ambiguity	Role Prescription and Role Taking	Role Clarification and Role Making
2. Role Overload	Prioritization	Role Slimming
3. Role-Role Distance	Role Boundness (Efficient Isolation)	Role Negotiation
4. Role Erosion	Fight for Rights and Rules	Role Enrichment

From Interrole Exploration by Udai Pareek. Reproduced from J. William Pfeiffer and John E. Jones (Eds.), *The 1976 Annual Handbook for Group Facilitators*. La Jolla, California: University Associates, 1976. Used with permission.

he noted that rewards such as "getting around and meeting lots of people, gaining prestige because of the many contacts that are made, availability of resources gained in one role for us in other roles, self growth . . . definitely accrued to the extension agents in the Pilot State program."

Our own experience over seven years is consistent with these observations. Recognizing these potential payoffs and building in ways to induce them offers one of the most effective support strategies to enhance role satisfaction. Such rewards are one of the reasons people "put up with" the job of linking agent and love it. (Of course, you can burn out from an overbundance of pleasant, motivating stimuli, too.)

Linking agents, their managers and host agencies should recognize the many problems inherent in the linking agent role, actively and consciously should anticipate the inevitable conflicts, explicitly address them initially, and confront them in the course of work. At the minimum, doing so requires some sort of periodic reflection and analysis by relevant parties and, under optimal conditions, includes the use of some of the same strategies and tactics proposed for linking agents to use with their own clients, perhaps with the assistance of an outsider.

This brief discussion of the importance of a support structure for the functioning of a linking agent would not be complete without mentioning the need for professional development. In-service training of professionals all too frequently bears an unhappy resemblance to the adoption of innovations, with much attention at the front end and little or no attention after the initial training is provided. Professional development in the form of formal learning through college courses, access to the ideas of others through the literature, participation in training workshops and other short-term professional growth opportunities, sponsorship and legitimization at professional organization conferences, and "annual celebrations," are all a vital part of the support needed by linking agents. It is becoming increasingly probable that the number of linking agents will increase, and it is reasonable to hope that some of the formal and informal networking which has characterized other phenomena of equal vitality, e.g., the teacher center movement, will be used with linking agents. Further, it is possible and necessary to organize a training program which specifies free-standing clusters of skills to be developed, as well as an integrative framework which allows the clusters to be melded into dynamic roles for individual linkers. The section which follows attempts to provide an initial blueprint for doing so.

THE LINKING AGENT — A SPECIALIZED GENERALIST

As we focus on the individual linking agent, it is well to remember that we are talking about an abstraction. There is certainly no single idealized type of linking agent on which everyone could agree. The linking agent is commonly thought of as an amalgam of the information linker described by Farr (1971) and of the change agent discussed by Havelock and others in the general literature of change. Havelock, whose linkage model synthesized the dominant approaches to educational program improvement in the late 1960s, outlines at least four different roles — those of catalyst, resource linker, process helper, and solution giver. At no point, even in some of our own writings, has the term "linking agent" been accorded any operational definition. A broad description that can accommodate a range of particular roles is:

> A *linking agent* is an individual who helps others engaged in problem-solving by connecting them to appropriate resources.

This generic description is deliberately broad; on balance such breadth is an asset rather than a liability. Other terms which could be applied — change agent, program improvement specialist, human relations specialist — risk negative connotation on the part of the potential client. Linking agent, on the other hand, carries almost no connotation one way or the other for most people, and that fact allows clients to focus on the actual behaviors of an individual linking agent. For that reason, the label linking agent is preferred although other modifiers are needed to facilitate examination of the training requirements of such individuals. In this section some of the common variants of the generic role will be described, and a range of related issues will be explored.

Most observers of the current scene agree that the multitude of functions the complete linking agent could be called upon to perform require something of a super-person to execute. It seems to follow that one cannot talk in terms of single individuals but rather needs to consider teams or combinations of individuals. Indeed, the concept of the *linking agency* seems a fruitful avenue for exploration. In the preceding chapter, Lieberman has touched on the processes which may occur between linking agencies and client systems. Our own organization has been referred to as a linking agency since its inception. However, there seems little hope for the development and support of linking agencies over the next several years, given the state of the field. More specifically, I do not believe that sufficient "risk capital" will be available in the short-run (five years) at either the federal or state levels to plan and build brand-new organizational entities or convert existing entities, i.e., intermediate service agencies, into agencies which consciously and primarily view themselves as linking agencies. Such entities may expand their functions to include an array of linking functions and many are doing so with much promise. But there is no tradition in education, much less the technology required, of building *organizations* purposefully. With luck, there will be support for emergent units within "existing" agencies which have linking as their primary mission. Since these will be small at first, relatively few individuals will be involved in any given unit. Given this reality, it is highly probable and certainly realistic to expect renewed attention given to the creation and training of linking agents, so the linking agent is treated as an individual in this chapter.

Those who work in this field tend to function on a daily basis largely on their own, even if they have a range of colleagues or consultants to assist them. Most training that is feasible economically and logistically is likely to be designed and conducted with a focus on individual participants, not on total organizations, even if the individuals are team members drawn from a single agency. The organizational supports and resources clearly cannot be ignored, but focusing on the individual is more promising for our present purposes.

An array of "archetypal" roles can be used initially to provide a way of specifying narrower definitions and required skills for the roles will be outlined. The array in the following subsections represents personal conclusions drawn from observations of the current reality and each of the roles identified is one which I believe to exist in fact. None is as elusive as "Big Foot"; all can be sighted easily; each can be adequately distinguished from the others. While acknowledging that a range of roles exists at the present time and will continue to exist in the future, we need to set our long-range sights on a somewhat "full" role. This "full" role would have linking agents armed with a full array of skills to be employed as needed by the particular client situation and relationship. However, a series of iterations will be necessary before we can point to anything approaching an army of full-scale linking agents at work around the country.

For the first iteration we should concentrate on recruiting and training generalists who, with ongoing support and continued training based on their own experiences, can play an increasingly broad range of roles as appropriate in a given situation. There are some who will choose (and this should be a conscious choice) to limit themselves. Fine, so long as there remain those committed to expanding their repertoire and so long as new recruits can be attracted while we continue to refine our vision.

Each of the roles has different features and different requirements. Planners and managers should refine their selection procedures to better match potential linking agents with the roles they project they will hold and then begin to train them in a variety of skills, as well as in ways of matching the skills to individual client situations. The client who needs a lesson for Thursday's class won't be helped by a diagnosis of his/her organization, and linking agents need to develop skill in using the optimal combination of personal and other resources in diverse client situations. This necessity of responding to contingencies on an *ad hoc* basis argues for acknowledging that there is a *range* of acceptable role types which can be articulated and employed as organizers for training designs. Or the differential skill requirements for working through longterm relationships with various client systems can be used as organizers.

The Multiple Roles of the Linking Agent and Their Distinguishing Features.

As noted in the earlier discussion, the process of program improvement in schools is likely to involve the use of a variety of resources. When linking agents are involved in this process, they will find that they and the resources to which they can link the client, including themselves, will represent innovations with a variety of perceived attributes. Clients' perceptions of them and their resources may change in relative importance depending on what substage of the innovation process they are in. This innovation process and its substages, though it can be usefully presented and analyzed as a single linear sequence, is clearly not so straightforward in practice. Rather, an observer of the scene in a typical school would see some preliminary exploration, perhaps an initial public decision to go forward, an initial flurry of activity, pauses, reverses, restarts, and so on. This dynamic cycling and recycling, the making and remaking of decisions, is the reality of change in human systems.

At the risk of being overly simplistic in light of this reality, and to make the presentation a bit more manageable, readers might think of the innovation (or program improvement) process as having a *front-end* and a *back-end*. Probably, observers of any setting where a planned effort is underway would reliably assign its relative progress to one sector or the other, and allow for the inevitable disagreement as to just where front-

Training and Supporting Linking Agents 219

end shifts to back-end. For our purposes, readers need only accept the simple distinction between front-end and back-end as an heuristic device.

There are people now working in the field who concentrate their energies as linking agents on the front-end of the innovation process — that concerned with creating initial awareness of resources (be they information, programs, people, or potentials), with provoking interest, assisting in some way (even if indirectly) in some kind of initial choice/ decision which eliminates some options and sets the stage for the early phase of any implementation efforts. In the pages which follow, five front-end roles will be described, and examples of their action-settings and principal strategies cited.

The five front-end roles are:

- The Product Peddler

- The Information Linker

- The Program Facilitator

- The Process Enabler

- The Provocateur/Doer

Similarly, there are five back-end roles which will be discussed. Linking agents playing these roles concentrate on the later stages of the program improvement process following some initial direction-setting decision (e.g., "Let's go with Program X," "Let's implement Program Y," "Let's pursue line-of-inquiry Z"). Generally described as the implementation → institutionalization phase, it has only recently received attention in the field. Nonetheless, readers will easily recognize themselves and their colleagues and perhaps will find this simple mapping helpful.

Linking agents who concentrate on the back-end of the process must deal with the messy cycling and recycling, starting and stopping, diverting and aborting which characterize most efforts to do something different in human systems, i.e., schools. I have labeled these roles as follows:

- The Resource Arranger

- The Information Linker

- The Technical Assister

- The Action Researcher/Data Feedbacker

- The Educateur/Capacity Builder

Let me stress that there are, can, and should be, single individuals who can ply multiple linking agent roles, including special blends of the roles. They have been teased apart in this atomistic fashion in much the same way as the innovation process is segmented, so more bite-sized chunks can be inspected as a means of comprehending the *gestalt*.

Distinguishing Features. Before presenting the ten linking agent roles in more detail, several features will be presented to distinguish the roles one from the other. These features will subsequently be related to each of the roles within the two (front-end/back-end) subsets. Later sections of the paper will present specific attributes and skills required of linking agents and apply them to each of the ten roles. First the distinguishing features, case as questions:

Who does the diagnosis?

Who is the source of help?

What is being advocated?

What is the focus of the change effort?

What is the target of the change effort?

What is the degree of client targetedness?

What is the extent of emphasis on long-term problem-solving capability?

1. WHO DOES THE DIAGNOSIS? The extent to which the client is involved in the diagnosis of the problem situation is an early and crucial element in any program improvement effort. There is not a best answer to who *should* do the diagnosis in a given situation; rather, it is a function of the match among the client, the linking agent, and the particular situation. The various roles tend to represent a range on this dimension from total reliance on the client's assessment of the problem through some collaborative problem identification to a situation in which the linking agent alone makes the diagnosis. In the latter case, data provided by the

client may be used but typically are not shared so much as answered by a particular solution. Thus, for purposes of distinguishing between the three points, they are *client, joint, linking agent*.

2. WHO IS THE SOURCE OF HELP? Related to the preceding discussion regarding the locus of the diagnosis is the question of the source of help once the diagnosis is made. The twin concerns of diagnosis and assistance are included in the discussion in order to highlight the probable symmetry between the two factors. In many cases the operating assumption, simply stated, is that the linking agent or outsider is the only possible source of assistance (and/or through him or her other outsiders). Conversely, there are other perspectives which would demand that the client function as the source of help for the problem once a clear diagnosis has been made. In a collaborative or joint situation, the discussion as to the source of help would likely be an open question framed by the parameters of the problem situation. The simple distinctions, then, are between *client, joint,* and *linking agent*.

3. WHAT IS BEING ADVOCATED? Another dimension which distinguishes the roles is the nature of the advocacy. Historically, many of the roles have been viewed as essentially non-advocate positions; however, a recent insight is that each of the roles does have a posture of advocacy, but that *what* is being advocated distinguishes one from another. The main distinctions are among advocacy of the *client's inherent potential* or capacity; advocacy of a particular *process*, e.g., the use of a rational problem-solving process; advocacy of the *use of information* as an aid to decision-making; or advocacy of a particular *product or solution* as an answer to a problem situation.

4. WHAT IS THE FOCUS OF THE CHANGE EFFORT? Next, it is important to recognize that the primary focus is different for each of the roles. These range across a focus on the *curriculum or program content* (typically including instructional methodology), on the *decision-making process* and its relative rationality, and on the *organizational processes*, especially relationships between working units and congruence between individual and organizational goals.

5. WHAT IS THE TARGET OF THE CHANGE EFFORT? Similarly, there is a range related to the level at which the intervention is targeted. For present purposes, these range from the *individual*, through the *group*, to the *organization*.

6. WHAT IS THE DEGREE OF MUTUAL GOAL-SETTING? Related to the target of the intervention is the degree to which linking agents derive the direction for their efforts from the perceptions, needs, requirements, et cetera, of the client versus direction from their own needs or preferred solutions. While some might wonder how professionals could

not be responsive to the client's needs and situation, a realistic assessment suggests that the extent of mutual goal-setting is a distinction worth noting explicitly. The range is from *low* to *medium* to *high*.

7. WHAT IS THE EXTENT OF EMPHASIS ON LONG-TERM PROBLEM-SOLVING CAPABILITY? The majority of linking agent roles focuses on solving short-term, here-and-now problems. The press of day-to-day business and the number and diversity of real problems justifies and explains the attention given to these problems. However, there is growing acknowledgement that it is not enough for a client to simply "experience" a particular solution. There is no guarantee that the next time around the client will be in any better position to diagnose the situation or explore alternatives independent of the linking agent. Thus, when possible and appropriate, there needs to be explicit attention given to the development of a long-term problem-solving capacity in the client system. Different roles place different emphases on the development of this capability. The range is from *little* to *some* to *much* on this dimension.

Front-End Roles. The linking agent roles which focus on the early stages of a program improvement process, which lead up to and include an active decision about a particular problem or program change, will not be addressed. Following the descriptions of the roles, they will be arrayed against the distinguishing features just presented and their relative emphasis on each feature noted. The five front-end roles follow.

1. PRODUCT PEDDLER. The exemplar of this role is the commercial book salesperson. Interaction with potential clients is directed solely toward the closing of the sale in such a way that repeat business will occur. Actual face-to-face contact is relatively infrequent. Principal strategies are the use of aesthetically appealing promotional materials. These are typically one-way, rather elemental presentations of features, bolstered by references to other adopting organizations or individuals which are believed to have credibility with the potential buyer. Often the salesperson is able to offer quantity or prepublication discounts and bonus materials with certain combination purchases. In many cases, his/her contact with the individual client ceases as soon as the order is taken. In others, (s)he may follow through to be sure that materials have arrived in good order and that the instructions for their use are clear.

2. INFORMATION LINKER. These individuals are typified by the information specialists housed in various ERIC Clearinghouses and Information Centers around the country. The typical interaction with clients is by phone and generally at the client's initiative. They seek to clarify the information needs of the client or the question the client is attempting to answer so that a strategy for searching a variety of data bases, either by hand or by computer, can be developed. In many cases the work of the

Information Linker is facilitated by an arrangement between the Information Center and the school district which eliminates most discussion about cost and related items, depending on the nature of the request. The product is delivered to the client in an information packet which may contain abstracts derived from a computer search, bibliographies compiled by the Information Linker, copies of journal articles retrieved, or sample microfiche of highly relevant documents. Though in most transactions the Information Linker engages in a dialogue with the client by phone, frequently the only communication is through a written request form. Where dialogue does occur, its purpose is focusing and defining the question in such a way that it is manageable for the Information Linker as well as on-target with respect to the interests of the client.

The questioning by the Information Linker is designed to elicit enough information to enable an efficient and focused search to be conducted. Under optimal conditions, there is a mid-point check with the client to refocus or refine the inquiry. This practice adds substantially to the cost and is probably not employed on a regular basis by most Information Centers. Given a reservoir of experience and/or some organizational history, the Information Linker typically builds up a file of searches, bibliographies, and relevant materials which can be quickly and easily assembled to meet many information requests, therefore precluding the need for an individualized solution to every inquiry. This improves the turnaround time and offers the possibility of focusing the client's request by putting stimulus materials in their hands early in their decision cycle. The goal of most Information Linkers is to improve the quality of decision-making in schools by stimulating the use of relevant research and other information. Their efforts are grounded in the belief that individuals can become increasingly rational in their work and should draw upon the experience of others, as captured in information documents, in solving their day-to-day problems.

3. PROGRAM FACILITATOR. A relatively new arrival on the scene is the Program Facilitator, exemplified by the State Facilitators of the USOE-sponsored National Diffusion Network (NDN). These individuals offer schools a wide range of tested programs which have undergone the scrutiny of a Federal and/or State Review Panel. Unlike the Product Peddler, the Program Facilitator presents the client with a broad variety of different curricular and instructional approaches, often grounded in different philosophical assumptions about learning and tested under differing conditions. The vast majority of the offerings call for some kind of in-service training in order to implement them effectively, in contrast to a simple product choice and use.

The typical operating strategy of a Program Facilitator is to alert a wide variety of schools in a given area to the availability of a range of programs, arrange for them to attend awareness conferences where a number of programs are introduced, provide opportunities for them to inspect further either the materials or the programs themselves in operation, and then arrange for initial training while being available to make phone calls, collect additional information, and so on, as requested.

By and large, Program Facilitators are not explicitly concerned with the quality of the decision or the manner in which it is made; rather, they assume that these are the province of the individual school district. Their stance is generally neutral with respect to particular programs; instead they promote the notion of choice from among many alternatives. Some may delimit their offerings based on state or regional priorities. On the one hand, their pool is broad and covers a range of subject matter at many grade levels, but, on the other hand, it is not all inclusive. Occasionally, these Program Facilitators are housed in agencies which also function as Information Centers, thus offering an enriched situation for the client system's decision-making and choice of programs. This situation is not, however, widespread at the present time.

4. PROCESS ENABLER. This role in its broadest form, is content-free and concentrates on communication, decision-making, leadership, and organizational structure problems which inevitably arise in attempts to upgrade the efficiency and/or effectiveness of schools. Generally, the Process Enabler begins "where the client is" and attempts, through several iterations, to assist the client in a clear definition of the problem and development of appropriate action plans for solving it. In most cases, the relationship with the client is one that extends over time and includes a range of diagnostic conversations and/or group meetings, sometimes complemented by formal data collection. For the purposes of this discussion, their emphasis is still on the front-end. A common function of such a person is to conduct or to critique faculty meetings or curriculum committee deliberations. Teacher evaluation or program review issues also may become the focus of the Process Enabler. Typically the initiator of the relationship is a decision-maker in the system, and relationship issues between faculty and administration almost inevitably constitute a component of the intervention. Their concern is on helping the system do its currently defined job better or more efficiently depending on the decision-makers. However, they typically have a value orientation which favors widespread participation by those potentially affected by any decision. This concentration usually results in greater involvement of teaching personnel in assessing the current situation and delineating action alternatives.

The OD consultant, communications specialist, process consultant, and group facilitator are typical examples of this role in action. Their general goal is to work themselves out of a job and to leave the client with some increased comfort and — perhaps — skill in solving the kind of problem which precipitated the initial request for help. These individuals are not necessarily well-received by school faculties whose primary concerns, at least on the surface, are less related to organizational process than to the teaching of kids. This means that a "pure" process approach employed by individuals unfamiliar or inexperienced with the content of schooling will face certain difficulties from the outset.

5. PROVOCATEUR/DOER. All of the foregoing roles generally proceed from an acceptance of the status quo of the client system, engaging in various degrees of adjustment to improve its functioning without modifying its general structure and direction. There is a role, though only dimly conceived at this time, for individuals who have a vision of alternative futures in which they have confidence and who have enough concern for the state of human systems that they attempt to initiate a more fundamental inspection on the part of school people of what is possible. They may scare or confuse most school people, but their position in the *constellation* should not be ignored. The critics of today's schools such as Holt, Kozol, Illich, and Hentoff probably come to mind most readily. It seems clear, however, that as interesting and provocative as these individuals' ideas are, these individuals have not functioned as leaders *implementing* major changes except in a very few locations.

This has occurred, in large part, because of their inability to provide concrete and workable alternatives which can be seen as practicable by a large enough number of school people. They have been unsuccessful in "helping the organization to make sense of its experiences so that it has a confident basis for future action," (Pondy, 1976b). They have not created the hope that leads to action guided and energized by its initial but changing vision. We could identify "Provocateurs" who are somewhat less shrill than the critics noted above and who have the linguist's skill in creating and using metaphors and myths to sustain individuals in ambiguous settings. Some of the more effective exemplars who both talk about new ways of educating and act on their beliefs include Dwight Allen, who was able to produce a major transformation of a large component of a major university within a very short period of time, Warren Bennis who, with the assistance of Hendrick Gideonse, has made major strides at the University of Cincinnati, and Per Dalin, whose International Management Training for Educational Change efforts in promoting functional temporary structures bridging entire continents should be better known and emulated by the American school people. That few if any "Provocateur/Doers" come to mind when thinking about elementary and secondary schooling is a sad commentary about the present state of affairs.

How these five roles relate to the distinguishing features noted earlier is delineated in Figure 6.

Back-end Roles. Similarly, there are five roles which are evident in the later phases of a program improvement effort.

1. RESOURCE ARRANGER. The first role which comes into play when planned program improvement effort or change gets underway is that of Resource Arranger. In its simplest form, this individual simply assures that the box of books or materials actually arrives, is the proper quantity, and so forth. In more elaborate situations logistical arrangements for introductory training or construction or modification of facilities may be called for. In some cases, the Resource Arranger may bring in additional people as consultants. Although any of the roles described in the preceding section might find themselves functioning as a Resource Arranger, it has been placed on the back-end side of the line to insure symmetry.

2. INFORMATION LINKER. This role mirrors the role of the Information Linker in the early phase, as there is likely to be continued need for information following the decision to adopt a particular program or course of action. Thus, the nature of the relationship with the client remains the same, and the transactions would look virtually identical. However, the substance or nature of the questions will differ. Typical questions might include, "How do I maintain records for this individualized program which I have adopted?" "How do I keep the community informed of my progress?" "How can I best evaluate this program and present the findings to the school board?" "My teachers seem to need additional training in order to use this curriculum; where can I get consultants?" Again, many of the questions will elicit a response drawn from research or other printed material. Oftentimes the Information Linker will go to a human resource file or other roster of person resources.

The nature of the questions which will emerge during the later phases calls for linking agents to extend themselves a bit more, to inject their own knowledge and experience into transactions, and to be slightly more aggressive in order to achieve maximum effect. For example, knowing the context of the program effort, the information linker can *anticipate* problems and provide information in advance of a formal request. The linkers are likely to be caught up more in solving problems flowing from implementation activities than in generating alternatives for action as they did in the earlier phase of their relationship. Of course, they may be just entering the process at this point and not have firsthand knowledge of what has come before.

3. TECHNICAL ASSISTER. The role of technical assister is one that is

FIGURE 6
RELATIONSHIP OF DISTINGUISHING FEATURES TO FRONT-END ROLES OF LINKING AGENTS

LINKING AGENT ROLES	Diagnosis	Source of Help	Advocacy	Change Effort Focus	Change Effort Target	Mutual Goal-Setting	Long Term Problem-Solving Capability
Product Peddler	Linking Agent	Linking Agent	Solution	Curriculum	Individual	Low	Little
Information Linker	Linking Agent	Linking Agent	Information	Decision-Making	Individual	Medium	Little
Program Facilitator	Client	Linking Agent	Solution/Process	Curriculum	Individual/Group	Medium	Little
Process Enabler	Joint	Joint	Process	Organizational Processes	Group/Organization	High	Some
Provocateur-Doer	Joint	Joint	Client's Potential	All	Organization	High	Much

increasingly seen as vital to the successful implementation of a program. The type of technical assistance offered can be of two types: First, there is that which is concerned with getting the kinks out of the particular program and which requires a certain amount of content knowledge, either of the program itself or of the subject matter, e.g., reading, math, science. Equally important is general problem-solving assistance. This type is employed as the school personnel begin the process of trying to change their prior modus operandi to meet the requirements of the new program. In this type of technical assistance, technical assisters convene faculty groups to look at the difficulties they're having in their individual classrooms, to share successes and failure and alternative strategies for coping, and the like. They also may marshall other adopters of similar programs for exchange sessions and provide the psychological support necessary to get adopters over the bumps of any substantial change effort.

4. ACTION RESEARCHER/DATA FEEDBACKER. Going one step beyond technical assisters who are primarily concerned with the success of the individual programs they are facilitating, the action researcher is concerned with learning and with helping the school learn the way in which the current experience can help solve future problems. The focus is on studying what is going on, while assisting its implementation in order to generalize from it to similar situations which may emerge later. Typical techniques include feedback sessions based on observation, survey feedback procedures incorporating information drawn from formal instruments completed by respondents in the school, and combinations of the foregoing. Typically, there is some attempt to learn more about the current situation. Such inquiries often provide the fodder for spinoff efforts directed at the generic processes of the school or system, e.g., curriculum development procedures, staff development, community relations, and decision-making, among others.

5. EDUCATEUR/CAPACITY BUILDER. To accommodate the long-term potential of schools as organizations capable of growth themselves and capable of promoting growth for their members one must envision an expanding linking agent role. In Western Europe, there are individuals called "Educateurs" who are essentially roving systems improvement specialists (Barnes, 1975). They are legitimized as generalists in the instructional process who engage with a particular school for a period of time and assist it in making a substantial leap forward from its current plateau. In the contemporary American scene, the parallel notion at the system level is that of "building capacity." This generally entails pushing beyond routine responses to specific here-and-now problems and establishing a capacity or reserve to cope with anticipated and unanticipated problems in the future.

The number of organizations which are prepared to engage in this kind of process and which are located in environments which will support capacity building efforts is rather small. It is clear that the short-term requirements for linking agents are likely to be in areas other than this one. That we should strive to establish the capacity for capacity building in our linking agents seems a worthy goal, however. These individuals need to bring together the vision and perspectives of the futurist, the comprehensive knowledge of available human informational resources, a wide repertoire of interpersonal and technical skills, and diversified experience in a number of organizational settings such that a range of alternatives can be presented to any given client for consideration and modification. The operational parameters of capacity building are unknown at this time even if the terminology is widely used.

How these five roles relate to the other distinguishing features is delineated in Figure 7 on page 228.

Linking Agent Types. The ten roles presented in the foregoing pages constitute two functional subsets which can be observed in the field. Each successive role in each subset could overlap its predecessor, and in that sense they represent a possible continuum increasing in "fullness" and complexity. From my observations and a belief that most external agents would agree to the importance of continuity with respect to the client relationship, the ten roles lend themselves to combination of symmetrical "types." That is, each of the roles arrayed on the front-end continuum is mirrored by a role on the back-end continuum. If a linking agent functions primarily as an information linker in early transactions with the client, (s)he is more likely to play a similar role in later phases of the relationship. A graphic view of these idealized symmetrical types is illustrated in Figure 8. Naturally, reality is probably not as tidy as that. However, it does show us some logical directions in which to proceed when training linking agents whose current role could be complemented by expansion.

Prerequisite Attributes of Effective Linking Agents (Adapted from Crandall and Eiseman, 1971; Eiseman, 1974; and Crandall *et al.*, 1974.)

Each of the roles described in the preceding subsections requires a mix of skills, many of which will not be possessed by potential linking agents and therefore will become the foci of training programs for them. Additionally, it is worth stressing that the roles are not for everyone. Matching the potential linker to the requirements of the job is every bit as crucial as the need to match the proposed program to the client's needs

FIGURE 7
RELATIONSHIP OF DISTINGUISHING FEATURES TO BACK-END ROLES OF LINKING AGENTS

LINKING AGENT ROLES	Diagnosis	Source of Help	Advocacy	Change Effort Focus	Change Effort Target	Mutual Goal-Setting	Long Term Problem-Solving Capability
Resource Arranger	NA	Linking Agent	Solution	NA	NA	Low	NA
Information Linker	Linking Agent	Linking Agent	Information	Decision-Making	Individual	Medium	Little
Technical Assister	Joint	Linking Agent/ Joint	Solution/ Process	Curriculum	Individual/ Group	High	Some
Action Researcher/ Data Feedbacker	Joint	Joint	Process	Process/ Organization	Group/ Organization	Medium/ High	Some
Educateur/Capacity Builder	Joint	Joint	Client's Potential	All	Organization	High	Much

Training and Supporting Linking Agents 231

FIGURE 8
COMPLEMENTARY AND SYMMETRICAL LINKING AGENT ROLES

FRONT END

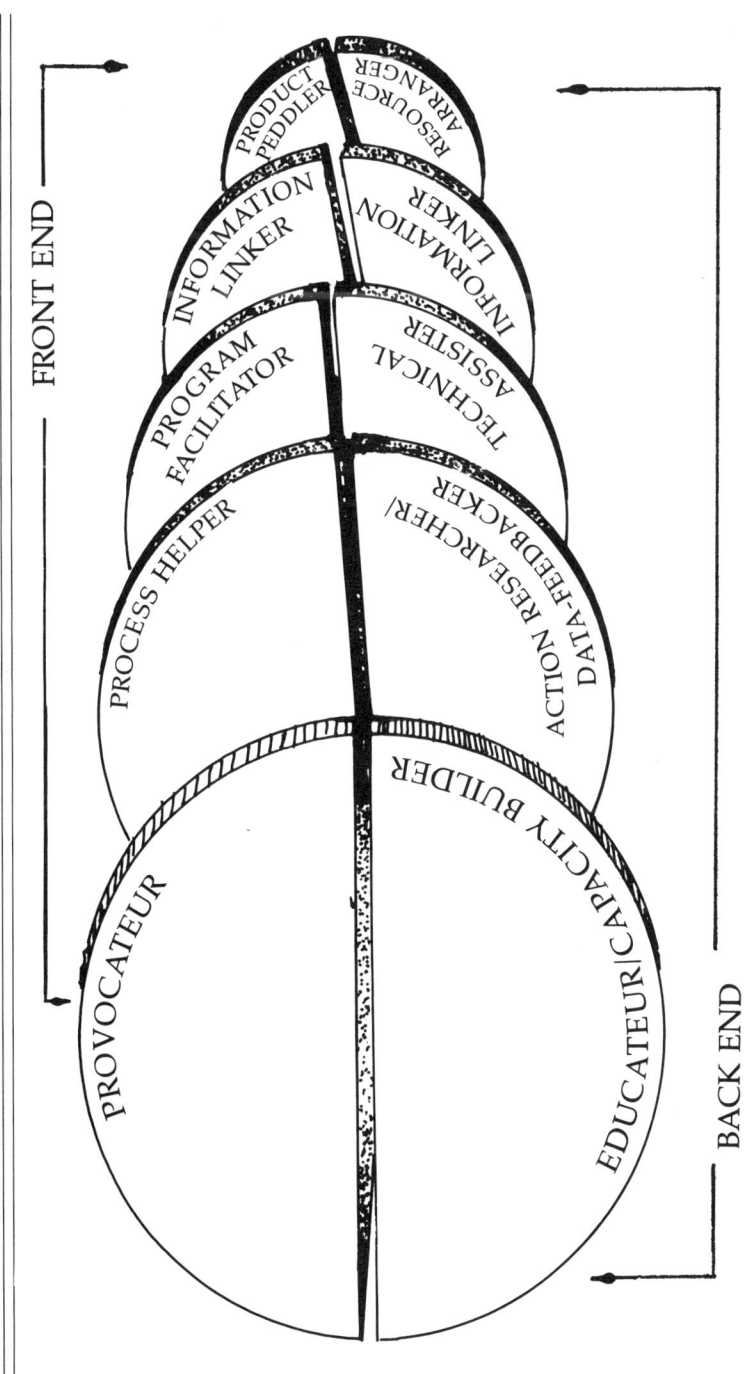

- PRODUCT PEDDLER / RESOURCE ARRANGER
- INFORMATION LINKER / INFORMATION LINKER
- PROGRAM FACILITATOR / TECHNICAL ASSISTER
- PROCESS HELPER / ACTION RESEARCHER / DATA-FEEDBACKER
- PROVOCATEUR / EDUCATEUR / CAPACITY BUILDER

BACK END

and requirements. Selecting linking agents is not simple, whether an agency is choosing from among already existing staff or whether it is hiring new staff from the outside. Half of the battle is won or lost at the point of initial selection.

It is also worth distinguishing between education and training. Stated most simply, the distinction is that training is job-specific while education is person-specific. In this context, the preceding sections have addressed components of the universe within which the linking agent will work and suggested a need for extensive and ongoing understanding of these classes of entities and their dynamic interrelationships. Much of this knowledge should be the subject of an ongoing educational effort initiated for or by linking agents. But many of these topics are ones in which any highly competent educational professional desires a thorough grounding. As such, they are the proper focus of education for the individual and are not exclusively related to the requirements of a particular linking agent job or role.

With respect to job-specific training, it is necessary first to determine the particular roles one desires to take or recruit for, to assess existing skill levels, and then to design and implement a training program to fill in whatever gaps exist in an individual's repertoire of skills. Training, then, is concerned primarily with skill development, though most training designs will also incorporate segments which are of a general educational nature.

At The NETWORK, we have found that many of the attributes necessary for success are not amenable to the type of training efforts that can be mounted feasibly. A rather careful and systematic assessment of the potential linking agent's capabilities has proven essential.

We have devised and refined a rather complicated, multi-stepped selection process based on the work of the Office of Strategic Services and detailed in *Assessment of Men: Selection of Personnel for the Office of Strategic Services (1969)*. It includes the design and structuring of simulated experiences in which the candidate is called upon to exhibit certain behavior reflecting his/her current level of skill or understanding in specified areas. We have employed the procedure a number of times over the last several years, and it has been used in at least two other settings, one of which was an agency hiring a team to work in the NIE-sponsored State Capacity Building Program.

Our experience has resulted in our being much more pessimistic about the possibility of training in the non-technical areas and verified the importance of selecting (versus training) for certain personal and interpersonal attributes. I believe that the successful linking agent, operating in an environment as complex as that suggested in this document, is a very special person indeed. In particular it calls for an individual who, Lippitt has suggested, needs to possess an "increased awareness of self, others, and the larger environment," allowing "for a more conscious use of self . . . as a professional tool rather than relying on actions stemming from an unexamined, intuitive base." (Lippitt, 1975a, p. 217).

In this subsection those prerequisite attributes which we have considered in selecting linking agents will be sketched and followed by descriptions of basic skill clusters amenable to training.

Cognitive Habits and Abilities. The requirements listed below are those we have found to bear on an individual's ability to operate in a complex environment. They should be understood to be measurable only indirectly by means that are yet incomplete, imperfect, and generally subjective. A good linking agent:

1. abstracts and conceptualizes the basic elements of a problem.

2. responds constructively to new information.

3. provides original ideas and fresh perspectives.

4. brings theory to bear on problems occurring in action settings.

5. resists premature closure but proceeds toward closure when appropriate.

These items should be taken as suggestive; they reflect the writer's bias toward a problem-solving orientation for linking agents.

Intrapersonal Competencies. These are general "life" competencies which undergird one's actions and reactions. They are reflected, if not necessarily demonstrated, in interpersonal transactions.

1. PROACTIVITY. This is related to how one perceives decisions, consequences, relationships, problems, and options. The distinction is between sitting back (mentally) at any stage in an intellectual situation versus taking the initiative to structure the circumstances or create a situation that will provoke some outcome in a particular direction. It is the difference between either accepting the status quo or waiting for new events to impinge upon one and, on the other hand, creating one's own reality.

Other manifestations of proactivity are the extent to which one actively seeks problems versus waiting for them to arise. The point here is that many problems will announce themselves to the linking agent, but in any given setting there will be those relevant and worthy problems which, if actively sought out, may hold more promise than those that announce themselves. The proactive person is in greater control of the overall setting than the reactive person who simply passively responds to the environment.

Related to the problem-seeking notion is the practice of *expanding boundaries*. This requires challenging assumptions and testing whether or not apparent givens are actually givens in a situation. One does this by making observations, asking questions, performing experiments or exerting influence to alter those things initially intended as givens.

We increasingly find ourselves encouraged by our culture to accept certain things as givens without testing them explicitly. Perhaps the simplest illustration of this phenomenon at work is the following simple puzzle:

a. Given the nine dots below:

```
    •   •   •

    •   •   •

    •   •   •
```

b. Take a pencil and draw four straight connected lines which pass through all nine dots without lifting your pencil from the paper or retracting any lines. Try to solve this puzzle before looking at the answer on page 242.

George Peabody, who has developed an exceptionally useful simulation called *Powerplay* (1973), uses the puzzle above to illustrate the shortcomings inherent in the typical tactics employed by individuals in situations where they are called upon to grapple with power issues.

He says:

> Most people are unable to solve this problem. The probable reason for this is an assumption that one must

conform to implied boundaries (or rules) which in fact do not exist. By playing *within* these imagined boundaries, a person is powerless to solve this puzzle or *the more important puzzles of how to get what you want or to get done what you want to get done in life.* (Emphasis added)

It is self destructive to accept as the limits of your behavior the real or implied rules, the real or implied expectations that others have of you, or other such boundaries. Imagined boundaries can unnecessarily limit your freedom and power if you let them. If, for instance, you accept the fact that the world is flat, you won't get around very much.

Real boundaries, however, necessarily limit your freedom because they are maintained by real rewards and punishments. There is a price to pay for crossing them.

Thus the primary questions are:

a. Are the boundaries real or just in my imagination? What are the realities?

b. How might I test them?

c. Do they restrict or sustain my freedom and power?

d. What are the costs and payoffs to me if I:
   1. play the game, conform to expectations?
   2. go outside the boundaries?
   3. change them?

As soon as you start asking these questions, you have freedom to select from a greater number of tactical options. You can cross boundaries or stay within them as you choose. (Peabody and Dietterich, 1973, pp. 11-12)

2. MATURITY. Given the context within which they are working, linking agents must make decisions and solve problems that result in actions consistent with mature attitudes and values. Jung, in developing a schema for the Preparing Educational Training Consultants (PETC) program at the Northwest Lab, has given considerable thought to the concept of maturity for individuals and organizations. Figure 9, excerpted from those materials, illustrates his view of the phases of maturity.

While at first glance it might seem that the desirable definition of maturity would be that associated with either the existential or the creative phase as labeled by Jung, it is probably more useful to work toward helping individuals be demonstrably conscious of where they are on the continuum in each particular situation, since the boundaries (between

236   David P. Crandall

FIGURE 9
GROWTH AND MATURITY POSSIBILITIES
FOR A HUMAN SYSTEM

STAGES OF GROWTH (In terms of inclusivenes and sophistication of functional capability)					
	Death				
	Senility				
	Old Age	Structure and procedures are rigidly maintained on the basis of *stereotypes* of how a system "such as ours" should be.	Structure and procedures have evolved on the basis of the system's *own experience*. They are strongly defended and maintained.	Structure and procedures change easily in response to the opportunity for *new experiences*, but improvements are difficult to maintain.	System maintains clear mechanisms for negotiating change in procedures or structure to respond to *changing needs, objectives or resources*.
	Middlescence				
	Adulthood				
	Adolescence				
	Childhood				
	Infancy				
	Birth				
		Stereotypic Phase	Opinionated Phase	Existential Phase	Creative Phase

↑

HUMAN →
SYSTEM

PHASES OF MATURITY
(In terms of phase of "self" identity and consequent orientation toward experiencing the world)

(from *Preparing Educational Training Consultants,* Northwest Lab)

phases and stages) are relatively permeable and may well be situation-specific. There is no "best" position, only an "informed" one. The notion of dynamic movement presented by Jung is consistent with the familiar Maslovian hierarchy of needs in that it describes a constantly expanding set of goals toward which one is striving.

3. SYSTEMATIC REFLECTIVITY. This competency refers to the way an individual regularly uses past experience to influence and inform the

nature of the subsequent experience. It is the notion of living life as a set of working hypotheses which, as an action researcher, one tests on an ongoing basis, using each set of results to formulate additional working hypotheses to be tested. Viewing problem situations from a long-term perspective is also central. This long-term perspective entails moving periodically from a relatively low level of analysis to a higher level of analysis, stepping back from the trees in order to see the forest, periodically reminding oneself of the ultimate objectives and viewing the gains or losses that might accrue in the short run from taking certain action within the larger context.

The reflective person challenges the common practice of organizing the world into logic-tight compartments where we often don't know what we know. A Persian proverb expresses the point beautifully:

> There are four kinds of men:
> He who knows not and knows not he knows not; he is a fool, shun him.
> He who knows not and knows he knows not; he is simple, teach him.
> He who knows and knows not he knows; he is asleep, wake him.
> He who knows and knows he knows; he is wise, follow him.

These three broad categories of intrapersonal competence — proactivity, maturity and systematic reflectivity — are among those on which we can assess potential candidates and about which they can be educated and supported in refining.

Work-Related Characteristics. While the following items many might consider to be self-evident, they are included because it is essential that we be explicit about our expectations of people. Those hiring, training, and supporting linking agents should test their assumptions about the characteristics they believe are important. Some suggested characteristics which are work-related then, are that the linking agent —

1. takes initiative.

2. can be depended upon to follow through.

3. is productive, can be described as having high output.

4. exhibits competence, accomplishes tasks effectively.

5. displays loyalty to the groups with which (s)he is associated and the organization for which (s)he works.

Evidence regarding these attributes is usually available from one's own experience or from previous employers.

Personal Qualities. There might be some argument as to the legitimacy of including personal qualities in any consideration of competencies or skills. They are important in the way in which professional staff are assessed by their superiors and colleagues, as well as the way in which they are perceived and received by clients. It appears to be helpful to be explicit about some of these qualities, and sharing them with potential staff gives them a clearer picture of our values and expectations for them in their interactions with us and our clients. They are included as suggestive of the type of things to be considered. A good linking agent —

1. expresses him/herself in an open, straight-forward, and candid manner.

2. appears self-directed, autonomous.

3. conveys that his/her prior experience has been varied, meaningful, and useful and that from it (s)he has developed a sense of perspective.

4. displays a sense of and concern for justice.

5. exhibits integrity.

6. demonstrates a concern for his/her own growth.

7. triggers enthusiasm in and energizes others.

8. exhibits a sense of humor.

9. displays social behavior appropriate to the client system.

Sieber, based on his extensive study of the Pilot State extension agents, suggests adding:

10. has low ego needs:

11. possesses high tolerance for frustration.

12. exhibits orderliness.

13. has the ability to enjoy new experience.

14. can exploit multiple role relationships for achievement of tasks.

* 15. maintains professional aloofness from internal politics.

16. has the ability to assess and exploit situations for achievement of tasks.

In the preceding paragraphs, four classes of competencies or characteristics seen as prerequisites to any technical training for linking agents have been outlined. When selection decisions are being made, such attributes and appropriate others should be consciously explicated, considered, modified, and ranked to conform to the requirements in an individual situation. These attributes are not the sort of thing easily modified by training interventions. Of course, it is possible and desirable to provide an environment the norms of which reinforce and support these attributes in linking agents. If one can secure a group of linking agents who possess these attributes in appropriate measure, then the chances for successful training in the technical skills required, the focus of the next subsection, will be greatly enhanced. Figure 10 arrays these distinguishing features in relationship to the ten linking agent roles described and denotes the author's estimate of the relative importance of each cluster of prerequisite attributes to each role.

Technical Skill Clusters for Linking Agents

We are all familiar with the *phenomena* embodied in the statement of "The best laid plans of mice and men . . .," and "The road to hell is paved with good intentions." Once we have a bead on the particular job of a given linking agent, we can then be more precise in delineating the skills needed to execute the job and in assessing the extent to which they are present or need to be developed. Skills can be defined as *"effective behavioral implementation of goals, intentions and plans, and affectively appropriate expression of feelings, values, ideas, opinions, and sensitivities."* (Schindler-Rainman and Lippitt, 1975, p. 226.) Those who bemoan

FIGURE 10
RELATIVE IMPORTANCE OF PREREQUISITE ATTRIBUTES
FOR VARIOUS LINKING AGENT ROLES

PREREQUISITE ATTRIBUTES

LINKING AGENT ROLES	Cognitive Skills and Abilities	Intra-Personal Competencies	Work-Related Characteristics	Personal Qualities
Product Peddler			++	
Information Linker	++	+	++	
Program Facilitator	++		++	+
Process Enabler	+++	+++	+++	+++
Provocatuer	+++	+++	++	+++
Educateur/Capacity Builder	+++	+++	++	+++
Action Researcher/ Data Feedbacker	+++	++	+++	+++
Technical Assister	++	++	++	++
Information Linker	++	+	++	
Resource Arranger			++	

KEY: (blank) unimportant
    +   minor importance
   ++   moderate importance
  +++ critical importance

the lack of a curriculum focusing on behavioral skill development in social relations and social problem-solving, especially in school settings, have a good point. That a broad repertoire of behavioral skills or implementation competencies is required of linking agents is not likely to receive argument from the readers of this chapter. What is needed is a series of training episodes combined with multiple support systems where linking agents can discover and be confronted by the incongruities between their action-intentions and their action effects. (Readers interested in an in-depth treatment of the difficulties involved in helping professionals perceive the gap between their espoused theory-of-action and their actual theory-in-use so as to enhance their professional effectiveness should read Argyris 1964, 1976a; Argyris and Schon, 1974.)

The laboratory approach has been an exceptionally useful vehicle for such skill development. It provides the kind of feedback and motivation to re-practice and to try, try again in order to develop greater clarity and behavioral competence. The laboratory method of experiential learning, in a simplified form, can be portrayed as follows:

FIGURE 11
ELEMENTARY CONSTRUCTS OF EXPERIENTIAL LEARNING

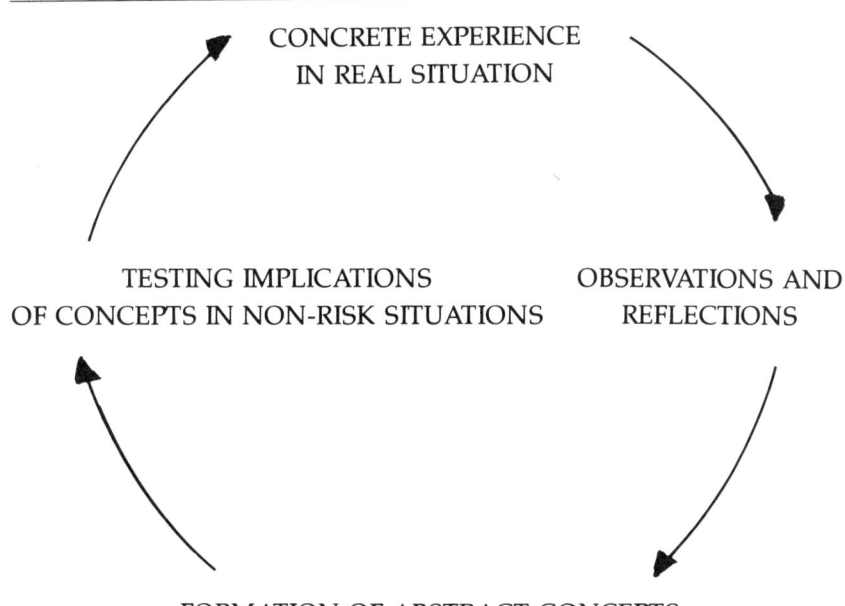

CONCRETE EXPERIENCE
IN REAL SITUATION

OBSERVATIONS AND
REFLECTIONS

FORMATION OF ABSTRACT CONCEPTS
AND GENERALIZATIONS

TESTING IMPLICATIONS
OF CONCEPTS IN NON-RISK SITUATIONS

This approach is put forward here as one recommended mode for training, where appropriate. It has the advantage of offering participants a chance to try things out in settings where they are not "playing for keeps," to receive helpful feedback and critique about their performance, to practice a new iteration of the skill, and to develop increasing confidence before going out to the real world. If the linking agent's support system is designed appropriately, the concept of laboratory education can be applied at the level of the actual job itself, with each transaction of episode with a client being viewed as a trial situation to be learned from.

Naturally, the learning process is somewhat more complicated than the elementary diagram above might suggest. See Lippitt's formulation of the elements below in Figure 12 for added detail. It is useful in designing training events and in focusing the specification of requisite skill clusters.

In addition to the prerequisite competencies and attributes already noted, and against the backdrop of a preferred method of providing training and education for linking agents, nine skill clusters will be described briefly, clusters which need operationalization and incorporation in a training program, depending upon the specific job of a given linking agent.

The nine are:
- Problem-Solving Skills
- Communication Skills
- Resource Utilization Skills
- Planning Skills
- Process Helping Skills
- Implementation Skills
- Content/Subject Matter Knowledge
- Evaluation and Documentation Skills
- Survival Skills

Problem-Solving Skills. There are many generic approaches to problem-solving, and the linking agent has an array of tools which might

---

Answer to problem posed on page 234:

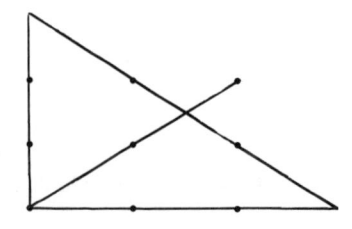

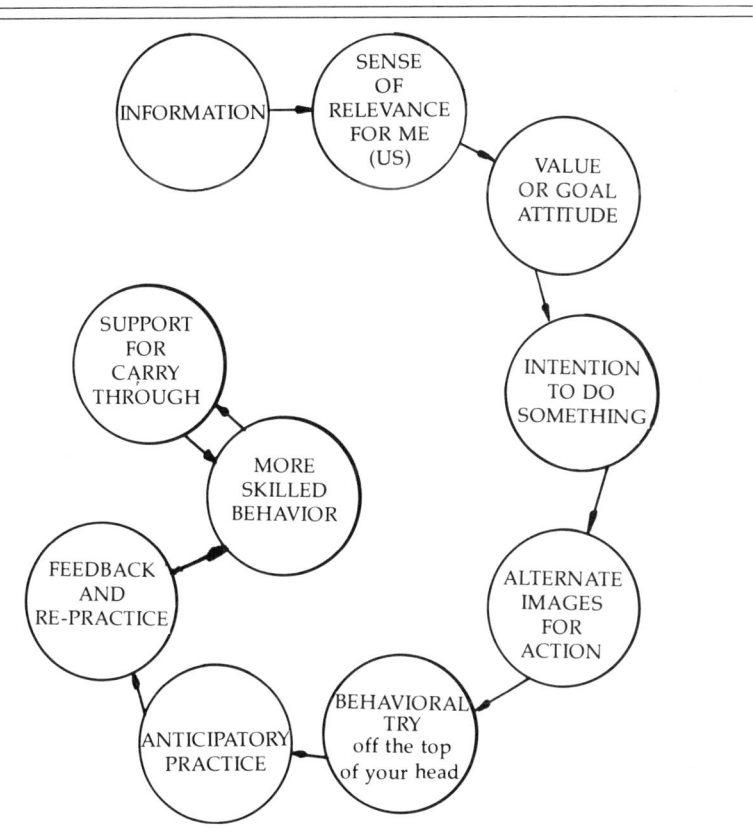

FIGURE 12
PARTS OF LEARNING PROCESS INSIDE THE LEARNER OR LEARNING SYSTEM

[Diagram: A circular flow of connected bubbles showing: INFORMATION → SENSE OF RELEVANCE FOR ME (US) → VALUE OR GOAL ATTITUDE → INTENTION TO DO SOMETHING → ALTERNATE IMAGES FOR ACTION → BEHAVIORAL TRY off the top of your head → ANTICIPATORY PRACTICE → FEEDBACK AND RE-PRACTICE → MORE SKILLED BEHAVIOR → SUPPORT FOR CARRY THROUGH]

Commentary on Diagram

One of the ingredients inside of us that has to get linked somehow to behavior is some kind of cognitive content; *information* or *knowledge* it is often called. A second ingredient is a belief that the bit of information has *relevance* for the self. The sense of relevance may be connected to or help generate a *goal* or a *value* or *belief.* And often, a *goal* or *value* helps generate an *intention* and *commitment to act* – at this point the internal processes of the self are sneaking up on action, but we still have no guarantee that ideas will be converted into overt action.

Reprinted by permission of the publisher from R. Lippitt, Linkage Problems and Process in Laboratory Education. In K. Benne, L. Bradford, J. Gibb, and R. Lippitt (Eds.), The Laboratory Method of Changing and Learning: Theory and Application. Palo Alto, California: Science and Behavior, 1975, p. 181. © 1975 by Science and Behavior.

be of assistance in any given situation (see NTL's Problem-Solving Booklet, Kauffman's *Systematic Problem Solving,* Northwest Lab's *Research Utilization Problem-Solving,* Schmuck's Situation-Target-Path (STP process). The rational problem-solving sequence generally includes:

1. defining the problem (or diagnosing the situation),

2. assessing the conditions surrounding the problem and their relative weight (This is typically done using some form of force field analysis),

3. generating some set of action alternatives

4. choosing from among them and instituting an action plan,

5. monitoring the implementation of the plan in such a way that a feedback loop exists.

This is a linear problem-solving approach. Within it, or as a substitute for it, there are various non-linear (so-called "creative") strategies which can be incorporated: Brainstorming, images of potentiality, Synectics, divergent thinking — these are labels for some of the main variations.

It is crucial that linking agents get a solid grip on the general problem situation. Only by delimiting their efforts can they hope to succeed. Classifying problem situations in some way so as to reduce the area of inquiry is called for. Recent work at the Northwest Lab has made a rather useful distinction among three types of problems that might call for different sorts of problem-solving techniques. First is *technical problem-solving,* wherein both the current state of affairs and the desired end point are known and able to be specified. In this instance a systems analysis or operations research mode is an appropriate problem-solving approach. Second is so-called *theoretical problem-solving,* where the current state of affairs can be limited, but the desired end state cannot be specified. This type calls for an action research approach which will develop a series of iterations leading to an agreeable end point (the RUPS process is one operational version of this action research approach). The third type is *philosophical problem-solving,* where there is clarity as to the current state of affairs as well as desired multiple end states, but fundamental disagreement as to the desirability of one or more of the possible end states. In this instance, the problem-solving approach of choice is conflict resolution and negotiation procedures.

Eiseman (1974) suggests that virtually any situation in a human system can be viewed and addressed as a potentially solvable problem or set of problems of one of the following types:

1. Distorted or non-existent perceptions of relevant reality

2. Distorted or non-existent communications among subsystems that need to collaborate

3. Feelings of frustration

4. Feelings of impotence

5. Undifferentiated dissatisfaction with the situation as it is.

6. Vagueness or confusion regarding direction of major objectives.

7. Minimal or non-existent commitment to explicitly stated high priority goals

8. Inadequate ability to formulate plans to achieve explicitly stated high priority goals

9. Inadequate ability to make decisions relating to explicitly stated high priority goals

10. Inadequate ability to implement high priority action plans

11. Inadequate attention devoted to the maintenance of the system

12. Existence of untapped, surplus, valuable resources

Koberg and Bagnall provide several hundred useful tools and techniques in a compendium entitled *The Universal Traveler: A Companion for Those on Problem-Solving Journeys*.

There is a need for linking agents to develop a repertoire of usable problem-solving approaches, to be able to classify problem situations so that the appropriate technology can be employed, and to know when to call for help in any one of the substages of the problem-solving process.

Communication Skills. This cluster of skills concentrates on generic communication processes. Linking agents need to have well-developed oral, written, and other (mediated) communication skills. In certain situations they will be called upon to make presentations to individuals or groups that will require the use of presentation aids. There will be situations where *questioning skills* are necessary in order to move productively forward on an agenda. In most situations, *active listening skills* are imperative for effective communication. There are situations where a one-way mode of communication, though not the preferred mode for many linking agents given their likely value set, will be called for. Various aids are available for developing and refining *oral communication skills;* there are several excellent resources for developing and refining skills in written communication (see *Writing for Results,* 1974; Far West Lab's Module on Technical Writing, 1974). The subcomponents of effective *interpersonal communication* have also been captured in various training programs, including those developed by Northwest Lab and the Center for Educational Policy and Management.

Resource Utilization Skills. At several points in the process of interacting with a client group, linking agents are likely to need to call upon resources other than themselves. Sensitivity in knowing when to "refer" as opposed to offering oneself as the resource is an essential ingredient in successful resource utilization and is likely to be enhanced to the extent that the linking agent is fully conversant with the resources available and the circumstances under which their use would be appropriate.

The backbone of the linking agent's formal information resources remains the ERIC data base and its companions, now accessible by computer in locations in almost every state. The more than thirty data bases (in addition to ERIC) which can now be accessed via computer add immeasurably to the information that the linking agent can bring to the client. Unfortunately, these sources are not free; cost may become a factor as well as turnaround time. Linking agents need not develop retrieval skills to the point where they would qualify as full-time retrieval specialists, but introductory training in the use of a computer terminal and familiarity with the main indexes used in education, RIE (Resources in Education) and CIJE (Current Index to Journals in Education), as well as some actual experience fingering microfiche and using a microfiche reader and/or reader printer will be invaluable to effective functioning. A recent compendium, *A Guide to Sources of Educational Information,* by Woodbury (1976), should be on the shelf of every linking agent. It is the best to date, though not absolutely current as of this writing.

In addition to formal information resources, the linking agent should be able to access *other programmatic resources,* either products or programs themselves or information about projects in which products have been used. Most large scale information centers have developed procedures for cataloguing so-called "fugitive" data of this sort. There are specialized centers which inventory a variety of curricular materials. EPIE (Educational Products Information Exchange, New York, NY) is an exemplary source of "consumer-oriented" information on products of interest to educators. Additionally, the linking agent would do well to either develop or gain access to some bank of *human resources.* The maintenance of such files is an almost overwhelming task, and initially linking agents will probably rely on their personal contacts. But as one's clientele expands, it becomes necessary to draw upon a larger and larger pool of human talent to supplement one's own resources. Various means have been employed for this purpose. RISE in Pennsylvania has published a directory of human resources for their state. The National Learning Disabilities Assistance Project (NaLDAP) at The Network maintains an active file on McBee cards of several hundred consultants in various areas.

Based on our own experience, the difficulties with using human resource files effectively, other than the normal storage, currency, and quality control issues, extend to such difficult matters as: How to provide adequate incentives to the consultants who make up the pool when any one of them may be used very little if at all? How to share in the success of a referral that really succeeds yet disown the failures. Most knotty of all, how to get people (i.e., linking agents) who are rather good consultants in their own right to avoid feeling less than successful if they have to refer to an outsider, especially one who couldn't possibly be as good as they would be — if they only had time.

To date, the most complete training program directly related to resource utilization in education remains the Educational Information Consultant (EIC) developed by Far West Lab.

Planning Skills. The cluster of skills associated with planning focuses on the "getting ready" work necessary to assure success during implementation of an improvement effort. It calls for a systematic and cautious look at the job ahead and a *delineation of the action steps* to be taken, the resources required at each point, the *anticipation of probable pitfalls* and "crunch" points, determination of budget and other *resource allocation* requirements, the ability to move from global statements of intent to operational statements that are actionable. It is helpful for linking agents to have at least a rudimentary knowledge of various *systematic charting procedures,* including flow charting, PERT charting, fault-free analysis, and the like, in order to array a picture of the impending effort for their own use and/or the clients. Abilities in "organizing for work" those who will be implementing a program are also desirable. Examples might include engaging in review and reflection sessions concerning the plan or engaging in role plays related to anticipated dilemmas (in order to practice the behaviors that may be needed in the real situation in a simulation where failure will not jeopardize the actual effort). The preceding three skill clusters obviously are integral parts of this cluster.

Linking agents able to employ systematic planning will also benefit by using various means of diagnosing relevant organizational components so as to locate the optimal entry points and discern the best path for the ultimate change effort. Though there are a number of tools available to the linking agent, all require some understanding of their underlying principles and practice in their use in order to be used effectively.[2]

Process Helping Skills. At virtually every point of contact with a client group, use of certain process skills holds the promise of vastly improving the effectiveness and degree of satisfaction of the overall effort. The linking agent should strive to develop a complex of skills including: *communicating feelings* appropriately; *active listening* and *feeding back* of implicit and explicit cues regarding understanding and satisfaction; *providing affective support* and legitimizing openness when appropriate; *confronting* when necessary to resolve problems or surface underlying issues; and

---

[2] Among the most helpful sources which should be inspected by the interested reader are *Diagnosing the Professional Climate of Schools* by Fox et al. (1973), a series of instruments developed for use in the COPED Project and the series of checklists developed by Havelock to accompany *A Guide to Innovation* (available only in ERIC ED056256).

A group of reference tools of immense utility to those with a behavioral science orientation or inclination are the *Annual Handbooks for Group Facilitators* and *Handbooks of Structured Experiences for Human Relations Training* by Pfeiffer and Jones. There are now six volumes of the former and seven volumes of the latter. The Schmuck and Runkel *Handbook of Organization Development in Schools* (1972) is also a valuable source of diagnostic instruments. Lake and Miles, in their recent compendium, *Measuring Human Behavior* (1973), bring together and review a vast array of instruments useful to change practitioners, as do Pfeiffer and Heslin in their *Instrumentation in Human Relations Training* (1973, 1976).

There are other sources of particular instruments with varying degrees of focus, including the principal instruments developed by the I/D/E/A-sponsored League of Cooperating Schools in Southern California headed by Goodlad, and the Organizational Needs Inventory (ONI) developed at The NETWORK and based on Havelock's early work. Some of these can be easily used and hand-scored while others, depending on the number of respondents and the perseverance of the linking agents, require access to computer facilities.

For those with access to a computer, there are at least two computerized programs which profess to measure organizational characteristics in a comprehensive way: the CHAMPUS Program under development by Bowers and his colleagues at Michigan and the PROFILE Procedure developed by Bass. Both utilize a questionnaire as input to a program and both are based on factor analytically developed models of organizational variables which must be taken into account in a major change effort.

role-taking, in the sense of developing empathy, coupled with the ability to portray the position of others in a way that does not make them feel as if they are being psychoanalyzed.

More specifically, it's very desirable that the linking agent develop the ability to make a "process intervention" directed at increasing the clients' awareness of what they are doing and enhancing their sense of control over their actions. This calls for *observational sensitivity* and the *ability to induce reflectivity* in others so that they can examine their actions in a way that is not threatening. Question-asking directed at checking progress and focus are ingredients in process interventions. Recent work in education has highlighted the importance of values and their centrality to individuals' attitudes and actions. Thus, it would be useful for linking agents to develop a familiarity with *values clarification techniques* and exercises. A wide range of useful tools for process helping is available, including many from the Pfeiffer and Jones series and the CEPM "Strategies of Organizational Change" program reports.

Sometimes, process problems arise which require far more than well-timed interpretations of ongoing behavior or data collection and feedback cycles. For example, the teachers and principal may find themselves repeatedly engaging in patterns of interactions which everyone agrees are debilitating. Eiseman (in preparation) has developed procedures which take linking agents step-by-step through the process of designing a full-fledged intervention plan to cope with such counter-productive interaction patterns. Because of their usefulness in resolving the kinds of conflict which school people continually encounter, his 'transition' procedures are especially relevant to linking agents.

Implementation Skills. As has been noted by recent observers of the scene (e.g., Fullan, 1975b), the bulk of attention in both research and practice has been related to the steps leading up to and including the decision to adopt a program. Some preplanning may occur and be more or less systematic, but it is increasingly obvious (Berman and McLaughlin, 1974) that the implementation phase is critical to the success of a program improvement effort. Runkel (personal communication) called attention to the striking convergence of these findings with some in other fields as reported by Coleman (1971), Fairweather (1972), Glaser and Taylor (1973), and the National Institute of Mental Health (1971).

The linking agent, in order to be of assistance at this stage of the process, needs to be able to employ the skills listed above in situations that will, in all likelihood, be more hectic than those that preceded the actual implementation. During implementation, questions of logistics and resource allocation, often shrouding emerging value issues, etc., come to the fore in a way often difficult to deal with. Hall and his colleagues have empirically derived a hierarchy of concerns which need to be taken into account during implementation (Hall et al., 1976). It is most probable that power and status issues (Giacquinta, 1973) will also come to the fore during implementation and require prompt attention by the linking agent.

A compelling case can be made for including the collection of data through relatively formal means as a central component in program improvement efforts, whether or not such efforts involve linking agents. Miles et al., (1969) have described the utility of a survey feedback approach to organizational change, and Bowers (1973) has demonstrated its effectiveness.

It is useful for the linking agent to develop a perspective on organizations' capacity for growth. Some of the more promising approaches to this are those developed by Jung and his colleagues at Northwest Lab and presented as part of their PETC III Training, wherein organizations are characterized as to their relative maturity in a schema paralleling that of developmental psychology for individuals. Likert's Systems 1-4 Framework (1975) presents a well known continuum of organization types. Eiseman (1974) presents an outline for an optimally functioning organization which is determined by the extent to which it is "dynamically homeostatic," "rational," "autonomous," "collaborative," and "committed to improving the quality of life."

Each of these schemas offers a useful way for viewing organizations as whole creatures having dynamic capabilities. Each offers the advantage of being applicable whether the unit of analysis is the district, the building, or the subunit within a building. Unfortunately, Likert's is the only one that to date has specific instrumentation keyed to the model.

During implementation it is probable that one or more people will need to assume a leadership role in order to assure the effort's forward progress. Familiarity with *leadership style* and issues related to it should be in the store of knowledge of the linking agent. Reviewing the work of Hersey and Blanchard (1972) is perhaps the most efficient way for the interested agent to develop a greater understanding of the function leadership style can play in the success of an effort. Further, it is probable that someone, in many cases the linking agent, will need to play a *coordination* function, engaging in activities such as division of labor, adjustment of resources, and clarification of roles. Also important are *providing support for the action efforts* through communication to individuals in the hierarchy who can endorse or applaud the effort, as well as to those who can facilitate movement to or from the desired direction; *soliciting feedback* regarding interim success as well as expressions of concern about emerging problems; *orchestrating periodic "celebrations"* so that participants feel a sense of dynamic movement toward the desired goals; and *facilitating goal restatement* and adjustment.

Content/Subject Matter Knowledge. This cluster of skills relates to content or subject matter as typically defined. It is important to view *process as content* at appropriate points, and in many cases the only content expertise that the linking agent must be sure to be on top of is that related to process. The biggest danger for linking agents is the creation of expectations on the part of the client as to the content expertise of the linking agent, expertise on which delivery cannot ultimately be relied. One must convey clearly that one is an expert in identifying and drawing on resources in reading, not that one is a reading expert (unless one is). For the Product Peddler knowledge of only a specific set of tangibles is called for. For the Information Linker, the content is typically of formal data bases and collections of information. The Program Facilitator is expected to possess a range of superficial knowledge about a variety of programs and may have in-depth knowledge in knowing where to get it, by employing skills which would be classified in the preceding Resource Utilization skill cluster.

When linking agents find themselves in situations with both long-term potential (e.g., multi-year efforts), and a particular content focus such as reading or special education, it is essential that they develop, as a minimum, *familiarity with the main issues* in the field, an understanding of the historical trends and roots which have led up to the current state of the art, a grasp of the distinguishing features of particular approaches or conceptual subdivisions in the content area, and knowledge of the acknowledged experts who have name recognition with practitioners and other audiences.

Given that the work of the linking agent is going to occur in school settings where the curriculum is the ranking priority, a cluster of elemental knowledge and skills related to the generic *process of curriculum development* is essential.[3] Additionally, it is well to have some sense of the distinction between curriculum as the content of education and instruction as the process. *Instructional practice* and technology is an area where much work has been done that the linking agent can take ready advantage of. The work of Ely and others in the Instructional Development Institute project is exemplary in this regard.

Not all the work of the linking agent will be focused on the classroom as an isolated unit. Therefore, knowledge of, and sensitivity to, the reality

---

[3] As an initial text, Tyler's classic *Basic Principles of Curriculum and Instruction* (1969) remains as good a starting point as any. Goodlad (1966) has extended the early work of Tyler in a useful way.

of administrators is desirable. Lipham's work in the field is well known, and the 1964 yearbook of NSSE, *Behavioral Science and Educational Administration*, presents a reasonable perspective on developments, as well as tracing the history of the field. Since many linking agents will themselves have been former teachers or administrators, the issue of perceived homophily or heterophily should not be ignored in their preparation. These terms refer to the extent to which they are likely to be seen as "more like," i.e., homophilous with, or "more unlike," i.e., heterophilous with, their potential clients. (These terms and their variations should probably head the list of jargon which linking agents should commit to memory for use at professional meetings.)

In addition to the sets of content knowledge noted, given the requirements of most full-bore program improvement efforts, the linking agents should develop a basic understanding of the process of *planned change* in education.[4]

---

[4]Seminal works reflecting the dominant social psychological perspective include Lippitt, Watson, and Westley's *Dynamics of Planned Change* (1958); Miles' *Innovations in Education* (1964); and Bennis, Benne, and Chin's *The Planning of Change*, Volume I (1961), Volume II (1969), Volume III (1976). Another important entry in this tradition is *The Laboratory Method of Changing and Learning: Theory and Application* (1975) by Benne, Bradford, Gibb, and Lippitt.

In terms of research specifically directed at program improvement efforts in schools, the most notable are Sieber and Seashore's study of the Pilot State Dissemination effort (1972); Goodlad's study of the Pilot State Dissemination effort (1972); Goodlad's I/D/E/A series (1975) based on the five years of the League of Cooperating Schools in Southern California, and the Rand Change Agent Studies (1975) of federally-sponsored innovative projects. Related entries are the oft-ignored *Oregon Studies* (Schalock et al., 1972) and Schmuck et al., *Handbook of Organizational Development in Schools* (1972). Piele's recent summary is also of particular interest to linking agents.

There are also a few useful educational or training packages or programs. Virtually all have been supported with federal money. Havelock's *Change Agent's Guide to Innovation in Education* (1973) and Havelock and Havelock's *Training for Change Agents* (1973) draw upon the vast compendium of research conducted by him and his colleagues at the Institute for Social Research in its Center for Research on Utilization of Scientific Knowledge (CRUSK). Mick, Paisley, et al., produced three volumes as a part of an early (aborted) effort to establish a training program for educational extension agents (1973). Banathy et al., at the Far West Lab, developed an extensive six-volume modular series directed at paraprofessionals in Development, Dissemination, and Evaluation (1972). Previously noted is the output of Northwest Regional Laboratories Improving Teacher Competencies Program, presently packaged as the PODS Program (Preparing OD Specialists). The Lab's products constitute an extensive sequential training effort for individuals who wish to work as change agents in educational settings.

Fortunately, a current effort funded by NIE will enable these products to be modularized and tailored to the specific needs of linking agents. The Center for Educational Policy and Management (CEPM, formerly CASEA) as well as Research for Better Schools, Inc., (RBS) have also produced publications or training materials of interest to linking agents. A useful guide to these and other materials developed by the Labs and Centers is the *Educational Dissemination and Linking Agent Source Book* (1976), a product of the Cooperative Interlab Project currently sponsored by NIE.

Evaluation and Documentation Skills. In this cluster are skills related to: designing and conducting *formative evaluations*, producing data useful to the redirection of the project effort; (occasionally) providing for some sort of summative or *impact assessment* of outcomes; and documenting the work effort.

Evaluation tends to be viewed negatively by many practitioners. Most of their experiences are bad ones: evaluation activities are disruptive, insensitive to instructional needs and time-consuming, taking time away from teaching; the information provided is over their heads, technically and rarely self-evidently useful to the system, building, or teachers; evaluation is used for "political" purposes, i.e., "proving" minorities are inferior. But increasingly, external agents are able to neutralize these historically negative connotations. Close work with clients has enabled them to elevate the level of discourse, usefully explore ongoing project activities and ultimate impact as well as fruitfully examining the implications of one effort to others.

Linking agents do not need to have an advanced degree in evaluation or research methodology but should possess some fundamental understanding of evaluation concepts, alternative approaches, emergent issues in the field, *sources of technical assistance*, and tools or instruments for use at various points in the process.[5]

Documentation calls for designing, in appropriate detail, some standardized way of describing events of interest in the effort, analyzing them for insights, teasing out critical incidents which have special relevance for the various audiences of the project, producing written reports at different stages of the process, and identifying potential components of the project which might be more fully described in some kind of packaged material. Some of the foregoing skill clusters are interrelated, as there are ingredients of communication, planning, and problem-solving involved in any evaluation and documentation work.

Survival Skills. This cluster is, as much as anything else, directed at increasing the level of awareness and legitimizing the everpresent need to "stay alive" in a professional situation. For many people the focus in the short-run will be on coping with crises and foul-ups in the program or dealing with hostile group members in a school. In the long-run, survival takes on a professional development focus on ongoing training and education and of expanding the group of colleagues and friends to whom one

---

[5] The 1969 yearbook of the National Society for the Study of Education, edited by Ralph W. Tyler, *Educational Evaluation: New Roles, New Means,* provides a useful introduction. The Office of Planning, Budgeting and Evaluation of USOE has recently published two very helpful monographs, *A Practical Guide to Measuring Project Impact on Student Achievement,* numbers 1 and 2.

can turn for counsel and solace about various matters in one's work and life. Survival also requires maintaining appropriate communication with different levels of the client system, the resource system, and one's own host agency as to one's progress and plans (cf. Arends, 1976).

Herb Shepherd, in a delightful article, "Rules of Thumb for Change Agents," offers the following statement:

> Staying alive means staying in touch with your purpose. It means using your skills, your emotions, your labels and positions, rather than being used by them. It means not being trapped in other people's games. It means turning yourself on and off rather than being dependent on the situation. It means choosing with a view to the consequences as well as the impulse. It means going with the flow even while swimming against it. It means living in several worlds without being swallowed up in any. It means seeing dilemmas as opportunities for creativity. It means greeting absurdity with laughter while trying to unscramble it. It means capturing the moment in the light of the future. It means seeing the environment through the eyes of your purpose.

He offers several corollaries under a "GENERAL RULE NO. 3: NEVER WORK UPHILL." These are:

1. Don't build hills as you go.

2. Work in the most promising arena.

3. Don't use one when two could do it.

4. Don't overorganize.

5. Don't argue if you can't win.

6. Play God a little.

For linking agents, who will generally view themselves and be viewed by others as the expendable factor in the equation, the importance of developing and refining survival skills should be underscored. Naturally, their importance is related to the type of situation in which one is working, but awareness of their existence and importance is critical.

These nine primary technical skill clusters — Problem-Solving Skills;

Communication Skills; Resource Utilization Skills; Planning Skills; Process Helping Skills; Implementation Skills; Content/Subject Matter Knowledge; Evaluation and Documentation Skills; Survival Skills — have differential importance for the various linking agent roles previously described. Figure 13 summarizes the writer's best guess of the relative primacy of the skill clusters for effective performance of the ten linking agent roles. In virtually every area, adequate materials exist to provide the *knowledge and understanding* linking agents need, and suitable *training* materials can be adapted from existing elements and combined in ways most pertinent to needed *skill development* for a given linking agent's role(s). Reconceptualization of the elements and their interrelationships by those with an optimistic vision will move us toward the creative blend solutions which are within our reach.

Just as was illustrated earlier by the overlap of the ten roles noted in Figure 8 which concluded the third part of the chapter, an inspection of Figures 10 and 13 shows the complementarity of the attributes and requirements for effective performance of the roles. Thus, linking agents should be able to discern qualities and skills in their colleagues which are incorporated in their own primary role(s), that is, there is a bit of them in each of their counterparts. Understanding and appreciating how this connects all linking agents together is a subtle piece of the reconceptualization needed for the contraption to work.

The Linking Agent in Action.

In the preceding subsections, a number of issues related to the multiple roles of linking agents, attributes to be assessed in their initial selection, and primary technical skill clusters to be developed through an ongoing training program have been presented. Sections I and II painted the larger context in broad strokes and called for attention to knowing the resource system; diagnosing and comprehending a complex client system; and functioning in a productive way within a host agency whose primary mission was not likely to be that of linking. It would be possible at this point for us to have a squadron of fully-knowledgeable and well-trained linking agents ready to work with an array of client systems and able to draw on a rich reservoir of resources. Even with a squadron, "the whole thing" could never come together in an integrated effort.

The contraption *can* work, both in particular program improvement efforts and in larger systems for preparing and supporting such individuals and efforts (see Culbertson's chapter which follows). At this point in

FIGURE 13
RELATIVE PRIMACY OF TECHNICAL SKILL CLUSTERS FOR VARIOUS LINKING AGENT ROLES

TECHNICAL SKILL CLUSTERS

LINKING AGENT ROLES	Problem Solving	Communication	Resource Utilization	Planning	Process Helping	Implementation	Content/ Subject Matter	Evaluation/ Documentation	Survival
Product Peddler		+++							+
Information Linker	+	++	+++				++		++
Program Facilitator	+	+++	+	+		+			++
Process Enabler	+++	+++	++	+++	+++	++		+	++
Provocateur	++	+++	+	++	++	+	+	+	
Educateur/Capacity Builder	+++	+++	++	+++	++	+++	+	++	
Action Researcher / Data Feedbacker	+++	+++	++	++	+++	+++		+++	
Technical Assister	++	++	++	++	++	++	++		++
Information Linker	+	++	+++						
Resource Arranger		+							+

KEY: (blank) skill not essential for effective role performance
  +   tertiary skill for effective role performance
  ++ secondary skill for effective role performance
  +++ primary skill for effective role performance

the document it may be helpful to discuss four issues relating to putting the schema in motion and maximizing its chance for success. These four issues are:

1. Assessing why action-intents do not lead to action-effects

2. The function of collaboration and the development of an inside/outside team

3. The phases of the relationship with the client system

4. The complexity of the implementation process.

Each of these issues could, in itself, be the subject of an entire chapter, and so they will simply be sketched out here. They constitute matters which need attention by the linking agent and those concerned with both management and policy.

Assessing Why Action-Intents Do Not Lead to Action-Effects. This phenomenon characterizes more of human endeavor than most of us would care to acknowledge. Despite the most well-conceived and carefully articulated plan on the part of linking agents, the intended outcomes will almost never be achieved. Rather than lowering our expectations and resigning ourselves to never achieving our goals, it is more productive to refine the ways we examine what is going on so that adjustments can be made from one time to the next. Eiseman (in preparation) has formulated the following diagram to explain this phenomenon.

In the corners of Figure 14 are four primary clusters into which virtually all aspects of a transaction involving one or more people can be assigned. The three generic problems that result in *intention-effects discrepancies* are,

1. There may be a *lack of clarity* with respect to the elements of any one of the four major clusters.

2. There may be a *conflict within a cluster* between its elements.

3. If there is clarity and no within-cluster conflict, there may be *lack of congruence* between any of the four clusters.

FIGURE 14
WHY ACTION-INTENTS DO NOT LEAD TO ACTION-EFFECTS

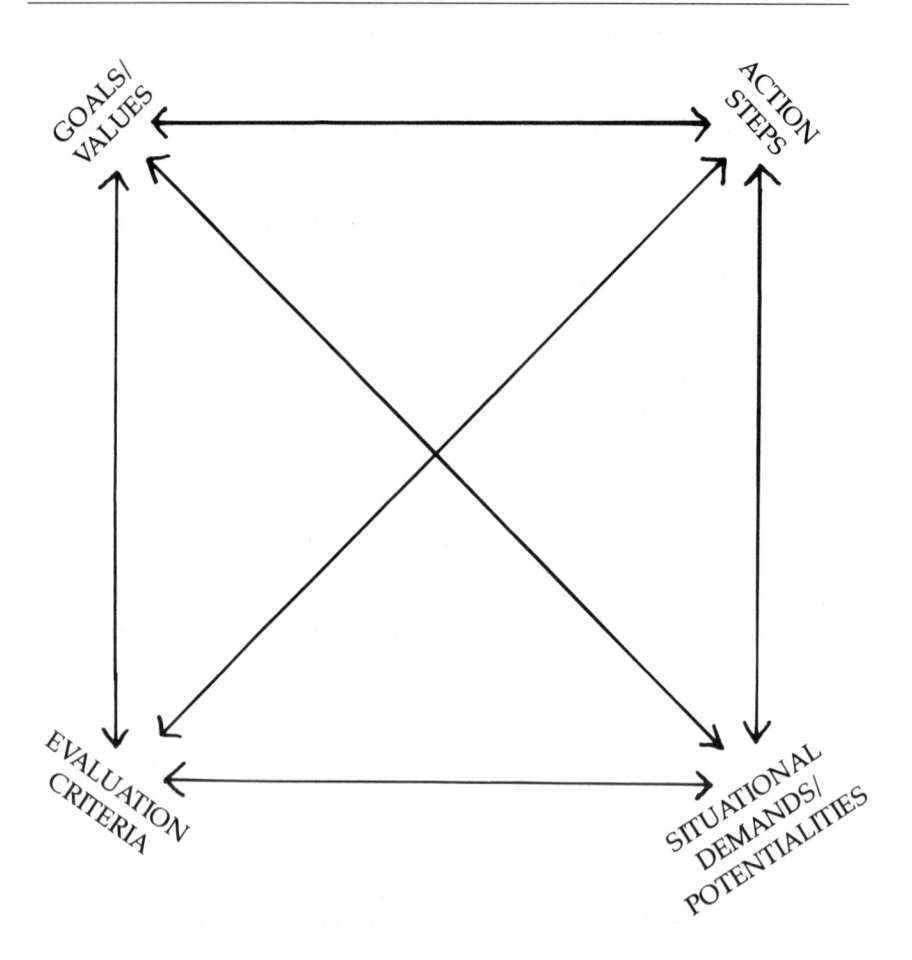

(Diagram: four clusters arranged at the corners of a square, connected by double-headed arrows along the sides and diagonals:)

- GOALS/VALUES (top left)
- ACTION STEPS (top right)
- EVALUATION CRITERIA (bottom left)
- SITUATIONAL DEMANDS/POTENTIALITIES (bottom right)

In order for action-intents to lead to the desired action-effects, all four clusters must be clear, internally consistent, and congruent. If one views them in a logical sequence, while recognizing that in any given instance their interactions do not necessarily follow this sequence, one can see that the *goals and values* underlying an effort provide the momentum leading to the *action steps*. These, when taken, push up against the *situational demands and potentialities* in a way which, depending on the feedback mechanisms, may modify any of the preceding steps. As the action steps are inevitably transformed by the situational factors, the explicit and implicit *evaluation criteria* influence the perception of relative success or achievement of the desired outcome(s) for the actor as well as the observer. Any breakdown or lack of congruence between or within any of the four clusters as they interact in a dynamic process will, in more cases than not, produce a shortfall. And, of course, we can only have an imperfect knowledge of the future.

Like all elementary paradigms, this one can serve as an easy-to-employ checklist which linking agents can use to review the completeness of each cluster and of the probable interaction of the essential elements, or at least their (and relevant others') understanding of each cluster. Procedures drawn from the skill clusters noted earlier could be employed to produce clarity on the content of each cluster, as well as to check and recheck for congruence between clusters.

Developing an Inside-Outside Team. Virtually all of the major writers in the field and observers of the educational change process encourage the development of an inside-outside team in any intervention. (Havelock, 1973; Jung, d.u.; Schindler-Rainman and Lippitt, 1975). In most cases the linking agent is the outsider to the system; the insiders are those participants relevant to a particular effort. These authors discuss the advantages and disadvantages of the insider versus the outsider as a change agent; they suggest that the optimal solution is one which combines both so as to derive the benefits and avoid the disadvantages of each.

Among the operational difficulties for linking agents will be identifying appropriate members of the team, assisting them in becoming more skillful in using external resources (including the linking agent), expanding or contracting the composition of the team to take into account changing requirements of the ongoing process, maintaining communication with the constituencies represented by the inside members so that the inside team does not become viewed as a special interest group bent on achieving its own individual purposes, guarding against the group becoming captivated by its own good relations in a way that effectively impedes active work on the original purpose, and shifting the linking agents' role within the group as the relationship develops in order to maximize its long-term effectiveness (see Cartwright and Zander, 1968).

In our own work at The NETWORK, we have been confronted with a reality related to participation. Like many of our colleagues, we believe in increased involvement of teachers and parent/community members in educational decision-making. Thus, in a number of our projects we have specified involvement of representative members of these constituencies as a *quid pro quo* for our engagement with the school. Our experience has demonstrated the necessity of being flexible on this point. Many program innovations are of such modest scope that either extensive involvement with a number of teachers or any involvement at all by parents or community members is dysfunctional. These publics simply do not have a meaningful role if the matter under consideration is an innovation or a set of possible innovations which can be adopted by a single teacher and implemented without any fundamental shift in the values promoted by the program. Hence, conscious reflection upon one's values and the extent to which they impose inappropriate conditions on a given situation should be urged.

The notion that the inside-outside team is a tremendously useful vehicle for ensuring the success of change effort is usually accompanied by a belief that collaboration is a preferable mode of behavior between professionals engaged in such efforts. Many of us espouse collaboration in our work with schools and try to promote it. What is increasingly clear is that there is substantial ambiguity about exactly what collaboration is.[6]

Collaboration seems to aim for a win-win situation as opposed to one in which there is a single victor or everyone loses. The winning or losing can apply to goals (of a project) or any other components or activities. As such, it is a phenomenon at work at several different levels simultaneously, and a favorite forum for promoting it is decision-making settings or group meetings. Here, most professionals attempt to effect "consensus." The "consensus," though rarely actually tested, is often ascribed to groups which produce near unanimous decisions on one or more issues. However, the main point to be made at this juncture, given the constraints of space, is that collaboration is not the strategy of choice in every instance; pros and cons can and should be articulated before it is promoted. Indeed, there are many instances where a collaborative strategy is counter-productive. Eiseman (JABS, forthcoming), drawing from Thomas, identifies five strategies (avoidance, competition, accommodation, compromise, and collaboration) and suggests they be employed selectively depending upon the favorability of "the collaborative climate." Peabody and Dietterich (1973) identify three strategies: collaboration, negotiation, and coercion, to be employed under different circumstances. Again, the primary point is that virtually all aspects of the individual situation, including explicit identification of the self-interests of relevant parties, especially the linking agent, need to be assessed before we develop collaborative skills for ourselves and our clients and work to develop conditions favorable to collaboration in our work. However, the

---

[6]Indeed, a recent search of the literature did not turn up any operational definition of the term, let alone good descriptions or analyses of it in practice.

realities in contemporary schools are simply not presently as rosy as we might wish.[7]

Phase of the Relationship with the Client System. Stressing that what is of critical importance is the awareness with which the linking agents view all aspects of their working situation, let us turn to the topic of the phases of the relationship. It is possible to look at any relationship between two people, break it into (either a few or a great many) component parts, and then array them in a chronological sequence. Awareness of where one is in one's relationship with a client will aid linking agents in determining the best move to make at a given point. The important thing is not what the particular framework is, but that it is a planful one, workable and useful for particular linking agents. Lippitt and Lippitt (1975) identify four major phases in the consultation process:

1. The phase of contact, entry, and relationship establishment.

2. The phase of contract formulation and establishment of a work relationship. (It should be noted here that contract does not necessarily imply a legal document only, but also includes the psychological contract.)

3. A phase of planning the goals and steps of problem-solving for the change effort.

4. A phase of the action-taking and continuity of effort.

Under each of these four major phases, the authors outline 14 specific "work foci" such as: Helping identify and clarify the need for change, exploring the readiness for change, planning for involvement. They discuss these in light of the advantages or disadvantages facing the inside or the outside consultant. In an earlier version (1973) of this document, the Lippitts delineated some 26 specific dilemmas and related them to 11 major phases of the relationship. These dilemmas include the power dilemma, legitimization dilemma, and entry dilemma.

---

[7]My recent case study of our experience with collaboration in The NETWORK, "An Executive Director's Struggle to Actualize His Commitment to Collaboration" reviews our frustration (JABS, forthcoming).

Havelock (1973) has described six major stages of the planned change process:

1. Building the relationship

2. Diagnosis

3. Acquiring relevant resources

4. Choosing the solution

5. Gaining acceptance

6. Stabilizing the innovation and generating self-renewal.

These stages are viewed as sequential but have permeable boundaries between them as suggested by Figure 15 on the next page.

Implementation Issues. The increasing importance being given to understanding the process of implementation was noted earlier. In part, this increased attention is due to the realization that often the innovation which is reported to be in place is not, upon inspection, being implemented. (Goodlad, 1975; Gross et al., 1971; Hall and Loucks, 1975). A related difficulty, not addressed here, lies in specifying exactly what the core components of the innovation are so that upon observation one knows what one should be seeing. Fullan (1975), in a useful paper commissioned by the International Management Training for Educational Change (IMTEC) Project in Europe, addressed the question of implementation as "The putting into practice of the essential characteristics of innovation." He identified four dimensions as related to determining the extent to which an innovation has been implemented:

1. The structure

2. The role and/or behavior of participants

3. Knowledge and understanding as related to the innovation

4. Value internalized

FIGURE 15
PHASES OF THE RELATIONSHIP

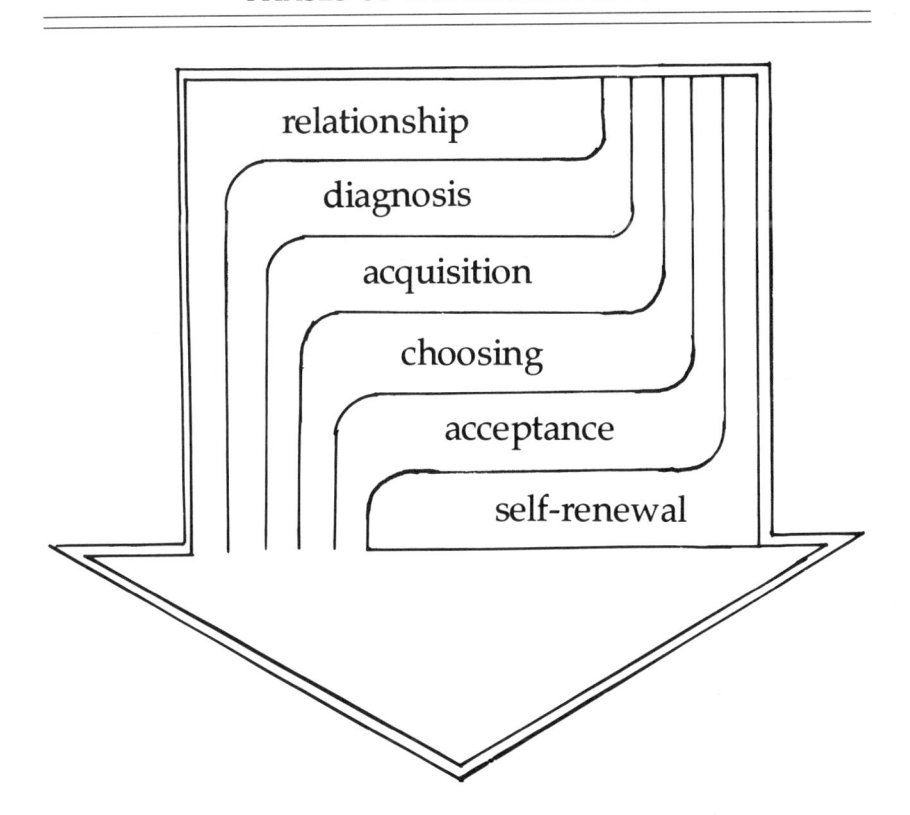

- relationship
- diagnosis
- acquisition
- choosing
- acceptance
- self-renewal

Reprinted by permission of the publisher from R. Havelock, The Change Agent's Guide to Innovation in Education. Englewood Cliffs, New Jersey: Educational Technology Publications, Inc., 1973, cover. © 1973 by Educational Technology Publications, Inc.

He notes that the first two dimensions are directly observable, while the second two require drawing inferences from observation or interrogation. Fullan makes the point that much attention to date has been on studying outcomes. These studies attempt to ascertain by observation or questioning whether the innovation, which is rarely defined fully in terms of the four dimensions noted above, can be said to be in place. What is not typically studied is the implementation process, leading up to or contributing to the attainment of the outcome.

Ten factors are important to implementation, according to Fullan and Pomfret. Worthy of special emphasis is the desirability of establishing mechanisms to

> co-define the nature of the innovation in practice, continuing in-service training during initial implementation, providing resource support during implementation as well as in the predecisional phase, establishing feedback mechanisms to allay anxiety and address power relationships between the givers and receivers of feedback, the importance of developing a capacity to use "the innovation," utilizing alternative evaluation approaches so that data facilitates implementation and involves clients in the process. (Fullan and Pomfret, 1975)

Also noted, and related to a recent study by Pincus (1974), is the matter of providing incentives. While Pincus has spoken to the need to provide incentives for school districts to do what they don't want to do, Gross (1971) as well as Fullan focus on creating explicit payoffs for teachers and adopters so that they will be motivated to go beyond a superficial or routine adoption (see Hall et al., 1975).

These issues, of course, will be of primary concern to linking agents who concentrate on later phases of program improvement efforts. But anyone entering the school setting should at least be cognizant of these issues to avoid being tripped up by fantasies about the rationality and realities of schools as innovating units.

WHERE DO WE GO FROM HERE?

In this chapter, I have attempted to present a relatively complete overview of the issues which, in my opinion, need to be considered in developing training programs and support mechanisms for an anticipated crop of linking agents. For some this paper will suffice; for others, concerned with the collection of materials and design of experiences related to creating new knowledge for themselves or for linking agents, attention should be focused on developing educational experiences based on any one of the subsystems discussed earlier.

For those concerned with recruiting and selecting linking agents, attention should be focused first on developing a tailored set of prerequisite attributes. These can then be related to selected technical skill clusters, chosen for their relevance to particular linking agent roles, e.g., those described previously or combinations thereof. For those concerned with skill development itself, attention should be directed to acquiring a thorough grasp of the available resources for those skill clusters that are pertinent to the given situation and designing training programs which build upon them. Individuals exist, who can themselves be categorized in one of the ten roles described and who can assist in any one or more of these ways. In all cases, purposeful efforts must be mounted to develop a support system for linking agents and to sustain it.

In this chapter, I have attempted to argue that our best opportunity lies in establishing a pragmatic, eclectic, and flexible framework which maximizes the adaptation of existing resources and induces tolerance for a range of suitable solutions to the problem of training and supporting linking agents. What we need are great groups of generalists who specialize in Resource Utilization, and among the critical resources which they must know how to utilize are blends of other technical skills drawn on as appropriate in given client situations. At a minimum, it is necessary to know what one does not know, and at the maximum, to begin working for oneself and others in order to expand one's repertoires of knowledge and of skill. So one who wishes to become the *complete linking agent* develops a plan to acquire a broad array of understandings and skills, including:

- A sense of history about the field of dissemination and educational program improvement.

- Knowledge of past, current, and emerging federal and state programs concerned with these topics.

- Knowledge of the literature of planned change, behavioral science, and curriculum theory.

- Knowledge of and access to sources of programs, products and information.

- Understanding of the quality control issues, ethical issues, and value issues inherent in such work.

- Understanding the many facets of an innovation as perceived by potential clients.

- Awareness of oneself as an innovation.

- Developing and using a systematic view of the client system.

- Developing and refining a knowledge of organizational dynamics, especially those peculiar to schools.

- Developing an understanding of, and skills in managing, the "mutual adaptation" process.

- Developing skills in diagnosing various aspects of organizations.

- Developing means of assessing and promoting the growth of the clients with whom they work.

- Fostering the development of a collaborative climate within which to work and be housed.

- Employing data collection and feedback procedures to guide an effort and to elevate the level of discourse.

- Developing a consciousness as to the presence and relevance of various personal and intrapersonal attributes of oneself and others.

- Developing mechanisms for clarifying, negotiating, and renegotiating one's own role(s).

- Securing and refining a range of technical skills appropriate to one's role.

- Developing and effectively using a range of formal and informal support mechanisms.

- STAYING ALIVE!

Clearly the arena is sufficiently large that it is impossible to describe one single solution. The means presently exist whereby those interested can move to action with somewhat greater clarity as to where they are headed. Leadership is needed to mobilize the available resources to take the next steps.

We may be on the verge of achieving a major breakthrough in the area of educational program improvement. From my vantage point, the true measure and significance of our efforts now will be determined by the extent to which we build on the best of the past. We must continue to work toward the ambitious goal of substantially improving the educational enterprise. Where there are surely places for linking agents of all sorts, I hold that we have an obligation to work toward a future where linking agents will be capable of:

> Interacting with client systems and their key members in ways that lead to
>
> Identifying/specifying high priority problems collaboratively, the solutions to which call for
>
> Mobilizing internal or external resources (people, programs, information, etc.) which are brought to bear on the problems by
>
> Implementing a collaboratively developed plan which takes into account
>
> 1. the history and current context of the organization
> 2. the interests of those affected by the change, even when unarticulated
> 3. the need for adequate documentation so that others may learn from the experience.
>
> Challenging the client system to reflect upon its experiences in such ways as are likely to endure a long-term problem-solving capacity.

With good fortune and concentrated efforts, we can create such a future. How to do so is a problem more complex than many, but every bit as solvable.

REFERENCES

Arends, R. *Assumptions about Linkers and Sets of Skills to be Considered Essential for Linkers To Be Effective on a Sustained Basis.* Portland: Northwest Regional Educational Laboratory, mimeographed, 1976.

Argyris, C. *Integrating the Individual and the Organization.* New York: Wiley, 1964.

Argyris, C. In Cooper, C. *Theories of Group Process.* New York: Wiley, 1975.

Argyris, C. *Increasing Leadership Effectiveness.* New York: Wiley, 1976(a).

Argyris, C. Theories of Action that Inhibit Individual Learning. *American Psychologist,* 1976, 31, (9), 638-654, (b).

Argyris, C. Leadership, Learning, and Changing the Status Quo. *Organizational Dynamics,* Winter 1976, 4 (3), 29-60, (c).

Argyris, C., & Schon, D. *Theory in Practice: Increasing Professional Effectiveness.* San Francisco: Jossey-Bass, 1974.

Baldridge, J. Deal, T., Ancell, M. (eds). *Managing Change in Educational Organizations.* Berkeley: McCutchan, 1975.

Barnes, F. *National Educateur Program: A proposal submitted for consideration to the U.S. Dept. of Justice.* New Canaan, N. Y.: Berkshire Farm Institute for Training and Research, 1975.

Bass, B. A Systems Survey Research Feedback for Management and Organizational Development. *Journal of Applied Behavioral Science,* April, May, June 1976, 12, (2), 215-229.

Benne, K., Bradford, L., Gibb, J., & Lippitt, R. (Eds.). *The Laboratory Method of Changing and Learning: Theory and Application.* Santa Clara: Science and Behavior, 1975.

Bennis, W., Benne, K., & Chin, R. (Eds.) *The Planning of Change* (1st ed.). New York: Holt Rinehart Winston, 1961.

Bennis, W., Benne, K., Chin, R. *The Planning of Change* (2nd ed). New York: Holt Rinehart Winston, 1969.

Bennis, W., Benne, K., Chin, R & Corey, K. *The Planning of Change, (3rd ed.).* New York: Holt Rinehart Winston, 1976.

Bentzen, M., et al. *Changing Schools: The Magic Feather Principle.* New York: McGraw Hill, 1974.

Berman, P., & McLaughlin, M. Federal Programs Supporting Educational Change. *Rand Change Agent Series.* Santa Monica, California: Rand Corporation, 1974.

Bowers, D. OD Techniques and Their Results in 23 Organizations: The Michigan ICL Study. *Journal of Applied Behavioral Science,* 1973, 9, (1), 21-42.

Cartwright, D., & Zander, A. (Eds.). *Group Dynamics.* New York: Harper Row, 1968.

Coleman, J. Conflicting Theories of Social Change. *American Behavioral Scientist,* May 1971, *14,* (5), 633-650.

Corwin, R. Models of Educational Organizations. In *Review of Research in Education, Vol. 2.* Itasca, Illinois: Peacock, 1974.

Crandall, D. An Executive Director's Struggle To Actualize His Commitment to Collaboration. Accepted manuscript to appear in *Journal of Applied Behavioral Science,* Spring 1977.

Crandall, D., et al. *Solving Today's Problems – Coping With Tomorrow's World: Developing New Approaches to Occupational Competence.* Merrimac, Massachusetts: Network of Innovative Schools, mimeographed, 1974.

Crandall, D., & Eiseman, J. *Criteria for the Selection of Linking Agents.* Merrimac, Massachusetts: The Network of Innovative Schools, mimeographed, 1971.

Dissemination Analysis Group. *Report of the Dissemination Analysis Group to the Dissemination Policy Council.* Washington, D.C.: HEW, Office of the Assistant Secretary of Education, 1976.

Educational Labs & R&D Centers for the National Institute of Education. *Educational Dissemination and Linking Agent Sourcebook.* San Francisco: Far West Lab, 1976.

Eiseman, J. *My Professional Focus.* Amherst, Massachusetts: Univ. of Mass., mimeographed, 1974.

Eiseman, J. A Third Party Consultation Model for Resolving Recurring Conflicts Collaboratively. Accepted manuscript to appear in *Journal of Applied Behavioral Science,* Spring 1977.

Engel, J., Wales, H., & Warshaw, M. *Promotional Strategy* (3rd ed.). Homewood, Illinois: Irwin, 1975.

Ewing, D. *Writing For Results: In Business, Government and the Professions.* New York: Wiley & Sons, 1974.

Fairweather, G. *Social Change: The Challenge to Survival.* Morristown, N. J.: General Learning Press, 1972.

Farr, R. Knowledge Linkers and the Flow of Educational Information. In Far West Lab, *The Educational Information Consultant: Skills in Disseminating Educational Information Training Manual.* Berkeley: Far West Lab, 1971.

Far West Labs. *Educational Programs That Work.* San Francisco: Far West Labs, 1976.

Far West Labs. *Technical writing: Informal Documents in Series 3, Section 3.3 A Training Program in Educational Development Dissemination, and Evaluation.* Berkeley: Far West Labs, 1974.

Far West Labs. *Technical Writing: Formal Documents in Series 3, Section 3.4 A Training Program in Educational Development Dissemination, and Evaluation.* Berkeley: Far West Labs, 1974.

Far West Labs. *A Training Program in Educational Development, Dissemination, and Evaluation.* Berkeley: Far West Labs, 1972.

Fox, R., Schmuck, R., Van Egmond, E., Ritvo, M. & Jung, C. *Diagnosing the Professional Climate of Schools*. Fairfax, Virginia: NTL Learning Resources Corp., 1973.

Fullan, M. Overview of the Innovative Process and the User. *Interchange*, 1972, 3, (2-3), 1-46.

Fullan, M. *IMTEC: Implementation: Its Nature and Determinants*. Oslo: Decentralised Project No. 4, (Special activity), International Management Training for Educational Change (IMTEC), 1975.

Fullan, M., & Pomfret, A. *Review of Research on Curriculum Implementation*. Washington: NIE Career Education Program, 1975.

Giacquinta, J. The Process of Organizational Change in Schools. In F. Kerlinger, (Ed.), *Review of Research in Education*, vol. 1. Itasca, Illinois.: Peacock, 1973.

Giacquinta, J. Status Risk-Taking: A Central Issue in the Initiation and Implementation of Public School Innovations. *Journal of Research and Development in Education*. 1975, 9, (1), 102-114.

Glaser, E., & Taylor, S. Factors Influencing the Success of Applied Research. *American Psychologist*, Feb. 1973, 140-146.

Goodlad, J. *School, Curriculum, and the Individual*. Waltham, Massachusetts: Blaisdell, 1966.

Goodlad, J. Institute for Development of Educational Activities *(I/D/E/A) Series on Educational Change:* 6 Volumes. New York: McGraw Hill, 1975.

Goodlad, J. *The Dynamics of Educational Change*. Part of I/D/E/A series. New York: McGraw Hill, 1975.

Greenfield, T. Organizations as Social Inventions: Rethinking Assumptions About Change. *Journal of Religion and Health*. 1973, 9, (5), 551-574.

Greenfield, T. Theory in the Study of Organizations and Administrative Structures. Presented at *Annual Meeting of the International Intervisitation Programme on Educational Administration* (3rd). Bristol, England: July, 1974.

Gross, N. et al. *Implementing Organizational Innovations*. New York: Basic Books, 1971.

Hall, G., Loucks, S, Rutherford, W., & Newlove, B. *Operational Definitions of the Levels of Use of the Innovation (LOU) Chart*. Austin, Texas: Teachers Education Center, Univ. of Texas, 1975.

Hall, G., Loucks, S. *A Developmental Model for Determining Whether or Not the Treatment Really is Implemented*. Austin, Texas: Research and Development Center for Teacher Education, Univ. of Texas, 1976.

Handy, C. *Understanding Organizations*. Harmondsworth, England: Penguin, 1976.

Harrison, R. Role Negotiation: A tough-minded Approach to Team Development. In Burke, W., & Hornstein, H. (Eds.), *The Social Technology of Organizational Development*. La Jolla: University Associates, 1972.

Havelock, R. *The Change Agent's Guide to Innovation in Education*. Englewood Cliffs, N.J.: Educ. Tech., 1973.

Havelock, R. *A Workbook of Checklists to Accompany A Guide to Innovation.* (ERIC Document Reproduction Service No. ED 056-256).

Havelock, R., & Guskin, A., et al. *Planning for Innovation.* Ann Arbor, Michigan: Center for Research on Utilization of Scientific Knowledge, Institute for Social Research, 1969.

Havelock, R., & Havelock, M. *Training for Change Agents.* Ann Arbor, Michigan: Center for Research on Utilization of Scientific Knowledge, 1973.

Hersey, P., & Blanchard, K. *Management of Organizational Behavior: Utilizing Human Resources,* (2nd ed.). Englewood Cliffs, N.J.: Prentice Hall, 1972.

Jackson, P. *Life in Classrooms.* New York, Wiley, 1968.

Kauffman, R. *Identifying and Solving Problems: A System Approach.* La Jolla, California: Univ. Assoc., 1976.

Jung, C., Pino, R., & Emory, R. *Research Utilization Problem Solving,* (RUPS). Portland, Oregon: Northwest Regional Educational Labs, 1970.

Koberg, D., & Bagnall, J. *The Universal Traveler.* Los Altos, California: William Kaufman, 1972.

Kotler, P. *Marketing for Nonprofit Organizations.* Englewood Cliffs, N.J.: Prentice-Hall, 1975.

Lake, D., & Miles, M. *Measuring Human Behavior.* New York: Teachers College Press, Columbia Univ., 1973.

Likert, R. Systems 1-4 Framework. In Likert, R. *New Ways of Managing Conflict.* New York: McGraw Hill, 1976. 20-34.

Lippitt, R. Linkage Problems and Process in Laboratory Education. In Benne, et al., (Eds.), *The Laboratory Method of Changing and Learning.* Palo Alto, California: Science and Behavior, 1975.

Lippitt, G. *Visualizing Change.* La Jolla, California: University Assoc., 1973.

Lippitt, R., & Lippitt, G. *Consulting Process in Action.* Washington, D.C.: Development, 1975.

Lippitt, R., Watson, J., & Westley, B. *The Dynamics of Planned Change.* New York: Harcourt, Brace and World, 1958.

Lortie, D. *School Teacher.* Chicago: Univ. of Chicago, 1975.

Mick, C., Paisley, M., & Paisley, W. *Developing Training Materials for Educational Extension Services Personnel.* Stanford, California: Stanford University & Systems Development Corp., 1973.

Miles, M. (Ed.). *Innovations in Education.* New York: Teachers College Press, Columbia Univ., 1964.

Miles, M. Planned Change and Organizational Health: Figure and Ground. In J. Baldridge, & T. Deal, et al., (Eds.)., *Managing Change in Educational Organizations.* Berkeley: McCutchan, 1975.

National Institute of Education. *A Dissemination Special Relationship Request for Proposal (RFP) to Establish an "R&D Dissemination and Feedforward System: A Consortium of R&D Producers Disseminating and Gathering Consumer Oriented Information About R&D Products and Outcomes."* Washington, D.C.: National Institute of Education, 1976.

National Institute of Education. *Catalog of NIE Educational Products,* 2 vols. Washington, D.C.: U.S. Government Printing Office, 1975.

National Institute of Mental Health. *Planning for Creative Change in Mental Health Services: A Manual on Research Utilization.* Washington, D.C.: U.S. Government Printing Office (DHEW No. HSM 71-9059), 1971.

National Society for the Study of Education (NSSE). *Educational Evaluation: New Roles, New Means.* R. Tyler (Ed.), Chicago: Univ. of Chicago, 1969.

National Society for the Study of Education (NSSE). *Behavioral Science and Educational Administration.* D. Griffiths (Ed.), Chicago: Univ. of Chicago, 1964.

National Special Media Institute. Selecting Instructional Strategies and Media. Part of *Instructional Development Institute Series.* Washington: National Special Media Institute, 1972.

National Training Laboratories. *Problem Solving* Bethel, Maine: National Training Laboratories.

Network of Innovative Schools. *Organizational Needs Inventory.* Merrimac, Massachusetts: The NETWORK, mimeographed, 1973.

Northeast/Mid-Atlantic PIP Diffusion Project. *Project Information Packages: Overview.* Merrimac, Massachusetts: The NETWORK, 1976.

Office of Strategic Services, *Assessment of Men: Selection of Personnel for the Office of Strategic Services* (reprint of 1948 edition). New York, N.Y.: Johnson Reprint Corporation, 1969.

Owens, R. *Organizational Behavior in Schools.* Englewood Cliffs, N.J.: Prentice Hall, 1970.

Pareek, U. Interrole Exploration. in J. Pfeiffer and J. Jones (Eds.), *The 1976 Handbook for Group Facilitators.* La Jolla, California: University Associates, 1976.

Peabody, G., & Dietterich, P. *Powerplay, a Simulation Dealing with Collaboration, Negotiation, and Coercion.* Naperville, Illinois: Powerplay, Inc., 1973.

Pfeiffer, J., & Jones, J. *Annual Handbooks for Group Facilitators,* 6 volumes. La Jolla, California: University Associates, 1971-1976.

Pfeiffer, J., & Jones, J. *A Handbook of Structured Experiences for Human Relations Training,* 7 volumes. La Jolla, California: University Associates, 1969, 1974.

Pfeiffer, J., Heslin, R., & Jones, J. *Instrumentation in Human Relations Training.* La Jolla, California: University Associates, 1973, 1976.

Piele, P. *Review and Analysis of the Role, Activities, and Training of Educational Linking Agents.* Final Report. Eugene, Oregon: ERIC Clearinghouse on Educational Management, 1975. (Ed. 128871)

Pincus, J. Incentives for Innovations in the Public Schools. *Review of Educational Research,* 1974, 44, (1), 114-138.

Pondy, L. Beyond Open System Models of Organization. Presented at *Annual Meeting of the Academy of Management*. Kansas City, Missouri: August 12, 1976. (a)

Pondy, L. Leadership as a Language Game. In M. McCall, and M. Lombardo, (Eds.), *Leadership, Where Else Can We Go?* Durham, N.C.: Duke University Press, 1976. (b).

Rogers, E. *Diffusion of Innovations*. New York: Free Press, 1962.

Rogers, E. M. & Shoemaker, F. F. *Communication of Innovations: A Cross-Cultural Approach*. New York: Free Press, 1971.

Runkel, P. & Schmuck, R. *Findings From the Research and Development Program on Strategies of Organizational Change at CEPM-CASEA*. Eugene: U Oregon, 1974.

Runkel, P., et al. *Strategies of Organizational Change Program, Bibliography on Organizational Change in Schools*. Eugene, Oregon: Center for Educational Policy and Management, 1974.

Sarason, S. B. *The Culture of the School and the Problem of Change*. Boston: Allyn Bacon, 1971.

Schalock, H., Thomas, G., Morse, K., Smith, C. & Ammerman, H. *The Oregon Studies in Educational Research, Development, Diffusion, and Evaluation*. Monmouth, Oregon: Teaching Research, 1972. Vol. I-V.

Schindler-Rainman, E. & Lippitt, R. Designing for Participative Learning and Changing. In Benne, et al., (Eds.), *The Laboratory Method of Changing and Learning*. Palo Alto: Science and Behavior Books, 1975.

CEPM: Schmuck, R. *Situation-Target-Path*. Eugene: Center for Educational Policy Management.

Schmuck, R. A., Runkel, P. J., Saturen, S. L., Martell, R. T. & Derr, C. B. *Handbook of Organizational Development in Schools*. Palo Alto: Mayfield, 1972.

Schmuck, R. & Miles, M. *Organization Development in Schools*. Palo Alto: National Press, 1971.

Sherwood, J. J. & Glidewell, J. C. *Planned Renegotiation: A Norm-Setting OD Intervention*. Lafayette: Purdue University, Institute for Research in the Behavioral, Economic, and Management Sciences, 1971.

Shepherd, H. Rules of Thumb for Change Agents. *The Staff Specialist as an Internal Consultant*. Washington, D.C.: Organization Renewal, Inc., 1973.

Smith, L. M. & Keith, P. M. *Anatomy of Educational Innovation: An Organizational Analysis of an Elementary School*. New York: Wiley, 1971.

Sieber, S. Organizational Influences on Innovative Roles. In J. V. Baldridge and T. Deal (Eds.), *Managing Change in Educational Organizations*. Berkeley: McCutchan, 1975. (article first appeared in 1968.)

Sieber, S., Seashore, K., & Metzger, L. *The Use of Educational Knowledge: Evaluation of the Pilot State Dissemination Program*. New York: Bureau of Applied Social Research, Columbia University, 1972.

Sieber, S. Toward a Theory of Role Accumulation. *American Sociological Review,* 1974(a) 39 (August): 567-78. A-621 of Bureau of Applied Social Research, Columbia University.

Sikorski, L. A. & Hutchins, C. L. *A Study of the Feasibility of Marketing Programming for Educational R&D Products*. San Francisco: Far West Labs, 1974.

Toffler, A. *Future Shock*. New York: Random House, 1970.

Turnbull, B. et al. *Exemplary Practice: A Report on Recent Searches*. Office of Dissemination and Resources, NIE, 1975.

Tyler, R. W. *Basic Principles of Curriculum and Instruction*. Chicago: Univ. of Chicago, 1969.

U.S. Office of CEPM: For Education, National Advisory Council on Supplementary Centers and Services National Association of State Advisory Council Chairmen, State Department of Education. Sharing Educational Success. mimeographed. USOE.

USOE. A Practical Guide to Measuring Project Impact on Student Achievement. Number 1 in a series of *Monographs on Evaluation in Education*. No. 1780-01460. Washington: U.S. Government Printing Office.

United States Office of Education. A Practical Guide to Measuring Project Impact on Student Achievement. Number 2 in a series of *Monographs on Evaluation in Education*. No. 017-080-01516. Washington: U.S. Government Printing Office.

Waller, W. *The Socioloy of Teaching*. New York: John Wiley and Sons, 1932.

Woodbury, M. *A Guide to Sources of Educational Information*. Washington, D.C.: Information Resources Press, 1976.

Zaltman, G., Duncan, R. & Holbek, J. *Innovations and Organizations*. New York: Wiley & Sons, 1973.

6

A Nationwide Training System for Linking Agents in Education

Jack Culbertson

> *The time is 1985. The place is Washington, D.C. The occasion is the conclusion of a conference on linking agent training and support for training. Leaders from a dozen nations attended the conference which examined the origins, development, structure and functioning of a nationwide training and support system for linking agents in the United States. Papers on the origins and development of the nationwide system during the 1965-85 period have been discussed, as have descriptions and analyses of the operational and organizational aspects of the nationwide system. Dr. Julia Courtney, the final speaker, has reached the podium and is ready to summarize the major findings and conclusions of the conference. The paper which follows represents an edited version of Dr. Courtney's presentation.*

The evidence presented at this conference shows that progress during the 1965-85 period in achieving a nationwide system for training linkers has been made; however, the system has emerged very slowly, is not yet complete, and is still evolving. In documenting these conclusions and in summarizing major conference findings, I shall organize my remarks around the following topics: The concept of the linking agent; the forces affecting linking agents and linking agencies; the structure and functions of the nationwide training system; and the structure and functions of the system to support training.

THE LINKING AGENT CONCEPT

Various writers shaped and transmitted the linking agent concept to the educational community in the 1960s and the early 1970s. Havelock's synthesis of pertinent concepts and findings had a major impact on those interested in educational change.[1] Sieber's pioneering documentary study in the early 1970s was also influential in helping leaders see the significance of linking concepts within the context of state dissemination programs (1972). Within several years, many scholars had accepted the linking agent concept (and refinements of it) and saw in it potential for advancing as well as shedding light on what was called "educational innovation" in the 1960s and "educational improvement" in the 1970s.

In the late 1960s and early 1970s, the linker tended to be defined in general terms as, for example, one who helps others engaged in educational improvement by connecting them with needed human and knowledge-based resources. Through the 1970s and into the 1980s, the concept became much more complex: Different types of linkers were postulated, various kinds of linking agencies were identified, and differing systems toward which linking agents could direct their efforts were defined. In fact, the key development during the 1965-85 period with regard to the concept of linking was its increased differentiation to encompass differing classes of linkers and a broad range of specialized functions.

External and Internal Linkers

During the late sixties and first part of the seventies, the distinction between internal and external linkers was clearly drawn. While both types of linkers pursued the same general goal of educational improvement, their bases of operation varied. Internal linkers resided within school systems, while external linkers worked from agencies outside these systems as, for example, intermediate service agencies and educational laboratories.

Most of the attention of scholars in the first half of the seventies was directed at defining the unique features of the external linker. The margi-

---

[1] For the most comprehensive synthesis see Ronald Havelock, *Planning for Innovation through Dissemination and Utilization of Knowledge*. Ann Arbor, Michigan: Center for Research on Utilization of Scientific Knowledge, 1974.

nality of the linking role, for example, was one of the features highlighted. It was argued that the effective external linker could bring to school systems an objectivity and a detachment which members of these systems could not display. Because external linkers were marginal, they were not seen as vested in situations in the same way others in the situation were. In contrast to internal linkers, the thinking and action of external linking agents could be less constrained or, at least, constrained differently. As a result, these agents had a special capacity to identify and help others identify potential for educational improvement and, in turn, the resources needed to realize potential.

While unique capacities were ascribed to external agents, there was also the view that the role was an extremely demanding one fraught with ambiguity, susceptible to conflicting expectations, and highly vulnerable to overload. Paradoxically, the relative objectivity associated with the role carried with it a lack of intimate knowledge of the organizations to which links were made. In addition, the linkers, in order to preserve the "external" role had to forego belongingness and to confront related emotional demands. Another special demand on external linkers stemmed from the great need for a base of both broad knowledge and skill. Because these agents used knowledge based products and services as the key instruments of improvement, they were pressed to acquire much information from many sources for application in a wide variety of contexts.

As the seventies unfolded, more and more attention was given to the concept of the "internal" linker. Studies conducted by James Becker, Gerald Marker, Carole Hahn, Ernest House, Richard Schmuck, Philip Runkel, and other scholars and leaders highlighted the significance of the internal linker role in improvement activities. Becker and Hahn, for example, in 1975 made the case for the "internal" linker as follows:

> Change agents are more likely to be helpful when they are a part of the system they are seeking to change. Understanding of particular situations and of specific needs of others in the system increases the likelihood that change agents will succeed. Being on hand to provide advice and support for teachers as they seek to implement an innovation also increases the likelihood of success.

The view that principals were in a highly strategic position to encourage and influence change through an internal linking role at the school level was documented in a range of studies. Highlighted in the studies were the legitimizing and gatekeeping roles of principals in change efforts.[2] Systematic literature reviews such as that conducted by Garth Jones (1969) bolstered such conclusions that the inside agent was somewhat more effective than the outside agent in bringing about change.

As the seventies ended and the eighties began, writers were giving more systematic attention to the concept of internal and external linking agents as *partners* in improvement. As the complementary capacities of the two linker types were recognized, advantages of joint endeavors became clearer. Linkers external to school systems, for example, brought both general commitment and a wide range of information resources to improvement activities; linkers inside school systems brought commitment to specific improvements and an intimate understanding of the change variables in schools and the communities in which the schools were embedded. While the external linker's power derived more from a specialized knowledge base than from organizational position, the internal linker, had the advantage of special or earned position in the organization to be changed. "External" linkers drew upon a wide range of knowledge-based products and services; the "internal" linkers had available a wide range of tacit or clinical knowledge related to educational improvement. Given an outside base and the need to perform a facilitative role, the external agent had a more limited capacity for advocating specific problems to be addressed or changes to be initiated. On the other hand, because of a base of established or emergent policy in the organization served and the growing availability of data from local needs assessment efforts, the internal linking agent had a greater capacity for advocacy of this type. In the late seventies and eighties, then, a growing number of improvement efforts which involved teaming efforts and which capitalized in more systematic ways upon the differing skills and capacities of internal and external linking agents were begun.

Subsystems to be Improved

In the sixties and most of the seventies, the sub-systems in school districts toward which linkers could direct their efforts had not been explicitly defined. However, in the early 1980s, educational improvement activities began to be defined more widely and more frequently in terms of activities in three sub-systems: those directed at improving teaching and learning systems in which principals, teachers, and teacher association leaders were key actors; those focused upon improving management

---

[2]See, for example, Paul Berman, Milbrey McLaughlin and others, *Federal Programs Supporting Educational Change*. Vol. I-V. Santa Monica: The Rand Corporation, 1975.

and leadership systems supportive of teaching and learning in which principals, superintendents, and other educational leaders played a role; and those directed at policy decisions designed to bring about educational improvement in which school board members, superintendents, directors of educational planning and other school and community leaders were central participants.

By 1985, internal and external linking agents were choosing to specialize in the sub-system activities much more frequently than in the 1970s. Thus, more clear cut sub-system emphases tended to increase the effectiveness of both internal and external linkers by making it easier to organize needs assessment information inventories of training materials, human resource banks, and other kinds of linker support in more efficient ways and in ways which served given classes of specialists more effectively.

Schema I summarizes information on linker specializations within the context of the three sub-systems noted above. It is worth emphasizing that the types listed in Schema I qualified as linkers only if they met all three of the following criteria: They were engaged in educational improvement activities, they used knowledge (e.g., ideas or products) as instruments of improvements, and they acquired knowledge from organizations external to school systems for use if they were internal linkers or provided knowledge to school system leaders if they were external linkers.

As linkers developed sub-system specializations and sought improvements from internal or external bases, their roles became more differentiated and more complex. Very few linkers, for example, could engage in activities designed to improve the many functions performed in the sub-systems of teaching-learning, management-leadership, and policy-making. In fact, linkers specializing in the improvement of only one sub-system often tended to concentrate upon selected, rather than all of, the pertinent functions.

The trend toward specialization contributed to the growth of linking agencies which housed personnel performing a variety of linkage functions. Stated differently, the practice of individuals performing varied linking functions on an independent and entrepreneurial basis — a pattern which dominated the 1960s and early 1970s — began to diminish slowly in the latter part of the seventies. In the eighties the number of linking agencies staffed by full-time specialists slowly increased. Schema II summarizes some of the developments leading to greater differentiation in linking agent roles and encouraging establishment of linking agencies staffed by specialists.

SCHEMA I
CLASSIFICATION OF LINKERS IN THE 1980s

	School District Sub-Systems to be Improved by Linkers		
	Teaching-Learning	Management-Leadership	Policy-Making
Types and Illustrations of Linkers	Internal Linkers (a) Teacher association leaders (b) Principals External Linkers (a) Trainer from an intermediate service agency (b) Developer of training materials from an educational laboratory	Internal Linkers (a) Principals (b) Directors of staff development External Linkers (a) Educational Laboratory specialist in linker strategies (b) Professor specializing in management strategies	Internal Linkers (a) Superintendents (b) Directors of research and planning External Linkers (a) Policy analyst from a university (b) Developer from an R and D center

SCHEMA II
DEVELOPMENTS LEADING TO GREATER DIFFERENTIATION IN LINKING AGENT ROLES:

1965 →	1970 →	1975 →	1980 →	1985
More attention given to the external linker role	External linker role studied by Sieber and others	More systematic efforts to define unique functions of external linker role	More systematic efforts to define unique functions of external linker role	Such specialized external linking functions as organizational entry, problem defining, information processing product diffusion and training highlighted
Limited attention given to internal linker role	Internal linker concept received growing attention	More systematic efforts to define unique functions of internal linker role	More systematic efforts to define unique functions of internal linker role	Such specialized internal linking functions as gatekeeping, legitimation, knowledge acquisition, training, and implementation highlighted
General concepts of linker publicized by Havelock and others	Some examination of relationships between internal and external linking concepts achieved	Some clarification of the complementary of internal and external linker roles		Internal and external linker partnerships defined and operationalized
Individuals tended to perform linkage agent roles on an entrepreneurial basis	Growth in the complexity of linking agent roles made it more difficult for all of the functions to be performed by given individuals	Growing emphasis placed upon linking agencies		The number of linking agencies staffed by linking specialists increased
Linking concepts applied to improvement efforts in undifferentiated ways	Differences in the sub-systems of teaching-learning, management-leadership, and policy-making and the implications for linking more clearly recognized	Linkers chose more frequently to specialize in linking vis-à-vis one sub-system (i.e., teaching, management, or policy-making)		**Training materials, exemplary practice, resource banks and other support products classified for use in teaching-learning, policy-making and management-leadership sub-systems**

FORCES AFFECTING LINKING AGENTS AND LINKING AGENCIES

Forces of Decline

During the 1965-85 period, the practice of linking agents and agencies was influenced by a variety of forces, only a few of which can be treated here. Perhaps, the most influential force promoting linking agentry was the shift from a long period of rapid enrollment growth and resource expansion in the late 1960s to a period of decline in the 1970s and 80s. The number of schools, for example, increased by more than 50 per cent in the 1960s. However, by 1985 thousands of schools present in 1970 had been closed. Educational leaders in the seventies and eighties had to deal with a new phenomenon in American education, the management of decline. Scholars such as Kenneth Boulding (1975) emphasized that the risks associated with decision making in a contracting environment were considerably greater than the risks in an expanding one. Further, in an environment of decline, it is much more difficult to correct for decision errors because of resource constraints.

The diminishing resource and client base caused policy makers and administrators to look at educational organizations and their improvement in new ways and to search for a wider range of viable responses to critical decision situations. Greater attention was given to planning, and the resulting search for alternatives caused educational leaders to link more frequently with individuals and information sources beyond their own educational institutions and, in turn, to place greater emphasis upon the internal linking role in improvement efforts. The external linking agent became more important to school systems, and opportunities for encouraging cooperation between internal and external linkers in improvement endeavors increased.

As the environment of decline became more pervasive in school districts, the attainment of organizational renewal through new positions and facilities and through personnel mobility was no longer feasible. Because the capacities of educational institutions to add new and younger personnel were limited, the staffs of school systems became smaller, older, and less mobile.

Many educational leaders recognized this problem and began a search for alternative modes of organizational renewal. A widely adopted strategy for renewal was the provision of increased staff development for school leaders already on the job. Consequently, many school systems in the seventies employed directors of staff development and gave them responsibility for promoting organizational renewal through the continuing learning of personnel — learning that was intended to cause educational improvement. Again, this strategy caused leaders in school systems to look outside for pertinent materials, ideas, and information and for personnel who could provide assistance in the design and/or implementation of staff development programs. External linkers proved to be a very important source of assistance to staff development directors who turned to them for help.

Mandates and Court Decisions

Another important influence on schools and their increasing reliance on linking agents was the growing number of legislative mandates and court decisions in the 1965-85 period — mandates which required special improvement efforts on the part of educational leaders. Some of these were directed at education generally as, for example, improvement programs for reading. However, most were concerned with improving education and learning opportunities for special groups in society. For example, in the first half of the seventies, most states enacted legislation to improve education for the handicapped, and these were extended and reinforced dramatically in the latter part of the decade by the far-reaching Public Law 94-142 directed at special education. Legislation, often buttressed by court decisions, addressed such areas as women's equity, school desegregation, and education for the poor. The unprecedented number of court decisions and legislative mandates placed demands upon schools to improve education and educational opportunity. Again, school leaders were forced to reach beyond their own institutions for ideas, services and products and this condition improved the climate for those functioning as internal and external linking agents.

Diffusion and Use of Linking Concepts

Havelock's concepts of linking agents and agencies not only affected the scholarly community but also impacted upon national educational policy. Leaders in federal agencies made policy and program decisions in the seventies which were strongly influenced by linking agent concepts. These decisions had a substantial impact upon programs affecting educational regional laboratories and research and development centers and they influenced efforts to improve education in leading school systems, state education agencies, intermediate service agencies, and institutions of higher education. Since many of the programs supported and encouraged by federal agencies were shaped by linking agent concepts, they had widespread influence on programs to improve education. In addition, national leaders were influential in the seventies and eighties in expanding the products and services available to linking agents engaged in educational improvement, an expansion which further enhanced the work of linking agents.

As the decades unfolded, the beneficial aspects of the linking agent role were more clearly recognized. In a society increasingly devoted to learning, linkers, as participants in improvement activities, were acquiring new learnings constantly. These learnings required contacts with diverse individuals, organizations, and subjects. Consequently, the role carried with it a certain challenge and excitement not often found in other roles during a period of decline, and this attractive feature was increasingly recognized in the 1980s. The status of linkers was also enhanced because of the growing number of full-time linkers in education and the growing attention to the concept of linking agencies in education. The support provided for the role by all levels of educational government was another positive factor adding to the status and competence of linkers. Finally, the technical demands on linkers to master a wide and growing body of information diminished because information systems to support their work were developed, and these had increasing use. In turn, this access to systematically organized information increased the effectiveness and status of linking agents.

The forces noted above also contributed to an expansion and a strengthening of linking agencies. In the 1970s, leaders in regional labs and R & D centers gave important intellectual and functional leadership to linkage efforts and programs. A key achievement, for example, was the creation of a regional exchange system in the late 1970s which served a growing number of internal linkers and other educational practitioners. In the mid-seventies, the state capacity building programs, supported by the National Institute of Education, created substantial press among state education agencies for advancing the role and functioning of linking agents. There was a visible trend during the 1965-85 period for states, especially the larger ones, to strengthen, expand, or create intermediate service agencies and, in the process, to add positions for linking agents.[3] Smaller states appointed agents within state education agencies to work with school district personnel in improvement efforts. States also gave encouragement and support to leagues, networks, and other inter-school

---

[3] See Robert Stephens, *Regional Educational Services*, Washington, D.C.: Educational Research Service, Inc., 1976.

district arrangements concerned with the use of linking agencies to facilitate educational improvement. As already noted, many school systems placed growing emphasis upon internal linker functions and the training of linkers. All of these developments increased the number and influence of linking agents.

An Enhanced Role for Higher Education Institutions

During the 1965-75 decade, relationships between school systems and universities, characterized by tension, became even more strained. School system leaders sometimes felt they were exploited because the research efforts in which universities were involved frequently required their cooperation, while the perceived benefits to them were limited. Some leaders also believed that they could not obtain the assistance they needed from institutions of higher education in confronting the unprecedented challenges before them. Still others concluded that the institutions of higher education were not providing them the kind of trained personnel needed for the new conditions in education. The dissatisfaction resulted in a tendency on the part of some school system leaders in the early 1970s to detach themselves from leading institutions of higher education. They began to carry out their own research, to conduct their own staff development, and to consider taking on the pre-service training of teachers, a development that was not unrelated to the fact that institutions of higher education in the late fifties and sixties had prepared some very versatile and able individuals who assumed influential leadership positions in school systems in the late sixties and seventies.

As school system leaders became more deeply involved in staff development and research in the seventies, they saw complexities involved in these functions and the limitations of independent efforts more clearly. As a result, in the latter part of the seventies they had powerful reasons to seek help from those institutions of higher education whose motivation and perceived need for cooperation with school systems in an environment of decline had also increased. Significantly, states such as Colorado, Texas, and Iowa required that personnel in intermediate service agencies work with institutions of higher education (Stephens, 1977). Governmental agencies became more supportive of institutions of higher education after such individuals as Ernest Boyer and Mary Berry accepted important educational leadership posts in the Carter administration in 1977 and went on record in support of improved research in universities. In addition, as state, local, and federal leaders became more involved in linkage endeavors, the need for new ideas to deal with the challenges of educational improvement became evident. Toward the end of the decade there was an increase in funds for university research, in part because leaders recognized that no class of organizations in society was as well equipped to generate ideas as higher education institutions, and because institutions serving society generally needed a continuing flow of new ideas. As described below, universities also adapted their research and development programs, to serve the needs of internal and external linkers more directly.

Even though the number of professors of education had dropped from 34,000 in 1977 to 30,000 in 1982 (Guba and Clark, 1977), hundreds still served as effective external linkers; however, most of these linkers functioned on an individual and entrepreneurial basis. At the same time, there was an increase in the number of external linkers in higher education with such institutional bases as R & D centers, school study councils, and other units which provided opportunities for competent individuals to perform full-time linking functions.

A major constraint affecting the use of linking strategies during the 1965-85 period was the limited number of truly outstanding linking agents and agencies. The cadre of linkers possessing the motivation, skill, and knowledge to perform with excellence, in other words, was a relatively small one. The more talented linkers were not limited to any one agency but were thinly distributed among intermediate service agencies, regional laboratories, state agencies, institutions of higher education and related organizations. During the 1975-85 period, representatives of differing groups in education advocated that some of the agencies just noted should assume the major responsibility for linking functions. However, by 1985 linking agents were operating in a variety of agencies, and no one type of linking agency clearly dominated efforts to improve education through linkage.

THE STRUCTURE AND FUNCTIONS OF THE NATIONWIDE TRAINING SYSTEM

As the number of internal and external linkers increased and their functions became more specialized, the demand for training also grew. Consequently, training activities of various kinds were initiated in the sixties and were expanded in the seventies. These activities and the needs toward which they were directed inevitably led to discussions about nationally-oriented training programs for linkers. As early as 1965, a proposal was made for a federally supported and centralized agency to prepare a selected cadre of leaders skilled in educational improvement (Culbertson, 1965). A decade later, the Interstate Project on Dissemination recommended (1976) that "a plan for a nationwide system for sharing educational knowledge be developed and implemented." A sub-recommendation of the Interstate Project was that programs of in-service and pre-service training should be developed and funded, an arrangement which, among other things, would provide trainees the concepts and skills needed to use "information from research, development, and practice in decision-making and in professional development." Other organizations recognized the need for more systematic training for linkers and proposed additional arrangements to meet training needs as, for example, regional consortia composed of state agencies. Various levels of educational government encouraged the systematic examination of training alternatives, and by the latter half of the 1970s, the nationwide decentralized system of training, buttressed by national support and leadership, was widely accepted as the most desirable alternative. Four assumptions provided support for this alternative:

1. Because the training needs of internal and external linking agents in the United States were highly diverse, a decentralized nationwide system of training could best capitalize upon and respond to that diversity;

2. Because a wide variety of training arrangements in education already existed in local settings, a strategy of adapting these arrangements to new uses seemed more viable than creating a totally new national system;

3. Because almost all potential trainers and linking agents worked in local or state settings across the nation, many more individuals could be trained for the same expenditures in a decentralized than in a centralized system;

4. Because more experimentation in linker agent training programs could be achieved through the use of many varied settings, the art and science of linker agent training could better be advanced in a decentralized than in a centralized approach.

Major Elements and Functions of the System

In the late seventies and early eighties, three somewhat distinct elements in the structure of the system became apparent. At the national level a number of federal agency and congressional leaders helped initiate and provided support for the nationwide training system, and their efforts were closely linked with that of leaders in state agencies and state legislatures. This element came to be called the federal-state sub-structure. A second element in the structure was responsible for the actual delivery of decentralized training. It was represented in such organizations as educational laboratories, intermediate service agencies, and institutions of higher education and was labeled the decentralized training sub-structure. The third element in the structure was interstitial in the sense that it was located between the training and the federal-state sub-structures. This element provided training for trainers and other system support; it was called the intermediary sub-structure.

The Federal-State Sub-Structure. The federal-state element in the late seventies and early eighties played an important role in bringing the nationwide system into being. Among other things, various agencies in the Department of Health, Education, and Welfare encouraged and supported early efforts to conceptualize the system, coordinated the efforts of leaders responsible for programs which supported training, supported proposals to train linkers through a variety of federal legislation directed at general objectives (women's equity, improved learning of students from backgrounds of poverty, better education for the handicapped, more effective vocational educational training and so forth), and invested in the improvement of state capacities to use knowledge and to achieve more effective linking agency endeavors. Congressional leaders contributed to the development of the system by passing pertinent legislation, by appropriating monies for a variety of federal programs requiring training, by providing special funds in the late 1970s for selected internal linkers through the "teacher center" legislation, and by passing legislation to support the training of external linkers in the early 1980s.

Leaders in the various states made substantial contributions to the emergence of the nationwide system of training, and their efforts were linked with, but not limited to, federal initiatives. In the years of the late seventies and early eighties, major leadership initiatives were unfolded in various states. In some cases, these were expressed through state education agencies and in other cases, through governors' offices and state legislatures.

In the sixties, state education agencies grew in size and strength as federal programs grew. By the seventies, the states were making effective use of federal "flow-through" monies for training. Some, by the mid-seventies, were also very effective in building their capacities for carrying out knowledge use strategies to improve education. Leadership was also expressed through the expansion and development of intermediate service agencies and through work with the state legislatures to interpret linker training needs and to acquire state and federal funds to support linkage strategies and linker training.

In the early 1980s, there were new initiatives at the highest levels of state government directed at the improvement of education. Selected governors, in cooperation with leading legislators in several mid-sized states, arrived at new designs and new resources for educational improvement. Those designs featured, among other things, educational improvement centers using linker strategies and serving differing regions within states. The centers facilitated both experimentation and training, and their design was influenced in certain ways by concepts and mechanisms drawn from knowledge-use strategies in the field of agriculture.

The Decentralized Training Sub-Structure. Since the nationwide system was a decentralized one, various agencies assumed responsibility for training. Prominent organizations engaged in training internal and/or external linkers were intermediate service agencies, institutions of higher education, educational laboratories, school systems with well organized staff development programs, and special associations concerned with linking as, for example, leagues, networks, and cooperatives made up of various school systems. Some states, particularly the smaller ones, offered training directly for linkers through state education agency personnel. However, the predominant pattern, especially in the 1980s, was for states to provide back-up support for intermediate agencies engaged in the training for linkers.

Agencies comprising the training sub-structure drew upon existing arrangements and upon training experiences gained during the 1965-75 period. The key functions performed through this sub-structure and directed at the design and delivery of training were:

1. Acquiring pertinent strategies, instruments or procedures for assessing the training needs of linkers;

2. Facilitating or conducting the assessment of the training needs of given linker populations;

3. Gathering information pertinent to the design of programs for linkers on such knowledge-based products and services as the following:

a. Training and/or learning strategies

b. Training content or processes

c. Inventories or catalogues on sources and types of pertinent training materials

d. Exemplary practices

e. Agencies or trainers with knowledge of training strategies, content materials, or processes and/or pertinent skills in training;

4. Designing training programs for linker groups

5. Implementing and managing training programs for linkers

6. Evaluating or ensuring that training programs offered were evaluated.

The Intermediary Sub-Structure. A third component in the structure of the nationwide training system, as already noted, was a class of organizations which was interstitial (i.e., linked both to the federal agencies and to units directly engaged in training).

These organizations performed important functions associated with the training of trainers and the provision of dissemination support for the training system. Illustrative organizations in this category were the Council of Chief State School Officers, the National Council for Staff Development, and the Council for Educational Development and Research. These and other organizations possessed communication channels that enabled them to reach linkers and linking agencies within their membership. The Council of Chief State School Officers, for example, in the late seventies provided training for selected linkers from various states across the nation. To take another example, the American Association of School Administrators in the late seventies established a special division of intermediate service agencies which provided dissemination and other support for linkers in these agencies. Schema III illustrates and summarizes the three structural elements of the system along with the major functions performed. An examination of the schema will likely make clear why those who subscribed to theories of "loosely coupled" organizations saw in the system an illustration of these theories (Weick, 1976).

SCHEMA III
STRUCTURES AND FUNCTIONS OF THE SYSTEM

Structures with Illustrative Components	Functions
Federal-State Sub-Structure	

A. HEW and state agencies using linking strategies
  1. Bureau of Education for the Handicapped
  2. National Institute of Education
  3. State Education Agencies
	Provided Leadership and Financial Support

B. National and State Legislatures
  1. Legislative programs
  2. Funds to support legislation	

Intermediary Sub-Structure	

A. Organizations with individual linkers as members
  1. The National Education Association
  2. National Academy for School Executives
	Provided Training for Trainers and Other Support Dissemination

B. Organizations with linking agencies as members
  1. American Association for the Accreditation of Teacher Education
  2. Council of Chief State School Officers	

Decentralized Training Sub-Structure	
A. Internal to School Systems 1. Staff Development Divisions	Provided Training for Linkers

B. External to School Districts
  1. Educational Laboratories and R&D centers
  2. Intermediate service agencies
  3. Institutions of higher education	

In sum, then, the nationwide system was made up of three key sub-structures, each of which performed important functions: the federal-state sub-structure, the training sub-structure, and the intermediary sub-structure. The specific functions performed through the federal-state and the intermediary sub-structures will be described in more detail later in this paper in the section entitled "The Support System for Training Linkers." The sub-structure which delivered training deserves a more detailed treatment at this point.

Goals and Objectives of the Nation-Wide Training System.

A primary question in establishing the nationwide system had to do with its training goals. What training outcomes, in other words, should the system seek? This question was discussed largely from two perspectives — types and numbers of clients to be trained, and the understandings, attitudes, and skills linkers needed to function more effectively. Although the question of goals received continuing debate, some consensus began to be achieved by the 1980s.

Clients to be Served

One major client issue had to do with whether both external and internal linkers should be trained through the system. As the key role of these two types of linkers came to be understood and as the potential for cooperative improvement efforts by them was more clearly identified, the argument to include both internal and external linkers in training became more persuasive.

Internal linkers, by definition, resided in school systems, and the largest population of potential trainees consisted of those teachers, principals, and other leaders engaged in improving teaching-learning through the use of linking strategies. The smallest population served was school board members and other leaders engaged in policy-making, and the middle-sized group was made up of principals and other school district personnel concerned with improving teaching and learning systems through more effective management and leadership.

For a variety of reasons, the actual number of principals, teachers, and other leaders served by the system was relatively small. First, the number of personnel systematically engaged at any one time in linking efforts to improve education in any of the sub-systems noted above was a relatively small per cent of the total number of personnel at work. Most of the personnel, in other words, spent their time in maintaining rather than in improving the system where they worked. Even those who sought to improve education did not always rely upon linkage strategies and did not seek knowledge-based products and practices external to their school systems. Many of them relied upon strategies of political influence to bring about change, rather than upon knowledge-based linking strategies. Finally, many of those who did use linkage strategies in educational improvement were not motivated or were not able to participate in formal training activities. Thus, the nationwide system during the 1965-85 period provided training to fewer than five per cent of the total number of teachers and administrators employed by school systems.

The potential number of external linkers in intermediate service agencies, educational laboratories, R & D centers, institutions of higher education, and related agencies to be trained was substantially fewer than the number of potential internal linkers. The largest groups of external linkers were in institutions of higher education and in intermediate service agencies. The smallest number of external linkers was located in educational laboratories, research and development centers, and associated agencies. Thus, the number of external linkers participating in the training offered by the nationwide system during the 1975-85 period was measured in thousands, in sharp contrast to the number of internal linkers measured in tens of thousands.

The Derivation of Goals from Sub-System Functions.

What were the goals which shaped the content of training programs for linkers? Throughout most of the seventies, the content used in programs for linkers was not derived from systematically developed goal statements. However, in the late seventies more careful attention was given to the use of explicitly articulated goals for content selection in training. Thinkers began to make more explicit the functions performed in the three sub-systems toward which improvement activities could be directed, and these functions provided one important base for systematically selecting content for training. Another source of goal statements was implicit in the three general functions performed by linkers: improving education; spanning the boundaries between one's own organization and another organization in order to acquire and/or provide knowledge-based products, ideas, or services for use in improvement activities; and using and/or helping others use knowledge-based products, ideas, or services for educational improvement. The general linker functions and the sub-systems through which education could be improved are summarized in Schema IV. The concepts presented in Schema IV provided one framework for deriving goals and objectives for the training of linkers.

Each of the three sub-systems in Schema IV offered linkers a means

SCHEMA IV
A FRAMEWORK FOR ANALYZING AND DERIVING
TRAINING GOALS FOR LINKERS

	Improving Education	Spanning Organizational Boundaries	Providing, Acquiring and Using Knowledge Based Products and Services
Teaching-Learning Systems			
Management-Leadership Systems			
Policy-Making Systems			

Systems to be improved

for improving education. In each system relatively discrete functions were performed. (See Schema V for a detailed listing of functions.) Since one strategy for linkers interested in improvement was to make the functions within the sub-systems more effective, these functions provided important bases for determining training objectives and content for internal and external linkers.

Schema V suggests that there were several differences in the various sub-systems which had implications for training. First, the functions performed by personnel in the three sub-systems differed. Second, by implication, the technologies and theory used to perform system functions were dissimilar. Third, the contexts in which the functions were performed and, in turn, the personnel involved were different as were the linking structures required. All these dissimilarities contained criteria for designing programs differentiated to linkers' needs in the differing sub-systems. Such criteria in the late seventies and eighties were used increasingly to articulate specialized training objectives and to select specific content related to the objectives.

As greater understanding about the differences developed in the 1980s and as training was differentiated accordingly, linking became more specialized and more effective. To be sure, training was not toally differentiated for linkers concerned with improving given functions in the various sub-systems. As both internal and external linkers sought improvements,

SCHEMA V
SUB-SYSTEM FUNCTIONS RELATED TO EDUCATIONAL IMPROVEMENT

Sub-System	Functions
Teaching-Learning System	1. Diagnosing students' needs and learning difficulties[4] 2. Devising learning objectives and programs to meet needs 3. Asking types of questions which require a different type of thought process 4. Effectively rewarding certain kinds of student behavior 5. Using various kinds of audio-visual and instructional aids 6. Evaluating student performance 7. Effectively using different kinds of knowledge to teach curriculum content 8. Instructing individuals, small groups and large groups
Management-Leadership System	1. Managing curriculum and instruction[5] 2. Managing staff personnel 3. Managing student personnel 4. Managing finance and business functions 5. Managing school facilities 6. Managing school community relations
Policy-Making System	1. Analyzing discrepancies between goals and accomplishments 2. Deducing objectives from discrepancy analysis 3. Assessing which objectives, if attained, would offer the best cost-benefit ratios 4. Determining policy objectives 5. Generating alternatives to achieve chosen objectives 6. Choosing the most effective alternative(s) 7. Developing plans to achieve chosen objective(s)

[4] Adapted from Commission on Public School Personnel Policies in Ohio, *Realities and Revolution in Teacher Education*. Cleveland: Greater Cleveland Associated Foundation, 1972, p. 15.
[5] Adapted from Lipman, J. M.; Hoeh, J. A., Jr., *The Principalship: Foundations and Functions*. New York: Harper & Row, 1974.

they confronted essentially the same philosophical, psychological, and educational issues in the making of decisions as well as a host of similar leadership issues. For example, a secondary school teacher concerned with using linking strategies to help teachers in the math department become more skillful in diagnosing learning difficulties encountered issues similar to those a principal encountered in using linking strategies to improve the management of curriculum and instruction in a school. An external linker providing resources to the two internal linkers (i.e., math teacher and the principal) confronted similar issues. While the issues confronted were similar and while their confrontation did result in common learnings for linkers, the applications had somewhat different meanings because of differences in the three sub-systems. Trainers generally recognized the need to produce learnings which would enable different specialists to understand and appreciate their respective roles and functions. This was particularly true in school districts which undertook, often in cooperation with external linkers, "whole-system" training for internal linkers.

The Derivation of Goals from General Linker Functions

Schema IV contains within it another rubric for examining training objectives, namely, the three general functions performed by linkers. Those functions focus on the use of knowledge, the spanning of organizational boundaries, and educational improvement. These general functions were critical ones both for internal and external linkers, but before specific training objectives based on these functions are articulated, they need further definition.

Within the three sub-systems toward which linkers could direct their efforts (see Schema V), indicators of educational improvement were reflected in improved system performance or, more specifically, in more effective or efficient carrying out of functions within the three sub-systems. In this approach, the outcomes sought through sub-system performance could remain the same, but the performance of the functions to produce the outcomes would be changed and improved. The other strategy of improvement was to change the objectives of the various sub-systems. In this approach there was the assumption that existing sub-system objectives were discrepant with client or societal needs.

Whether linkers were concerned more with improving the ends or the means of education, knowledge of, commitment to, and skill in educational and organizational change were required. From those requirements in the late seventies a range of goals to guide the training of linkers was developed (see Schema VI for one series of goals). These goals were used to generate change-related training content for both internal and external linkers.

Linking strategies also required the effective spanning of organizational boundaries. The initial purpose of such spanning was to increase the knowledge-based options available to those concerned with improving education in given sub-systems as the following illustration suggests.[6] In the early eighties a school superintendent concerned with the attainment of new policies and more effective desegregation looked beyond the school system she headed to a professor responsible for a desegregation center in a near-by university. The initial purpose was to achieve a larger number of knowledge-based options than those immediately available within the school system. The professor provided a range of options and later became an external linker to the school system. Through the external role, the professor helped the school superintendent and other internal linkers to get knowledge used and, as a result of a series of activities, to achieve new policies for the district.

There were some differences in boundary-spanning for internal and external linkers. The direction of initiation differed, for example, as external linkers directed communications toward internal linkers and vice-versa. An initial activity of the internal linker, to take another instance, tended to be the search for information and options, while an early activity of the external linker was often that of providing information and alternatives. More fundamentally, however, there were more similarities in the two boundary-spanning roles than differences. Schema VII sets forth a series of general understandings, attitudes, and skills required of those engaged in boundary-spanning activities.

The third general function of linkers was the acquisition and use of ideas, expert services, research findings, descriptions of practice, and other knowledge-based products and services in improvement activities. This function tended to be similar for both internal and external linkers. Stated in another way, linker differences which seemed marked on first examination, after careful examination often proved much less significant. Thus, internal linkers, as already noted, tended to search for products and services in initiating improvement activities from sources external to school districts. However, internal linkers, after acquiring knowledge, had an important role in transmitting knowledge to personnel in given

---

[6] In the late 1950s, Talcott Parsons postulated three key functions of the boundary spanner: mediating relations with those receiving an organization's outputs; controlling technical units of an organization; and procuring facilities or resources for organizational activities. (See Talcott Parsons, "General Theory in Sociology" in Leonard Broom and Leonard Cattrell (Eds.), *Sociology Today.* New York: Basic Books, 1959, pp. 3-38.) The third function (i.e., procuring knowledge resources) was emphasized in analyses of the internal linker role while the first function (i.e., mediating relations) received more attention by those examining the external linker role. The second function (i.e., controlling technical units) began to receive some study in the 1980s within the context of linking agencies.

SCHEMA VI[7]
LINKER UNDERSTANDINGS, ATTITUDES, AND SKILLS FOR IMPROVING EDUCATION

LINKER UNDERSTANDINGS

Models of change
Strategies of change
Barriers to change
Processes of change
Effects of change
Types and attributes of innovations
Levels or stages in innovation implementation
Educational and organizational goal-setting
Planning for change
Organizational development and health

LINKER ATTITUDES

Commitment to educational improvement
Favorable self-concept and low ego needs
Tolerance for ambiguity
Positive views toward risk
Acceptance of complexity
Flexible orientation to problem-solving

LINKER SKILLS

Helping clients conduct needs' assessments
Employing data collection and feedback procedures
Developing support and reinforcement systems
Diagnosing improvement problems
Helping clarify group or organizational goals
Fostering a climate for change
Generating alternative solutions to problems
Attaining and helping others attain effective planning
Provoking thought on new alternatives or new perspectives
Helping identify developmental potential in groups, individuals and organizations

---

[7]Ideas included in Schema VI were drawn from such writers as David Crandall, Ronald Havelock, Ann Lieberman, Douglas Paul, Philip Piele, Philip Runkel and Richard M. Schmuck.

SCHEMA VII[8]
LINKER UNDERSTANDINGS, ATTITUDES, AND SKILLS IN BOUNDARY-SPANNING

LINKER UNDERSTANDINGS

The nature of complex organizations
Organizational dependency and inter-dependency
Organization-environment relationships
Inter-organization communication
Types and attributes of relevant agencies
Organizational contact and entry
Problems of boundary-spanning
Tactics of boundary-spanning

LINKER ATTITUDES

Openness to ideas
Tolerance for diversity
Acceptance of uncertainty
Positive perspectives on conflict
Commitment to a search for alternatives

LINKER SKILLS

Selecting the organization to be spanned
Gaining entry and acceptance
Establishing trust relationships
Clarifying and negotiating organizational and individual roles
Achieving collaborative endeavors
Managing the "mutual adaptation" process
Handling critical aspects of inter-dependence
Coping with divided loyalties
Dealing with conflict

---

[8]Ideas included in Schema VII were drawn from such writers as George Ecker, Paul Hood, Matthew Miles, and James Thompson.

---

sub-systems and working with them to facilitate effective knowledge use. In the early stages of interaction external linkers tended to specialize in the transmission of information about many sources of knowledge-based products and services of potential use to internal linkers in various school systems. On the other hand, external linkers, in working more intensively with internal linkers to improve education continued to gather clinical knowledge as well as systematic knowledge related to improvement.

Thus, while there were some differences in the performance of the function by internal and external linkers which stemmed from differing contexts and perspectives, the differences were less fundamental than they often appeared at first glance. Schema VIII presents more specific training objectives related to the knowledge acquisition and use function.

SCHEMA VIII[9]
UNDERSTANDINGS, ATTITUDES, AND SKILLS IN USING KNOWLEDGE-BASED PRODUCTS AND SERVICES

LINKER UNDERSTANDINGS

Information science concepts
Sources of knowledge and its uses
Quality control and related professional issues
Origin and development of federal and state dissemination systems in education
On-going and emerging state and federal improvement programs
Inventories of human and information resources

LINKER ATTITUDES

Commitment to knowledge utilization as a means for improving education
Appreciation for diverse ideas and perspectives
Motivation to acquire new ideas and products
Positive views about applying theory to practice
Positive views both of producers and users of knowledge

LINKER SKILLS

Responding constructively to new information
Retrieving useful information from a wide range of sources
Describing and evaluating for clients relevant products and services
Linking participants engaged in inprovement processes with pertinent information sources
Providing technical assistance to those involved in improvement
Arranging the needed "mix" of resources
Advancing the learning and development of those seeking improvement

---

[9]Ideas included in Schema VIII were drawn from such writers as Launor Carter, David Clark, Ronald Havelock, Paul Hood, and Sam Sieber.

Commonality vs. Uniqueness in Training

The concepts in Schemas VI, VII, and VIII, as already implied, posed a major question to trainers and designers in the late seventies: To what degree should training for internal and external linkers be differentiated for the three linker functions, and to what degree should the content provided and the skills developed be similar for both groups? Since the level of knowledge development about the three functions was still limited even by 1985, the basic content in training programs designed to advance understandings tended to be similar for both internal and external linkers, even though the applications of the content differed as the organizational perspectives and contexts of these two types of linkers differed.

For example, those seeking understandings of change found syntheses of knowledge such as the ones developed by Douglas Paul and Joseph Giacquinta in the latter part of the seventies pertinent whether they were internal or external linkers.[10] Scholarly papers of this type and the many references encompassed in them provided on-the-job linkers an awareness of the different dimensions of change, alternative models of change, and insight into its processes and effects — among other things.

Because the contexts in which the three functions were performed differed both for internal and external linkers and because the knowledge available on the linker functions was general in nature, the applications of learnings acquired by linkers were often distinctive, both with regard to understandings and skills. Illustrative differences during the 1980-85 period in the application of relevant concepts can usefully be identified even at the risk of over-simplification. Schema IX highlights selected and illustrated differences related to the training of internal and external linkers.

Content such as that in Schema IX indicated that the context and the perspective of linkers were very important in determining the concepts chosen for application and the meaning attached to them. As differing applications of concepts and skills were made by external and internal linkers, and as they shared the differences with one another, they achieved a greater degree of common understandings and greater effectiveness in working with one another.

---

[10]See Douglas Paul, "Change Processes at the Elementary, Secondary, and Post Secondary Levels of Education" in this volume. Also see Joseph Giacquinta, "Organizational Change in Schools of Education: A Review of Several Models and Agents for Research" in D. Griffiths and D. McCarty (Eds.), *The Deanship in Higher Education* Danville, Ill.: Interstate Printers & Publishers, 1978.

SCHEMA IX
DIFFERENT APPLICATIONS OF LEARNINGS BY INTERNAL AND EXTERNAL LINKERS

Internal Linkers	External Linkers
1. Because internal linkers worked in more politicized environments, they made greater use of "normative re-educative" strategies of change than did external linkers.[11]	1. External linkers whose chief tools were knowledge-based products and services made greater use of the "empirical-rational" approach to change than did internal linkers.
2. Most internal linkers found the problem-solving model of change more meaningful than other models because it enabled them to address constraints and opportunities in their own situations.	2. External linkers valued linkage and social interaction models of change because they, in contrast to internal linkers, worked in varied settings and had opportunities to see the impact of knowledge diffusion processes in different school systems.
3. Internal linkers needed sources of information and search strategies which could help them locate products or services pertinent to specific improvement objectives.	3. External linkers needed to be familiar with a wide array of knowledge-based products and services so that they could respond to information requests related to varied improvement objectives.
4. Internal linkers used boundary-spanning skills to obtain relevant human or knowledge-based resources from organizations external to school systems.	4. External linkers applied boundary-spanning skills to provide information and services to diverse educational organizations engaged in improvement activities.
5. Since internal linkers brought commitment to specific improvement objectives and an intimate understanding of the change variables in local situations, they needed a general knowledge of resources external to the school system.	5. Since external linkers brought to bear a wide range of information, resources and improvement activities, they needed clinical knowledge about key variables affecting educational improvement in specific systems.
6. Internal linkers had special needs for knowlege and skill in goal setting because of their key legitimation roles.	6. External linkers needed knowledge and skill for use in bringing to bear a wide range of means to achieve goals.
7. Internal linkers needed greater knowledge about the types and attributes of agencies which could provide information on knowledge-based products and services.	7. External linkers needed greater knowledge of the types and attributes of agencies within which educational improvement activities take place.
8. Internal linkers needed greater understanding of information about the products emanating from knowledge uses so that they could apply them in improvement activities.	8. External linkers needed a greater understanding of the processes used to create knowedge-based products and systems.

[11]For distinctions between the "normative re-educative" and the "empirical-rational" see Robert Chin and Kenneth Benne, "General Strategies for Affecting Change Within Human Systems," in *The Planning of Change*. New York: Holt, Rinehart, & Winston, 1960, pp. 32-59.

Patterns of Training

The 1975-85 period was marked by much diversity in the training of linkers. However, as the nationwide system of training slowly emerged, certain patterns in training emerged. In 1975, for example, the typical pattern was to offer separate programs for internal and external linkers. In the late seventies and early eighties, a number of programs served both internal and external linkers simultaneously. This mix enabled internal linkers to understand educational improvement from the perspective of the external linker and vice-versa. Internal and external linkers, in attaining better understandings of their respective roles and resources, came to see more clearly why they should collaborate and how they could collaborate with one another in improvement efforts. Training sessions themselves frequently stimulated and facilitated cooperative follow-up activities on the part of internal and external linkers. State education agencies, large school systems, and institutions of higher education were important leaders in stimulating joint training patterns for internal and external linkers.

In the mid-seventies, training programs tended to concentrate more upon providing linkers information on useful training materials and on concepts of linkage. Towards the end of the seventies and eighties, greater emphasis was placed upon providing concepts and skills needed in undertaking change processes and, to a lesser degree, on skills and concepts needed to perform boundary-spanning roles effectively. Two major developments helped to account for this trend. First, information on training materials began to be presented in catalogues, inventories, and resource banks of various kinds, all of which made it feasible for linkers to acquire such information more easily outside training programs. Secondly, as educational organizations were confronted with declining enrollments, stable staffs and scarce resources, those seeking change were faced with major challenges. Consequently, the motivation among linkers to have greater understanding and skill in change processes grew, and those offering programs adapted them to meet the needs perceived by linkers.

In the seventies, the major emphasis was upon programs designed for those concerned with improving teaching-learning systems. This emphasis was reinforced by federal legislation in 1975 which supported teacher centers. In the late seventies and eighties, an increasing amount of attention was given to improving management-leadership and policy-making systems. This trend also was supported by the growing need for effective leadership. More specifically, the positive or negative roles which school principals and other administrators could play in helping teachers improve learning were documented in the 1970s, and the results were disseminated widely. One result was that principals participated increasingly with teachers in training programs for linkers offered through teacher centers.

The shift toward an increased emphasis on programs concerned with improving policy-making systems was clearly centered in needs for change. State and federal mandates, declining enrollments, retrenchment tendencies, desegregation decisions, energy shortages, and many other forces impinged upon school systems, and they in turn, created needs to assess and to change policy. A major challenge which confronted those designing programs was to offer learnings which would help improve policy-making in school systems. This required types of content and trainers different from those training linker specialists responsible for improving teaching-learning systems. Much of the content and many of the trainers came from policy centers in universities and from non-profit organizations specializing in policy studies.

In 1973, Ronald and Mary Havelock discussed "breadth of goal" alternatives bearing upon the training of linking agents. Alternatives posed were "specific skill learnings," skill sets and functions, "whole-role training," and "whole-system training." During the 1975-85 period, the trend was to deal with the "whole-role training" option in pre-service programs. It was not possible for linkers to learn all of the skill sets and understandings associated with a new occupational role in short-term, in-service programs or even in a series of planned sequential in-service programs offered through the nationwide training system. However, training programs offered through the nationwide system were very effective in dealing with "specific skill learning" and with "skill sets and functions." Both these alternatives could be dealt with within the context of sub-system functions (see Schema V) or the three general functions of linkers (see Schema IV). "Skill sets and functions" were more effectively dealt with through sequential programs. Through a series of 10 three-day training sessions, linkers could increase their competence in many of the skills associated with the general function of change, for example, as listed in Schema VI. The same goal was also achieved in some cases through intensive five-week summer workshops.

The option of "whole-system training" by 1985 still remained an ideal for almost all school districts where "whole-system" encompassed both central and school units. However, an increasing number of school systems during the 1975-85 period did undertake training directed at organizational change. However, these efforts, rather than concentrating upon the total system, tended to concentrate upon particular divisions within the central units of school districts or on given schools within a district.

In the late seventies and eighties, a growing number of the trainers participating in the system were outstanding linking specialists. All of these trainers brought tacit knowledge and clinical insights about linkage to the training situation; many brought extensive knowledge of the literature on linking.

Two kinds of teaching team patterns emerged in the eighties. The first was a linker team comprised of one internal and one external linker. This team operated principally in training sessions which involved both internal and external linkers where the focus was on skill learning. Another kind of team serving in a variety of training situations was comprised of a scholar versed in research and concepts on linkage and an articulate linker skilled in the technology of linkage. This latter team concentrated more on developing understandings than skills. Both teams noted drew upon additional resources beyond themselves. A number of the intermediate service agencies, for example, involved scholars and practitioners from the areas of manpower training, health, and welfare as they sponsored training sessions directed at issues of educational policy intertwined with other public policy issues.

As linking became more specialized, there was a trend toward distinguishing between training for generalists and specialists. Generalists in external agencies tended to be those who coordinated a staff performing varied and specialized linking functions as, for example, information processing, organizational entry and role negotiation, product diffusion, and training. Internal linkers serving generalists' roles tended to be principals, leaders in professional associations, department heads, superintendents, and others who were giving leadership to improvement efforts in the system in which they worked. One general set of objectives which guided the design of training programs for generalists was greater awareness of new developments in specializations, new products and services, and new findings about effective linking roles within and across organizational contexts. Training for those serving in specialized roles tended to be directed increasingly in the 1980s at functional skills and concepts in such areas as training, product diffusion, and organizational entry and role negotiations in the case of external linkers and knowledge acquisition, training, and implementation in the case of internal linkers. The content of such training was inevitably linked with more general content affecting all linkers as, for example, new knowledge of educational change processes.

THE SUPPORT SYSTEM FOR TRAINING LINKERS

As the nationwide system for training linkage agents developed, a series of functions and technologies emerged which were supportive of the training system. These helped to nurture and facilitate the growth of the nationwide system; significantly, the scope and quality of the functions and technologies expanded in the 1980s. Three general functions, all supportive of the training system, were established during the 1975-85 period:

1. Providing leadership to extend and improve the nationwide training and support system;

2. Providing funds for training innovations and for research and development to improve training;

3. Providing technical assistance to the system's program designers and implementers;

Schema X presents the functions and sub-functions of the system to support linker training which emerged during the 1975-85 period.[12] These various functions will be described in more detail as will the agencies which participated in the development and performance of particular functions and sub-functions.

The Leadership Function

Leadership for initiating and developing the nationwide training system, as already noted, had no single locus or expression but was evident in all parts of the system's structure, including the federal-state, the intermediary, and the training components. A brief summary of leadership functions performed in the 1970s is in order before comments about developments in the '80s are made.

---

[12]This schema is adapted from Paula Silver, "Summary, Conclusions, and Recommendations," in William Davis, Jack Culbertson, and Paula Silver (Eds.), *The Professional Development of Title I Principals: Concepts, Materials, and Strategies.* Washington: Ray Littlejohn Associates, 1977.

Nationwide Training System 307

SCHEMA X
FUNCTIONS SUPPORTIVE OF THE TRAINING SYSTEM

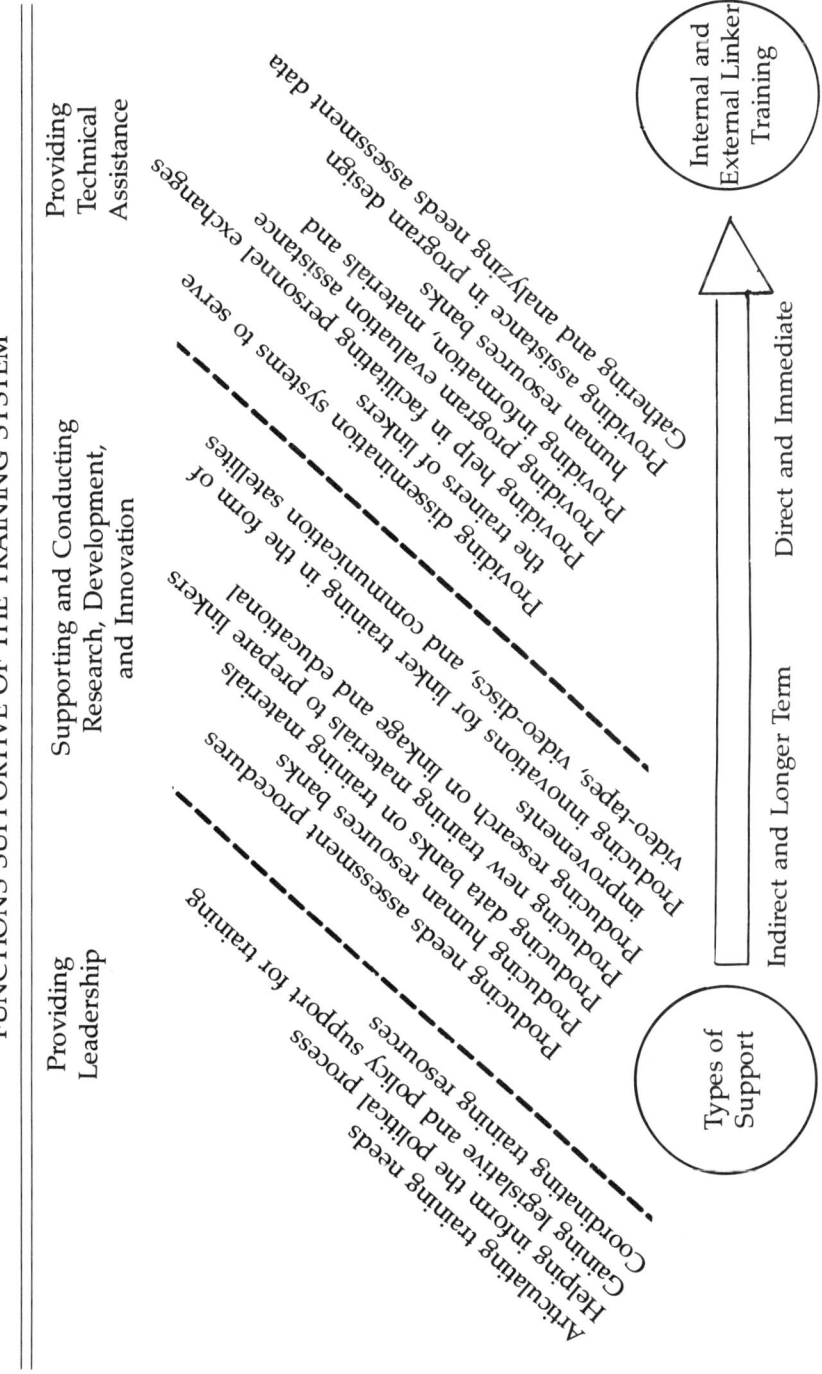

Providing Leadership
- Articulating training needs
- Helping inform the political process
- Gaining legislative and policy support for training
- Coordinating training resources

Supporting and Conducting Research, Development, and Innovation
- Producing needs assessment procedures
- Producing human resources data banks
- Producing data banks on training materials
- Producing new training materials
- Producing research on linkage and educational improvements
- Producing innovations for linker training materials
- Video-tapes, video-discs, and communication

Providing Technical Assistance
- Providing dissemination systems to serve the trainers of linkers
- Providing help in facilitating personnel exchanges
- Providing information, materials and human resources banks
- Providing assistance in program design
- Gathering and analyzing needs assessment data

Types of Support: Indirect and Longer Term → Direct and Immediate → Internal and External Linker Training

Initiatives to Develop the System. Leaders within the federal-state structure played key roles in helping legitimize the nationwide system during the 1975-80 period. State and Federal officials did this first by encouraging interested organizations and their leaders to define and explore the potential in the projected system and other support for those in federal-state arena concerned with legitimizing, interpreting, and obtaining financial support for the system. Leaders in the intermediary structure also played important roles in helping their respective members understand and, in some cases, to test out concepts related to the nationwide system of training.

Leaders in the training component of the system also provided important initiatives. School superintendents, especially in school districts with staff development divisions, were very persuasive in articulating the need for the training of internal linkers, and they obtained support from school boards in many cases to increase investments in training. In addition, many of them were successful in providing leaders at the state and federal levels support in articulating to legislatures the need for linker training and in gaining legislative action to expand the nationwide training system.

Funding the System. During the 1980-85 period, leaders committed to the development of the nationwide system achieved a number of important results, one of which was an increase in the funds available for linker training. By 1985, more than half of the states providing funds from their own resources to support linker training. Most were providing funds through intermediate service agencies, institutions of higher education, and through such newly established structures as educational improvement centers. A half dozen states provided support for state academies to conduct staff development programs in different regions and for different clients.

Federal resources for linker training increased during the 1980-85 period. The amount of "flow-through" dollars provided states which were used for training increased in the early '80s. In addition, the funds which were made available through teacher center legislation were increased substantially about the same time. As noted earlier, new federal legislation to train external linkers was enacted in the early 1980s and appropriations to implement the legislation increased annually during the 1981-85 period.

As federal and state funds increased, an implicit message was communicated to localities that linker training was valuable and significant. This message encouraged and helped leaders obtain more local monies to train internal linkers. Consequently, in many districts, there was some increase in training funds during the 1980-85 period for internal linkers.

Co-ordination Within the System. Another expression of leadership, especially during the 1980-85 period, was more effective coordination of training resources and activities at all levels of educational government. At the federal level, there was a distinct trend in the early eighties toward more effective coordination of education-related programs generally through the Office of the Assistant Secretary of Health, Education, and Welfare. This coordination was especially important for the nationwide training system, since a number of federal agencies provided financial support for the system.

Coordination of educational programs at the state level was positively affected by trends and actions at the federal level. In addition, there was press to coordinate public policies and programs more generally on such matters as manpower development, unemployment, welfare, education, and health. This press not only led to greater coordination of training for linkers in education, but also to more systematic coordination of the training of public servants more generally.

Coordination of training for linkers was improved in local schools for two reasons. In the first place, greater federal and state coordination required greater coordination locally, and secondly, as school systems established staff development divisions, one of their important functions was to coordinate the various training activities conducted, including those involving internal linking agents.

As the nationwide system emerged and as greater coordination was effected at the local, state, and federal levels, the need for coordination among the different levels of educational government became more apparent. Consequently, in the early 1980s, leaders in the executive branch of the federal government created a coordinating council for the nationwide system. This council was made up of representatives from all levels of educational government, from national professional associations and other agencies committed to the improvement of education through linking strategies, from leading citizens' groups, and from agencies actually involved in delivering training. This council helped to set directions and targets for improving the nationwide system and helped stimulate the system's leaders to undertake needed improvements. While the work of the council proved to be complex, leaders agreed that by 1985 it had performed significant leadership functions.

Providing Support for Improving the System

As the nationwide system grew, the perceived need for its improvement also grew. Consequently, three major improvement strategies were launched in the late seventies—attaining training innovations, producing research findings and creating new products and ideas. Three types of federal funds for implementing these strategies were provided: grants from specific agencies with capacities to support linker training as, for example, the Bureau of Education for the Handicapped; indirect funding in the form of "flow-through" dollars to states which, in some instances, supported linker training; and appropriations from teacher center legislation and from legislation designed to prepare external linkers.

State support was directed more at improving education in school systems through training than at producing research, development, and innovations in training for national diffusion. However, some state monies allocated to intermediate service agencies, institutions of higher education, and related agencies were used for the support of linker training. In addition, funds appropriated for educational improvement centers and related innovations in the eighties were also used to produce training innovation research and development supportive of training.

Institutions of higher education in the seventies and eighties allocated an increasing amount of their human and financial resources to support staff development programs in contrast to supporting pre-service programs for principals, teachers and others. Local school districts invested largely in the training of personnel through their own staff development program or through offerings by such external organizations as the National Academy for School Executives and the National Staff Development Council.

Achieving Training Innovations. Training innovations emerged in different settings as a result of the investments made.[13] During the 1975-80 period, for example, the first state academy for training educators was established. Supported and managed at the state level, the academy provided training to various leaders, including linkers in different regions of the state. By 1985, several states had developed such academies, and some served linkers concerned with interrelated public policy issues in different departments of state government.

In the late seventies and eighties a number of universities designed pre-service programs for preparing linkers which required on-campus study supplemented by field experience and a year's internship in a linking agency. These programs enabled participants to acquire not only a wider range of content and skills but also greater depth in learning than

---

[13]The emphasis in the discussion immediately following is on functional and structural innovations in the program. Innovations in training technologies are discussed later in the chapter.

was possible in in-service programs. They also produced a cadre of linkers who possessed a range of new skills and understandings which proved very useful to linking agencies in the 1980-85 period.

Federal agencies supported collaborative arrangements to produce innovations. In the late seventies, for example, grants were made to support collaborative programs for internal linkers through university-school system-state education agency partnerships. While this approach to training was complex and required major boundary-spanning efforts, it had two major advantages: It enabled trainers to draw upon a wide range of training resources in systematic ways, and it facilitated the establishment of "third parties" to assist in the attainment of innovations.

In the late seventies and early eighties, "travelling workshops" were packaged to achieve specific training objectives, and these were diffused widely by national associations and organizations for use in many states. The packages focused upon a specific topic as, for example, role negotiation by linking agents and could be adapted for use with both internal and external linkers. They were also sufficiently standardized to enable trainers to learn to use them efficiently.

As noted earlier, in the early 1980s, a variety of programs which were directed at the joint training of internal and external linkers emerged. Institutions of higher education in a number of instances were successful in designing programs for internal and external linkers, as were some directors of staff development in large city school districts and leaders in selected state education agencies. A major dynamic for learning in these workshops stemmed from the interaction of internal linkers and external linkers who shared different perspectives and possessed different experience bases.

Producing Research. The strategy of research support was carried out largely by professors and their graduate students from various disciplines in higher education institutions. Research not only illuminated aspects of teaching, management, and policy-making systems, but it also shed light on a range of questions bearing upon linkage processes. Only a few illustrations can be offered at this point.

In the late 1970s, almost no studies had been done directed at the internal dynamics of linking agencies, including the key variables which affected linker productivity and morale in these organizations. This area of study attracted a number of investigators in the 1980s. Studies of this type were especially important to those who had responsibilities for managing and leading linking agencies.

A question which continued to intrigue scholars and leaders during the 1980-85 period was the degree to which the performance of internal and external linkers was similar and the degree to which it was different. Both survey research and theoretically-guided inquiry unfolded on this subject. The findings had important implications not only for training but for the development of products to support the training of internal and external linkers.

As more attention was directed toward the training of linkers, questions arose about the recruitment and selection of individuals to enter this field of endeavor. Criteria of effectiveness as they related to linkage became a salient question. The question was raised not only for its implications for recruitment and selection but also for the performance appraisal of linkers and the definition of linker training needs. Both logical analyses of effectiveness and studies to test theoretically derived criteria were produced.

In the eighties, a number of studies were conducted to examine relationships between the technical units of linking agencies and defined aspects of their environments. For example, the relationship between information services of an agency and the clients the system served was investigated. The results of such inquiries began to illuminate ways agencies exercised control over the functioning of technical units, given specified demands and opportunities in the environment. Such research also began to shed light on organizational and environmental relationships and the boundary-spanning behavior of linkers.

Creating New Products. More funds were available for development than for research, although they were still limited. National intermediary organizations whose member units had developmental capabilities played an important role in creating new products to support training. For example, the Center for Development and Research (CEDaR) and its members joined together to create cooperatively a range of training materials to support the nationwide system for linkers. Another illustration was the American Educational Research Association which, in cooperation with its membership, produced developmental support for the nationwide system. Universities and other organizations with developmental capacities also produced a multiplicity of important products to support training. Only a few illustrations of pertinent development can be offered at this point.

Through the encouragement of the National Institute of Education and a number of regional educational laboratories and research development centers, a catalog *(Educational Dissemination and Linking Agent Source Book)* was developed in the latter part of the seventies. This and others which followed contained information supportive of those designing and implementing programs for linkers. As inventories of training materials were developed, greater attention was given to the attainment of more comprehensive and user-oriented systems for classifying those materials.

Another innovation which emerged in the late seventies was a product called human resource banks which supported linkers, linking agencies, and linker trainers. With the complexity of improvement activities and the need for expertise of various kinds, systematic and easily accessible information on human resources related to defined training needs proved useful to leaders in the system. Although problems were encountered in operationalizing and using these data banks, they provided information on a wide range of potential talent and expertise for designers and trainers.

In the seventies, needs assessment procedures tended to be based upon the perceptions of linkers and those responsible for training linkers. However, in the late seventies and eighties, more sophisticated approaches to the evaluation of training needs developed as a support to the training system. These included performance appraisal based upon job analyses, the identification of discrepancies between organizational objectives and performance, normative forecasting, theory-based models, and trend analysis.

Still another kind of product to support the nationwide system was new training materials. Many of these training materials were reality-oriented (e.g., cases, simulations and films) and were designed to facilitate skill learning and to offer knowledge application exercises. Other materials more conceptual in nature ranged from bibliographies to syntheses of information on exemplary practices and syntheses of knowledge on salient aspects of practice.

In the early 1980s, video-tape became prominent as the medium for communicating exemplary practice. The capacity of this medium for capturing and diffusing exemplary practice inexpensively made it an important support in linker training. Some of the tapes presented sequenced learning experiences. For example, one pattern involved first a trigger tape simulating a problem; second, a tape depicting an exemplary practice related to the problem; and, third, a tape discussing the concepts shaping the exemplary practice.

Recently, two additional technologies began to be used in the training of linkers. The first of these was communication satellites, able to reach large numbers of individuals in specified regions of the country. Certain universities developed the capability to utilize communication satellites in training and acquired the necessary equipment to do so. This approach proved to be cost-effective because of the large number of individuals who could be reached.

A second technology was the video-disc. In the late 1970s, a number of universities cooperated to test out the use of video-discs in transmitting ideas and information in training. This technology tended to be used initially in large urban settings where it proved to be effective, especially with small groups of various kinds. Later, it was diffused for use in suburban and rural areas and had been used in varied settings for the training of linkers by 1985.

To sum up, leaders in the late seventies and eighties increasingly agreed that the emergent nationwide system needed to be improved through programs of research, development, and training innovations. Limited resources were made available from various levels of educational development to fund these programs. The result was research findings, varied products, and a range of training innovations which impacted positively upon the nationwide system in the late seventies and eighties.

Providing Technical Assistance to Support Training Programs

As the nationwide system emerged and as training innovations, research findings, and development products were achieved, the demand for technical assistance to support the training of internal and external linking agents increased. The response to the request for technical assistance was provided partly by training units working with other units and partly by intermediary organizations with special links to trainers of linkers. As noted earlier, intermediary agencies were in direct contact with linkers through individual memberships in some cases and through institutional membership in others. The National Academy of School Executives, for example, had unique channels for reaching individual school superintendents practicing or desiring to practice linkage strategies in change, and such organizations as the American Association of Colleges for Teacher Education with institutional membership were able to reach a range of linkers in their member institutions.

Intermediary agencies were uniquely equipped to monitor the development of resources nationwide, to organize information on resources and to disseminate results to linker trainers and linkers through annual conferences, special seminars or workshops, and a variety of written and audiovisual media. As linker trainers in school systems, intermediate service agencies, institutions of higher education, and cooperatives of various kinds acquired information and knowledge-based products and services, and skills in their use, they utilized the information and skills in a variety of internal or external technical assistance activities.

Other kinds of technical assistance were also provided the educational community as, for example, the facilitation of personnel exchange for staff development purposes. In the early eighties, the trend to facilitate exchange between internal and external linkers in linking agencies developed. Internal linkers, by spending time in external linking agencies acquired, in a relatively efficient manner, information on a wide range of knowledge-based products and services relevant to school improvement. External linkers, by spending time in school systems on exchange arrangements, acquired clinical knowledge on problems of educational improvement related to policy-making, teaching, and management, all of which increased their competence and the competence of their agencies.

Summary

During the 1965-85 period, a nationwide system for the training of linkers emerged. By 1980, the major elements and functions of the system were relatively clear. The key elements were found in a federal-state structure involving leaders from both the executive and legislative branches of government; a training structure responsible for delivering learnings to linking agents; and an intermediary structure made up of organizations with special responsibilities for disseminating information and providing training to those with major responsibilities for training linkers.

During the 1975-85 period, a system to support the nationwide training system emerged. This system was based upon the functions of research, development, and training innovations. Technical assistance and dissemination systems were also created to communicate information and to facilitate the use of new products, services, training innovations, and research findings to improve for linkers and trainers of linkers. In 1985, both the nationwide system and its support system are firmly in place.

References

Becker, J. and Hahn, C. *Wingspread Workbook for Educational Change Agents.* Boulder, Colorado: Social Science Education Consortium, 1975, p. 27.

Berman, P., McLaughlin, M., et al. *Federal Programs Supporting Educational Change.* Vol. I-V. Santa Monica: The Rand Corporation, 1975.

Boulding, K. Introduction. In M. Rodekohr, *Adjustments of Colorado School Districts to Declining Enrollments.* Lincoln, Nebraska: University of Nebraska Printing and Duplication Service, 1975, 1-7.

Campbell, R. *Strengthening State Departments of Education.* Chicago: The University of Chicago, The Midwest Administration Center, 1967.

Chin, R. and Benne, K. General Strategies for Affecting Change within Human Systems, in *The Planning of Change.* New York: Holt, Rinehart & Winston, 1960, 32-59.

Commission on Public School Personnel Policies in Ohio. *Realities and Revolution in Teacher Education.* Cleveland: Greater Cleveland Associated Foundation, 1972, p. 15.

Culbertson, J. *Organizational Strategies for Planned Change in Education,* A paper presented to a Conference on Strategies for Educational Change, mimeographed, 1965.

Giacquinta, J. Organizational Change in Schools of Education: A Review of Several Models and Agents for Research in D. Griffiths and D. McCarty, (Eds.), *The Deanship in Higher Education,* Danville, Illinois: Interstate Printers & Publishers, Inc., (forthcoming).

Guba, E. and Clark, D. *Likely Near-Future Scenarios for Schools, Colleges, and Departments of Education.* Bloomington, Indiana: Indiana University, 2805 East Tenth Street, RITE Occasional Paper Series, 1977.

Havelock, R. *Planning for Innovation through Dissemination and Utilization of Knowledge.* Ann Arbor: Center for Research on Utilization of Scientific Knowledge, 1974.

Havelock, R. G. and Havelock, M. G. *Training for Change Agents.* Ann Arbor, Michigan: Center for Research on Utilization of Scientific Knowledge, 1973, pp. 39-43.

Interstate Project on Dissemination: Report and Recommendations. Washington, D.C.: The Council of Chief State School Officers, 1976.

Jones, G. N. *Planned Organizational Change: A Study in Change Dynamics.* New York: N.Y. Praeger, 1969.

Lipham, J. M. and Hoeh, J. A., Jr. *The Principalship: Foundations and Functions.* New York: Harper & Row, 1974.

Parsons, Talcott. General Theory in Sociology in L. Broom and L. Cattrell (Eds.), *Sociology Today.* New York: Basic Books, 1959, pp. 3-38.

Sieber, S. V., et al. *The Use of Educational Knowledge.* New York: Bureau of Applied Social Research, Columbia University, 1972, Vol. I-II.

Silver, P. Summary, Conclusions, and Recommendations. In W. Davis, J. Culbertson, and P. Silver (Eds.), *The Professional Development of Title I Principals: Concepts, Materials, and Strategies.* Washington: Ray Littlejohn Associates, 1977.

Stephens, R. *Regional Educational Services.* Washington, D.C.: Educational Research Service, Inc., 1976.

Stephens, R. *An Essay on the Future of Regionalism in Elementary and Secondary Education.* Arlington, Virginia: American Association of School Administrators, 1977.

Weick, K. Educational Organizations as Loosely Coupled Organizations, *Administrative Science Quarterly.* March, 1976, (**21**), 1-19.

ORDER BLANK

You may order additional copies of *Linking Processes in Educational Improvement* at $7.50 each, plus $1.25 postage and handling. Please complete the order blank, enclose a check payable to UCEA, and return both to the address shown on the other side of this card.

Name _____

Mailing Address _____

_____ Zip Code _____

Pre-payment is required.

ORDER BLANK

You may order additional copies of *Linking Processes in Educational Improvement* at $7.50 each, plus $1.25 postage and handling. Please complete the order blank, enclose a check payable to UCEA, and return both to the address shown on the other side of this card.

Name _____

Mailing Address _____

_____ Zip Code _____

Pre-payment is required.

Mail to:

The University Council for
Educational Administration
29 West Woodruff Avenue
Columbus, Ohio 43210

Mail to:

The University Council for
Educational Administration
29 West Woodruff Avenue
Columbus, Ohio 43210